RENEWALS 458-4574

DATE DUE

GAYLORD			PRINTED IN U.S.A.

Software Verification and Validation for Practitioners and Managers

Second Edition

For a listing of recent titles in the *Artech House Computing Library,*
turn to the back of this book.

Software Verification and Validation for Practitioners and Managers

Second Edition

Steven R. Rakitin

Artech House
Boston • London
www.artechhouse.com

Library of Congress Cataloging-in-Publication Data
Rakitin, Steven R.
    Software verification and validation for practitioners and managers /Steve Rakitin.—2nd ed.
      p.   cm.—Rev. ed. of: Software verification and validation.
    Includes bibliographical references and index.
    ISBN 1-58053-296-9 (alk. paper)
    1. Computer software—Verification.   2. Computer software—Validation.
    I. Rakitin, Steven R. Software verification and validation.   II. Title.
QA76.76.V47   R35   2001
005.1'4—dc21   2001022884

British Library Cataloguing in Publication Data
Rakitin, Steven R.
    Software verification and validation for practitioners and managers. — 2nd ed.
    1. Computer software—Validation   2. Computer software—Verification
    I. Title
    005.1'4
    ISBN 1-58053-296-9

Cover design by Igor Valdman

International Standard Book Number: 1-58053-296-9
Library of Congress Catalog Card Number: 2001022884

10 9 8 7 6 5 4 3 2 1

To Eileen, my wife, my best friend, my soul mate.

And to Jason and Sarah, who, in spite of me, have become independent, talented adults and from whom I've learned more than they know.

Contents

Preface to the Second Edition

This book contains a reasonable set of basic software verification and validation (V&V) activities. From firsthand experience working with many companies in several industries, I have found that basic software V&V activities are not well understood and are applied inconsistently. For example, several companies I worked with recently did not yet have a software quality assurance (QA) group, and a few had not even implemented basic configuration management (CM) practices. Further, in organizations that did have software QA, I found significant differences in effectiveness across the organizations and even across projects within the same organization. While my observations are not based on a statistically significant sample, I believe that my experiences are a fairly accurate reflection of the industry as a whole. In fact, Yourdon [1] reported recently that, while software quality has improved overall, the gap between those companies producing the best software and those producing the worst software has increased dramatically over the past decade.

As a consultant, I am frequently asked to help companies with "quality problems." Studying clients that experienced such problems, I found a common theme—they all behaved in an unpredictable manner. For example, it was not possible for these organizations to determine when major events, such as code freeze or first customer ship, would happen. (In some cases, it was not even possible to know if they would happen.) Because these organizations were unpredictable, marketing was unable to plan product rollout events, development and QA were unable to make effective use of expensive, scarce resources, and software V&V activities were not nearly as effective as they could be.

Len Race, a consultant and friend, observed that in order for businesses to become more efficient, they must learn how to behave in a more predictable manner. For me, this was a revelation. The connection between poor performance and unpredictable behavior became crystal clear. Unpredictable organizations exhibit many of the following symptoms:

- They consistently commit to more than they can deliver and consistently deliver less than was committed.

- They underestimate tasks and miss almost every schedule.

- People within the organization have goals and objectives that are not aligned with the overall business goals and objectives.

- There is a lack of accountability throughout the organization.

- There is no notion of using "best practices." If a written process exists, it is not followed consistently.

- There is a belief among employees that "we never have time to do things right but always have time to do things over."

When I help a company with quality problems, I start with the CEO and ask, "How are your people measured?" By looking at performance plans for individuals, you can understand why the organization behaves the way it does. Without fail, when looking at performance plans in companies with quality problems, I rarely come across the word "quality." Since behavior is directly related to how people are measured, why is it a surprise that these organizations have "quality problems"?

Once I made the connection between poor performance and unpredictable behavior, I realized that (1) management owns both the problem and the solution, and (2) to increase the effectiveness of software V&V techniques, organizations must learn to behave in a more predictable manner.

Clearly, management must take a leadership role in helping the organization behave in a more predictable way. It is for this reason that the title of this book has been changed to include managers. *Software Verification and Validation for Practitioners and Managers* includes specific actions that management can take to help the organization behave in a more predictable manner.

Who Is This Book For?

As the title states, this book is intended for two groups—practitioners and managers. Practitioners include software QA engineers, software engineers, and project managers who need a basic understanding of software V&V techniques.

Unfortunately, very little in the way of formal training in software V&V is offered in schools. As a result, there is a gap between the skills that many software quality practitioners have and the skills that are needed to produce high-quality software. This book is intended for those who have been given responsibility for performing software V&V tasks but who have not had the luxury of receiving training in this subject. Parts I through III are intended primarily for practitioners.

Managers include software QA managers, development managers, project managers, vice presidents of engineering and development, directors of quality, and CEOs. Management has the ability to change the behavior of the organization, by providing the leadership necessary to meet business goals and by aligning the way people are measured with those same business goals. Every management employee, from the CEO to first-line managers, must recognize that meeting business goals is easier when the organization is more predictable. Part IV of this book was written to provide managers and executives at all levels with specific strategies that they can use to help their organization behave in a more predictable manner.

To What Kinds of Software Are V&V Activities Applicable?

The software V&V activities described in this book are applicable to a wide range of software, a wide variety of products, and a wide range of industries. The best way to answer this question is with another question: "Is there a compelling business reason to develop good quality software and deliver it on time?" If the answer is yes, then many of the activities are applicable.

How Is the Book Organized and What Is New in This Edition?

Part I provides an introduction to software development and an overview of the software development process. Several software development life cycle models are presented in Chapter 2. The importance of a written software development process is outlined in Chapter 3. Economic motivation for many software V&V activities is discussed in Chapter 4.

In Chapter 1, a discussion of the international standard on life cycle models, ISO 12207, has been added. In Chapter 2, information on the Rational Unified Process has been included. References to software standards have been updated throughout Part I.

Part II provides an overview of software verification activities. Chapter 5 and 6 (along with Appendices A–D) provide details on the formal inspection process. Chapter 7 focuses on verification measures, and Chapter 8 contains an overview of configuration management.

Chapter 6 has been reorganized slightly to remove some redundant information. References to software standards have been updated throughout Part II.

Part III provides an overview of software validation activities. Chapter 9 provides an overview of testing. Testing measures are included in Chapter 10, and an introduction to software reliability growth is presented in Chapter 11.

Chapter 9 has been rewritten to include more details about types of tests that can be written and now includes information on the concurrent testing/development model, test planning, and test estimation techniques. Chapter 10 has been reworked to focus more specifically on validation measures.

Part IV is new and is focused on providing management with specific strategies that can be used to help the organization behave in a more predictable manner, thus significantly improving the effectiveness of software V&V activities. Chapter 12 provides an introduction and economic motivation. The topic of balancing quality, features, and schedule is discussed in Chapter 13. Chapter 14 presents the yellow sticky method—a technique for estimating tasks and building realistic schedules. Chapter 15 discusses issues related to balancing the needs of people, process, and product. Techniques for managing commitment and risk are discussed in Chapter 16.

In addition to Part IV, five new appendixes have been added.

Reference

[1]   Yourdon, E., *Rise and Resurrection of the American Programmer*, Upper Saddle River, NJ: Prentice-Hall PTR, 1998.

Acknowledgments

The notion of Predictable Software Development evolved from discussions I've had with my friend and colleague Len Race. His insight into business processes and his ability to "get things done" is simply uncanny.

I would also like to acknowledge the staff at Artech House. I am indebted to Tim Pitts, Ruth Young, Judi Stone, Jen Kelland, and others unbeknownst to me for helping me through the publishing process. They have provided a constant source of patience and encouragement.

Steven R. Rakitin
Upton, Massachusetts
July 2001

Part I
Introduction

The objective of Part I is to provide context for the situation that many software organizations find themselves in. Chapter 1 provides an overview of the so-called software crisis, and what has been and is being done about it. Chapter 1 also introduces a topic intended primarily for managers and executives—understanding the nature of software development. This topic is covered in depth in Part IV.

In Chapter 2, several life-cycle models are discussed. The objective of this discussion is to provide an overall framework for understanding how software V&V activities can be woven into the software development process.

The importance of having a written software development process is discussed in Chapter 3.

As with any business activity, verification and validation must be justified from an economic perspective. Chapter 4 concludes Part I with an economic justification of software V&V.

1

1

Software in Perspective

> We rely on software, and sometimes it fails us. Some of those failures are
> nuisances; some are disasters. It is not news that technology presents
> unique risks. Adding software to a system may make the service it pro-
> vides cheaper, more generally available, or more adaptable to change,
> but it will not make it more reliable. [1]

In the twentieth century we witnessed an explosion of technology based on
advanced hardware and exotic software. From implantable pacemakers to
Mars probes, this combination of hardware and software has led to some of
the most astonishing accomplishments and stunning failures over the past
half-century.

But has our seemingly insatiable appetite for technologically advanced
products outpaced our ability to produce such products? If so, how did this
happen and what has the software industry done to mitigate the conse-
quences of the situation?

1.1 The Software Crisis

The term "software crisis" was first used during the mid-1970s. The so-called
crisis was an acknowledgment that we had exceeded our capacity to develop
large, complex software-based systems with the software development technology of the time.

It was during the mid-1970s that, for the first time, the cost of software maintenance activities exceeded that of new software development. It was also during this time period that we saw the beginnings of what would become significant trends in later years: hardware costs declined dramatically while software costs continued to rise, and the number of projects that failed because of software grew substantially.

During this time, many people thought that if we only had better programming languages, we could pull ourselves out of the crisis. And so, the popularity of programming languages such as PL/1, Jovial, and APL increased. But still the failures persisted.

For example, there was the error in the navigation software used in the F-16 that caused the plane to flip over when it crossed the equator. There was the minuscule timing change made to the space shuttle software that caused the launch to abort in 1981 even after thousands of hours of testing by the most advanced software engineering team in the world. And sadly, there were at least two deaths from radiation overdoses directly attributable to a software bug in the Therac-25 Linear Accelerator [2].

In an attempt to avoid the problems associated with incorrectly translating requirements written in English into programs, much research was focused on formal languages for specifying requirements.

Formal specification languages (such as HAL/S) were developed to enable the creation of natural-language–based specifications. The idea was to develop requirements in the formal language and then feed the formal specification to a compiler, which would translate the formal specifications directly into a traditional programming language. Much of the software originally developed for the space shuttle orbiter was written in HAL/S.

Highly structured multitasking programming languages (such as Modula and Ada) were also developed to deal with those applications that had real-time, multitasking requirements.

In practice, the impact that programming languages have on overall software reliability is relatively small as compared with other factors. Programming languages such as PL/1, Jovial, and APL are not extensively used in commercial applications. Today, some of the most widely used programming languages include C, C++, and COBOL. Web applications are frequently developed using Java, Visual Basic, and variations of HTML. None of these languages were developed to address software reliability issues.

1.2 The Elusive Silver Bullet

By 1985, software engineering had come to be recognized as an engineering discipline unto itself. Many companies realized that they had to make significant improvements in the process they used to develop software if they were to remain competitive. By the mid-1980s, software had become an over-$300-billion industry.

Hardware costs continued to decline dramatically. New and powerful workstations were developed. These workstations and the networks of which they were a part provided the platform needed to commercialize computer-aided software engineering (CASE) tools. CASE tools implement a specific software development process (such as Yourdon's structured design, Ward-Mellor, or Hatley-Pirbhai). These tools provided software engineers with the ability to represent software designs in a graphical manner that is easy to maintain, cross-check, and most importantly, understand.

Many people thought that CASE tools were the silver bullet that would rescue the software industry from the software crisis. What happened instead was that many companies spent large sums of money on tools that were infrequently used. These tools implemented a process that frequently was not understood or was not consistent with the organization's software design process. We learned the hard way that there is no such thing as a silver bullet [3].

1.3 Other Attempts to Resolve the Crisis

There have been other attempts to resolve the software crisis, most of which have met with little or moderate success.

1.3.1 Formal Proof of Correctness

Formal proofs of correctness were an attempt to use mathematics to prove that programs were correct. By viewing a program as a mathematical object, it would be possible to demonstrate that a program was correct in a mathematical sense. This is possible since programming languages are based on rigorous rules of syntax and semantics.

This approach was most interesting to mathematicians. While it sounded good on paper, in practice its value was limited, because a formal proof cannot be applied until after the code is written. By then, it is usually too late. It was also very difficult to develop proofs for large programs.

1.3.2   Independent Verification and Validation

NASA and the U.S. Department of Defense (DoD) pioneered the use of an independent third party (usually a separate company) to review the software development work of the prime contractor on mission-critical projects. The independent verification and validation (IV&V) contractor reports directly to the customer, as does the prime contractor, and usually performs a variety of tasks, such as requirements analysis, requirements tracing, architecture review, design review, code inspections, and validation testing.

IV&V can be very effective, but it is prohibitively expensive on all but the most critical of applications, such as the flight control software for the space shuttle and software for implantable pacemakers.

1.3.3   Software Quality Assurance

For most software, it is not possible to justify the cost of an independent IV&V contractor. Many companies have established a software quality assurance (SQA) function as a sort of internal IV&V group. SQA groups typically perform many of the same types of activities performed as part of an IV&V effort.

SQA has been widely accepted as a practical, cost-effective way to improve software quality. Internal SQA groups have been shown to be effective in improving quality when SQA is viewed more broadly than as just a testing function. However, there is inconsistency in how SQA is implemented across companies, which has resulted in inconclusive results.

1.3.4   Cleanroom Process

Dr. Harlan Mills, formerly of IBM Federal Systems Division and a software process visionary, developed the cleanroom process. This process [4] combines formal program verification with statistical process control (SPC). Using this methodology, the first priority is defect prevention using mathematical proofs of correctness instead of debugging. Mean time between failures (MTBF) is used as a measure of software quality.

The cleanroom process is relatively new and has not yet gained wide acceptance. It requires significant changes in management and technical aspects of software development (specifically, knowledge of SPC as applied to software), which will further delay its acceptance.

1.4 Understanding the Nature of Software

The prevailing attitude that seems to exist in the executive ranks of many software organizations goes something like this: "We have been very successful (financially) by developing software the way we do. Why should we change? And besides, quality doesn't sell product. Features do."

As you may recall, automotive industry executives during the 1960s and 1970s had a similar attitude about their products. And we all know what happened in that industry.

> [A]chieving high software quality levels is one of the most effective business strategies that a company can follow. High quality will benefit user-satisfaction, employee morale, costs, schedules, and competitiveness. Nothing else is so pervasive. Conversely, poor quality is a drain on expenses, damages worker performance, annoys or alienates clients, and in extreme conditions can lead to litigation, bankruptcy, or both. [5]

The trend to increase productivity and quality in software development has begun to take hold—especially in those countries seeking to establish themselves as cost-effective alternatives to developing software in the United States. For example, Ed Yourdon reports that a division of Motorola in Bangalore, India, was one of the first organizations to achieve Level 5 on the Software Engineering Institute's (SEI) Capability Maturity Model (CMM^{SM}). Further, he reports that "[w]hile there have been good and bad software organizations in every corner of the world all along, many of the ambitious software organizations in countries like India are eager to obtain international recognition for their high-quality work so they can compete more effectively" [6].

Within the typical software organization, most senior executives do not fully understand how good software should be developed. More important, most senior executives and managers don't understand how the project team views the quality of the product they build. As described by DeMarco and Lister:

> We managers tend to think of quality as just another attribute of the product, something that may be supplied in varying degrees according to the needs of the marketplace.

The builders' view of quality, on the other hand, is very different. Since their self-esteem is strongly tied to the quality of the product, they tend to impose quality standards of their own. The minimum that will satisfy them is more or less the best quality they have achieved in the past. This is invariably a higher standard than what the market requires and is willing to pay for. [7]

As managers, we must rethink the importance of product quality and time to market. Quality is not only vitally important to our customers but it is important to employees as well as to the bottom line. Yes, features do sell products, but only if they actually work!

1.5   Software Process Improvement Initiatives

There have been significant strides made in improving software quality and reliability. Several initiatives aimed at improving the process of developing software are beginning to show positive results. Some of these initiatives are described here.

1.5.1   SEI Capability Maturity Model (CMM^{SM})

The CMM^{SM} provides a basis for appraising and improving software development. Through appraisals and assessments, the CMM^{SM} provides a model that organizations can use to improve their software development practices.

> The CMM supports measurement of the software process by providing a framework for performing reliable and consistent appraisals. Although humans cannot be removed from the appraisal process, the CMM provides a basis for objectivity.
>
> The CMM builds upon a set of processes and practices that have been developed in .0collaboration with a broad selection of practitioners.
>
> Basing improvement efforts on a model is not without its risks, however. In the words of George Box, "All models are wrong; some models are useful." Models are simplifications of the real world they represent, and the CMM is not an exhaustive description of the software development process. It is not comprehensive; it only touches on other, non-process factors, such as people and technology, that affect the success of software projects. [8]

Recognizing the need to address people-issues within the context of software development, Watts Humphrey [9] published his landmark work on the personal software process (PSP) and the SEI developed the Team Software Process (TSP^{SM}). In addition, the SEI has compared the CMM^{SM} to the ISO-9000 series of standards [10], and has reported on commonly applied methods for software process improvement [11].

1.5.2 ISO SPICE

The ISO SPICE project [12, 13] is an international collaboration involving 14 nations. The objective is to produce a standard for software process assessment based on rapid development program and industry trials.

The standard, ISO/IEC TR 15504, consists of nine parts and was published by the International Standards Organization (ISO) in July 1998/May 1999 as a technical report (type 2). It has since been adopted as a national standard by a number of countries, including the United Kingdom and Australia. Translations into French and Spanish have been published, and a translation into Japanese is in progress.

The standard provides a structure approach for the assessment of software processes for the following purposes:

a) by or on behalf of an organization with the objective of understanding the state of its own processes for process improvement

b) by or on behalf of an organization with the objective of determining the suitability of its own processes for a particular requirement or class of requirements

c) by or on behalf of an organization with the objective of determining the suitability of another organization's processes for a particular contract or class of contracts.

The framework for process assessment:

a) encourages self-assessment

b) takes into account the context in which the assessed processes operate

c) produces a set of process ratings (a process profile) rather than a pass/fail result

d) through the generic practices, addresses the adequacy of the management of the assessed processes

e) is appropriate across all application domains and sizes of organizations. [9]

1.5.3 Bootstrap

The Bootstrap project [14] is a European initiative aimed at overcoming the deficiencies in the SEI CMM^{SM}. The Bootstrap approach analyzes the current state of software technology used in industry and provides motivation for accepting new contexts for software engineering.

The Bootstrap methodology is fully aligned with ISO-9000 and is consistent with the SEI CMM^{SM}. However, it provides important profiles detailing the maturity of each major aspect of software development both at an organization and individual project level.

Bootstrap was designed to accommodate diversity in approaches and methods used by software organizations in different industries. It provides a framework for evaluation based on the priorities, type, and objectives of the organization, and provides a detailed plan for improving the development processes and overall software quality.

The focus of Bootstrap and the supported goals of the method are:

- Valuation of the capability level on the software producing unit (SPU) and project level;

- Comparison of capability levels between the projects and the SPU;

- Benchmarking the capability level against the European mean value;

- Identifying the main strengths and weaknesses of the company;

- Support for defining adequate business goals;

- Defining and implementing an improvement plan.

The main characteristics of the method are:

- It is suitable for small and big enterprises;

- It is supported by experienced assessors and adequate tools;

- Assessor qualification and knowledge is controlled by the Bootstrap Institute;

- Benchmarking is conducted against other companies in the same business sector;

- There is support in using the results to start with the process improvement.

To support efficient software process improvement, the Bootstrap methodology includes two major models to realize the assessment and the improvement process: (1) assessment scheme, and (2) process model. One result of a Bootstrap assessment is a detailed analysis of the capability level of the company and the projects. Based on this detailed analysis, the assessment generates the first-draft version of an improvement plan, which can be used to plan and realize the process improvement steps toward higher maturity.

1.5.4 ISO 12207

ISO 12207 is an international standard on software lifecycle processes. The purpose of the standard is to establish a "common framework for software life-cycle processes, with well-defined terminology, that can be referenced by the software industry" [15].

The standard identifies three groups of processes: Primary Life-cycle Processes, Supporting Life-cycle Processes, and Organizational Life-cycle Processes, as illustrated in Table 1.1.

The standard provides definitions of terminology and a process that can be used to define, control, and improve software life-cycle processes.

1.5.5 Trillium

Trillium [16] is a software assessment model developed by Bell Canada to assess the software product development processes of potential software suppliers in order to minimize risks and ensure timely delivery.

Table 1.1
ISO 12207 Life-cycle Processes [15]

Primary life-cycle processes	Supporting life-cycle processes	Organizational life-cycle processes
Acquisition	Documentation	Management
Supply	Configuration Management	Infrastructure
Development	Quality Assurance	Improvement
Operation	Verification	Training
Maintenance	Validation	
	Joint Review	
	Audit	
	Problem Resolution	

This model and its accompanying tools are not in themselves a product development process or life-cycle model. Rather, the Trillium model provides key industry practices that can be used to improve an existing process or life cycle.

The practices in the Trillium model are derived from a benchmarking exercise focused on all practices that would contribute to an organization's product development and support capability. Trillium:

- Has a telecommunications orientation;

- Provides a customer focus;

- Provides a product perspective;

- Covers ISO, Bellcore, Malcolm Baldrige, IEEE, and IEC standards;

- Includes technological maturity;

- Includes additional Trillium-specific practices;

- Provides a road map approach, which sequences improvements by maturity.

These are a few of the numerous software process improvement initiatives that are reshaping software engineering. Additional information on all of these initiatives can be found on the World Wide Web.

1.6   Summary

Now that the Software Crisis will soon celebrate its silver anniversary, it's time we recognized that this is not a crisis, it's a situation: software has bugs. It is in its nature to have bugs, and that fact is unlikely to change soon. [1]

The experience of the last 25 or so years has resulted in an overemphasis on programming skills to the detriment of such critical skills as requirements analysis and definition, architecture and design, and software verification and validation. What the software industry has (it is hoped) learned as a result of the software crisis is that the key to developing higher-quality software lies in a focus on the process. As observed by Dr. Edwards Deming, "The quality of a product is directly related to the quality of the process used to create it" [17].

References

[1] Weiner, L. R., *Digital Woes: Why We Should Not Depend on Software,* Reading, MA: Addison-Wesley, 1993, pp. 4–15.

[2] Leveson, N. G, and C. S. Turner, "An Investigation of the Therac-25 Accidents," *IEEE Computer,* July 1993, pp. 18–41.

[3] Brooks, F. P., "No Silver Bullet: Essence and Accidents of Software Engineering," *IEEE Computer,* April 1987, pp. 10–19.

[4] Dyer, M., *The Cleanroom Approach to Quality Software Development,* New York: Wiley, 1992.

[5] Jones, C., *Software Quality: Analysis and Guidelines for Success,* Boston, MA: International Thomson Computer Press, 1997.

[6] Yourdon, E., *Rise and Resurrection of the American Programmer,* Upper Saddle River, NJ: Prentice-Hall PTR, 1998.

[7] Marco, T., and T. Lister, *Peopleware: Productive Projects and Teams,* New York: Dorset House, 1977.

[8] Paulk, M. C., et al., *The Capability Maturity Model: Guidelines for Improving the Software Process,* Reading, MA: Addison-Wesley, 1995.

[9] Humphrey, W., *A Discipline for Software Engineering,* Reading, MA: Addison-Wesley, 1995.

[10] Paulk, M. C., "A Comparison of ISO 9001 and the Capability Maturity Model for Software," CMU/SEI-94-TR-12, SEI, 1994.

[11] Austin, R., and D. Paulish, "A Survey of Commonly Applied Methods for Software Improvement," CMU/SEI-93-TR-27, SEI, 1993.

[12] Dorling, A., "SPICE: Software Process Improvement and Capability Determination," *Software Quality Journal,* Vol. 2, 1993, pp. 209–224.

[13] SPICE Consolidated Product, Software Process Assessment, Part 1: Concepts and Introductory Guide, Version 1.00.

[14] Haase, V., et al., "Bootstrap: Fine-tuning Process Assessment," *IEEE Software,* July 1994, pp. 25–35.

[15] International Standard ISO/IEC 12207:1995, Information Technology—Software Life-cycle Processes, 1995.

[16] Coallier, F., "TRILLIUM: A Model for the Assessment of Telecom Product Development and Support Capability," *IEEE TCSE Software Process Newsletter,* Winter 1995.

[17] Deming, W. E., *Out of the Crisis,* Cambridge, MA: MIT Center for Advanced Engineering Study, 1982.

Web Resources

ISO SPICE Standard

For the most up-to-date information on SPICE and related topics, visit the following SPICE Web sites:

- http://www.sasqag.org/spice/index.html
- http://www.sqi.gu.edu.au/spice
- http://www.spiceworld.hm/

The nine parts of the SPICE standard are:

- ISO/IEC TR 15504-1:1998 Information technology—Software process assessment Part 1: Concepts and introductory guide;
- ISO/IEC TR 15504-2:1998 Information technology—Software process assessment Part 2: A reference model for processes and process capability;
- ISO/IEC TR 15504-3:1998 Information technology—Software process assessment Part 3: Performing an assessment;
- ISO/IEC TR 15504-4:1998 Information technology—Software process assessment Part 4: Guide to performing assessments;
- ISO/IEC TR 15504-5:1998 Information technology—Software process assessment Part 5: assessment model and indicator guidance;
- ISO/IEC TR 15504-6:1998 Information technology—Software process assessment Part 6: Guide to competency of assessors;
- ISO/IEC TR 15504-7:1998 Information technology—Software process assessment Part 7: Guide for use in process improvement;
- ISO/IEC TR 15504-8:1998 Information technology—Software process assessment Part 8: Guide for use in determining supplier process capability;
- ISO/IEC TR 15504-9:1998 Information technology—Software process assessment Part 9: Vocabulary.

Bootstrap Methodology

Visit the Bootstrap Institute Web site at:

- http://www.bootstrap-institute.com

TRILLIUM Model

Visit the TRILLIUM Web site at:

- http://www2.umassd.edu/swpi/BellCanada/trillium-html/trillium.html

Personal Software Process or Team Software Process

Visit the SEI Web site at:

- http://www.sei.cmu.edu/tsp/

Note: URLs cited were accurate as of April 2001.

2

Software Development Life-Cycle Models

Software development organizations all follow some process when developing a software product. In immature organizations, the process is usually dependent on a few individuals, it is not written down, or if it is written down, it is not followed. In more mature organizations, the process is written down, it is followed, and it is actively managed. Actively managing a process means that the process is dynamic rather than static, that its effectiveness is measured on a regular basis, and that the results of process effectiveness measures are used to drive process improvements. As discussed further in Chapter 15, a written software development process that is consistently followed and actively managed is a key component of predictable software development, a topic that is the focus of Part IV.

Selecting a life-cycle model is the most important aspect of creating a software development process. The life-cycle model selected has a significant impact on quality, time to market, initial development cost, and long-term support cost. Large applications can take hundreds of person-years of effort to develop and may remain in active use by customers for several years. As a result, costs incurred by the organization responsible for maintenance and support will be directly related to the robustness of the design and completeness of the documentation.

For the new generation of Web applications being developed on Internet time (weeks and months as opposed to months and years), the need for

17

the software development process is just as important as for large applications. As noted by Pressman:

> About every 10 years or so, a major new software-related technology captures the industry's consciousness. Avant garde software folks claim it as their own, and in so doing, become the darlings of the technological scene. High salaries, considerable prestige, and no small amount of hubris are sure to follow. The corps of avant garde adherents argue that the new technology is truly different, requiring a new paradigm. The ways of the past simply don't apply. In fact, the old ways can't possibly be adapted to a new set of business rules and technological realities. As a result, the avant garde reject the disciplines of the generation that preceded them, but ironically, adopt approaches that failed miserably a few generations back. The Internet and the vast array of applications that it has spawned are undoubtedly a major new software-related technology. I won't bore you with the obvious cliches; suffice it to say that the Internet and the WebApps that populate it are big—very big—and that their impact is profound. What worries me is that this major new technology has become a breeding ground for important WebApps that are hacked in much the same way as important application software was hacked a few generations back—in the 1960s and 1970s. [1]

In this chapter we will review several software development life-cycle models as a way of providing the context for software V&V activities and also to highlight some of the strengths and weaknesses of each model.

2.1 The Waterfall Model

The waterfall model, shown in Figure 2.1, is the most familiar model. During the requirements analysis phase, basic market research is performed and potential customer requirements are identified, evaluated, and refined. The result of this phase of the process is usually a marketing requirement or product concept specification (hereafter referred to as a concept specification). This document is usually prepared by product marketing with some participation from software engineering. Requirements in the concept specification are usually stated in the customer's language.

The concept specification is usually written at a very high level and requires further refinement and definition for it to be useful for software development. This is the focus of the requirements definition phase of the waterfall model. Requirements in the concept specification are reviewed and

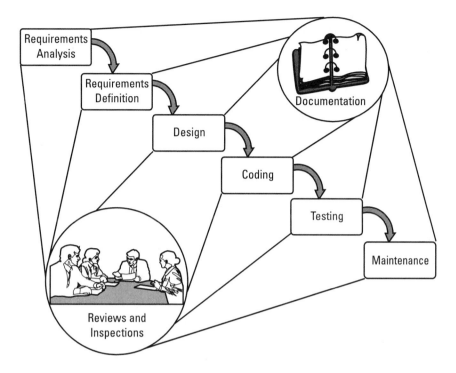

Figure 2.1 The waterfall life-cycle model.

analyzed by software engineers in order to more fully develop and refine the requirements contained in the concept specification.

Requirements from the concept specification must be restated in the software developer's language. For example, a requirement that frequently appears in concept specifications is that the "software must be user-friendly." This requirement must be restated into measurable terms meaningful to software engineers. It might be restated as: "An untrained user must be able to successfully perform [some function the software provides] within [some number of] minutes." The requirements definition phase results in a document called the software requirements specification (SRS) [2].

Once the SRS is developed, software engineers should have a complete description of the requirements the software must implement. This enables software engineers to begin the design phase. It is during this phase that the overall software architecture is defined and the high-level and detailed design work is performed. This work is documented in the software design description (SDD) [3].

The information contained in the SDD should be sufficient to begin to the coding phase. During this phase, the design is transformed or implemented in code. If the SDD is complete, the coding phase proceeds smoothly, since all of the information needed by software engineers is contained in the SDD.

According to the waterfall model, the testing phase begins when the coding phase is completed. Tests are developed based on information contained in the SRS and the SDD. These tests determine if the software meets defined requirements. A software validation test plan [4] is written which defines the overall validation testing process. Individual test procedures are developed based on a logical breakdown of requirements. The results of the testing activities are usually documented in a software validation test report. Following the successful completion of software validation testing, the product may be shipped to customers.

Once the product is being shipped, the maintenance phase begins. This phase lasts until the support for the product is discontinued. Many of the same activities performed during the development phases are also performed during the maintenance phase. It is a good idea to write a software maintenance plan to describe how these activities will be performed.

Some of the advantages of the waterfall model are:

- It is easy to understand.
- It is widely used.
- It reinforces the notions of define-before-design and design-before-code.
- It identifies when deliverables are produced and when reviews and inspections are held.

Some of the disadvantages of the waterfall model are:

- In reality, few projects ever follow the model.
- It does not reflect the iterative nature of software development.
- It is unrealistic to expect complete and accurate requirements early in the process.
- Working software is not available until relatively late in the process, thus delaying discovery of serious errors.
- It does not incorporate any kind of risk assessment.

2.2   Concurrent Development Model

The concurrent development model, shown in Figure 2.2, is well suited for rapid, flexible development. This model shares some attributes with the synchronize-and-stabilize [5] model that has evolved from companies such as Microsoft and Netscape.

In this model, the SRS is the starting point for development of both software and tests. Developers and software QA engineers work concurrently to develop and test the software. In the synchronize-and-stabilize model, the project team begins with the product vision, a vague description of what the product should do. An SRS evolves over the course of the project from this product vision.

The key attribute of this model is that developers and QA work concurrently. As bits of the product are developed, they are immediately tested and feedback is provided to developers. In the synchronize-and-stabilize model, this usually occurs about three times during the project. In the model illustrated in Figure 2.2, it can occur as many times as appropriate, determined by the project team. Also, the model illustrated in Figure 2.2 has something that the synchronize-and-stabilize model doesn't—the formal validation phase. During this phase, all of the tests that were run during the informal validation phase are repeated one more time on the completed product. The main difference between the informal and formal validation phases has to do with changes. During informal validation, developers are free to change whatever is required to meet the SRS. During formal validation, the only changes that are permitted are changes in response to bugs reported. No new features are allowed during this time. Why? Because adding new features at such a late stage would essentially invalidate all of the testing that was performed previously.

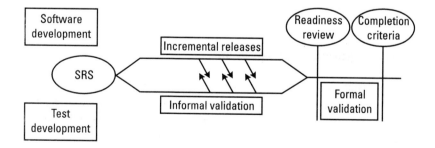

Figure 2.2 Concurrent development life-cycle model.

Another difference between the model illustrated in Figure 2.2 and the synchronize-and-stabilize model has to do with having objective criteria defined for starting formal validation testing and for completing formal validation testing.

Some of the more important differences between this model and the waterfall model are that:

- Development and testing are performed concurrently rather than sequentially.
- Multiple baselines are included as part of the process.
- There are defined criteria for starting and stopping formal validation testing.

Some of the advantages of the concurrent model are:

- It is flexible—the project team can decide when and how many incremental releases to create and test.
- Feedback from testing is immediate.
- No new features are added at the last minute.
- Formal validation testing is uneventful and predictable, since most of the bugs have already been found and fixed.

Some of the disadvantages of this model are:

- It requires that an SRS be written and maintained as the product features evolve.
- It requires discipline to ensure that features are not added late into the project.

2.3   The Rapid Prototyping Model

In many instances, companies build software for customers who are not exactly sure of what they want or need. By using a prototyping approach similar to that shown in Figure 2.3, the customer can assess the prototype and provide feedback as to its suitability for a particular application. The prototype can range from a paper schematic all the way to a working system that includes both hardware and software.

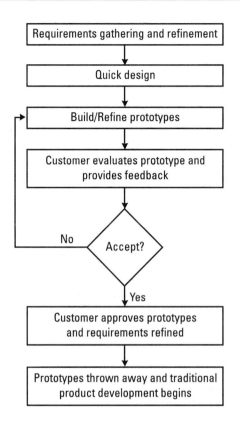

Figure 2.3 Rapid prototyping life-cycle model.

The rapid prototyping model begins with a requirements-gathering stage whereby the developers collect and refine product requirements based on whatever information or sources are available. Then, a rapid prototype is developed. This prototype is intended to be used for requirements exploration only. It is not intended to be the product. Little or no documentation may be produced for this prototype. Customers can then evaluate and critique the prototype, providing the developers with insight into what they really want. Based on this evaluation, the prototype may be refined and evaluated again. This process continues until the customer and developers agree that they have a good definition of the requirements.

The next step in the process requires that the prototype be thrown away; once the requirements are understood, the product can be developed using a more traditional, structured approach, such as the waterfall model.

Some of the advantages of this model are:

- Users own the requirements; this reduces the likelihood of misunderstanding or misinterpretation.
- It instills confidence that you are building the right product.
- For those situations where customers do not know exactly what they need, this model provides a means for requirements discovery.

Some of the disadvantages of this model are:

- Typically, instead of the prototype being thrown away, it becomes the product. Depending on how the prototype was developed, this can result in major problems for long-term support and maintenance of the product.
- This model requires extensive participation and involvement of customers, which isn't always possible.
- Software validation can be difficult, since requirements are not usually well documented.

2.4   The Spiral Model

The spiral model attempts to build on the benefits of the rapid prototyping and traditional structured development models, such as the waterfall model. Dr. Barry Boehm developed the model, shown in Figure 2.4. The spiral model adds two new concepts to software development models—risk analysis and cost.

The model can be viewed as consisting of four basic activities that correspond to the four quadrants of Figure 2.4. These are:

- Planning;
- Risk analysis;
- Development;
- Assessment.

The radial dimension of Figure 2.4 represents increasing costs. Each path around the spiral is indicative of increased costs. Also, many of the same activities are repeated during each trip around the spiral, which reflects the iterative nature of software development.

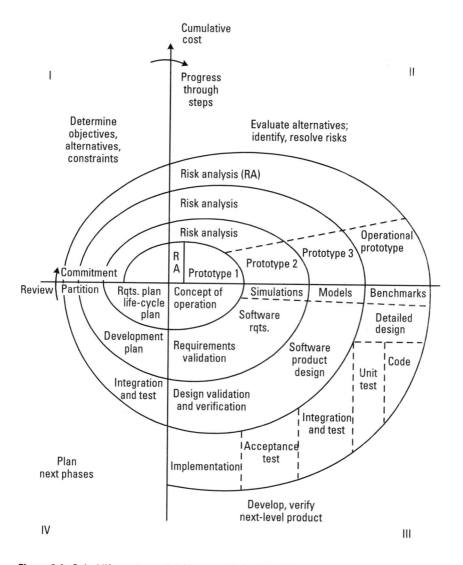

Figure 2.4 Spiral life-cycle model. (*Source*: [6] © 1988, IEEE. Reprinted with permission.)

During the first trip around the spiral, planning is performed, risks are analyzed, prototypes are built, and customers evaluate the prototype. Table 2.1 includes a summary by Boehm of the most commonly encountered risks and suggested risk-management techniques [6]. Risk management is discussed in more detail in Chapter 16.

Table 2.1
Commonly Encountered Risks and Risk-Management Techniques [6]

Risk	Risk-Management Technique
Personnel shortfalls	Staffing with top talent; job matching; team building; cross-training; prescheduling; key people; morale building
Unrealistic schedules and budgets	Detailed, multisource cost and schedule estimation; design to cost; incremental development; software reuse; requirements scrubbing
Developing the wrong software functions	Organization analysis; mission analysis; operational-concept formulation; user surveys; prototyping; early users' manuals
Developing the wrong user interface	Task analysis; prototyping; scenarios; user characterization (functionality, style, workload)
Gold plating	Requirements scrubbing; prototyping; cost-benefit analysis; design to cost
Continuing stream of requirement changes	High change threshold; information hiding; incremental development (defer changes to later increments)
Shortfalls in externally furnished components	Benchmarking; inspections; reference checking; compatibility analysis
Shortfalls in externally performed tasks	Reference checking; preaward audits; award-fee contracts; competitive design or prototyping; team building
Real-time performance shortfalls	Simulation; benchmarking; modeling; prototyping; instrumentation; tuning
Straining computer-science capabilities	Technical analysis; cost-benefit analysis; prototyping; reference checking

During the second trip around, a more refined prototype is built, requirements are documented and validated, and customers are involved in assessing the new prototype. By the time the third trip around begins, risks are known, and a somewhat more traditional development approach is taken.

Some of the advantages of this model are:

- It incorporates the iterative nature of software development, and therefore it represents the most realistic approach.
- It incorporates all of the advantages of both the waterfall model and the rapid prototyping model.

Some of the disadvantages are:

- It requires expertise in risk analysis.
- If a significant risk is overlooked, major problems could result.
- It is not well understood by nontechnical management and has not been widely used.

2.5   Hybrid Models

Hybrid models are based on combining aspects of two or more models. Many hybrid models, such as the one shown in Figure 2.5, are based on using so-called fourth-generation techniques (4GT), which consist of a wide array of tools that enable software engineers to depict software characteristics at a very high level.

In those instances where requirements are reasonably well known, developers can follow the left-most path of the model. Where requirements are not well known, developers can employ the rapid prototyping techniques. The hybrid model allows the flexibility to pick and choose the development model that best suits the particular situation.

Some of the advantages of this model are:

- It enables developers to choose the model that best fits the situation.
- It has all of the advantages of each model it encompasses.

Some of the disadvantages are:

- It is not widely understood or recognized.
- It has all of the disadvantages of each model it encompasses.

2.6   Model-Based Development

Several model-based development approaches have recently been introduced to help design and implement client/server and Graphical User Interface or GUI-based applications. An example of model-based development is shown in Figure 2.6. This approach is most applicable to a wide variety of business or information systems (IS) software.

Some of the advantages of this approach are:

- It is closely tied to specific business processes.

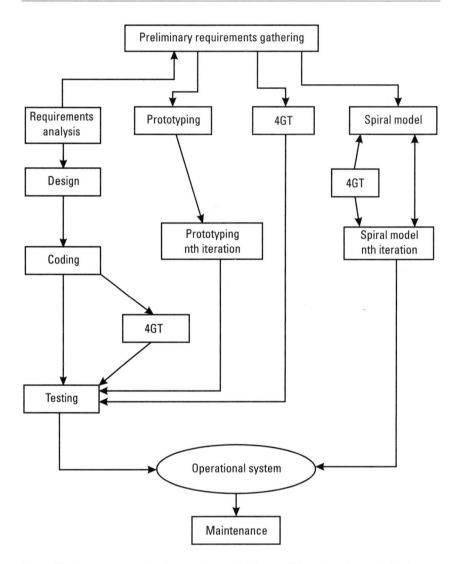

Figure 2.5 Fourth-generation life-cycle model. (*Source*: [7], used with permission.)

- It clearly delineates client and server applications.
- Tools are available to support the use of these models.
- It includes a style guide for the GUI.

Some of the disadvantages are:

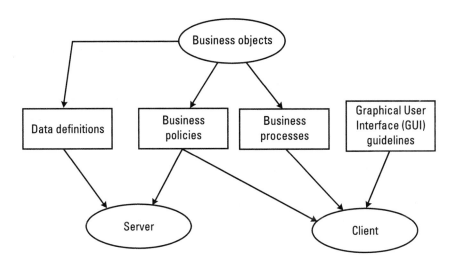

Figure 2.6 Model-based development.

- It does not include a structured development approach.
- It does not reference specific documents, deliverables, or reviews.

Further information on model-based development is available from the SEI [8].

2.7   Object-Oriented Models

When object-oriented (OO) techniques first appeared, the emphasis was on programming languages, followed by design and, later, analysis. Recently, attention has focused on OO lifecycle methodologies. While this work is still evolving, there are a few OO methodologies that are currently being used. Most of these methodologies emphasize the incremental, iterative, and concurrent nature of software development. Since classes and objects are used throughout the OO software development lifecycle, the process is "often referred to as seamless, meaning there is no conceptual gap between the phases as is often the case with other software development methodologies, such as the analysis (using Data Flow Diagrams) to design (structure charts) to programming gaps found in traditional structured analysis and design. Seamlessness together with naturalness is a big advantage for consistency"[9].

An example of a recently developed OO methodology is the Rational Unified Process (RUP). RUP is a product process developed by Rational Software Corporation [10] that provides project teams with a guide to more effective use of the industry-standard Unified Modeling Language (UML). RUP also provides software-engineering best practices through templates, guidelines, and tools. Most of the tools are, as you might guess, also provided by Rational. The RUP is based on four consecutive phases, as shown in Figure 2.7.

The purpose of the inception phase is to establish the business case for the project. This is done by creating several high-level use case diagrams, defining success criteria, risk assessment, resource estimate, and an overall plan showing the four phases and their approximate time frames. Some deliverables the inception phase might include are:

- A vision statement;
- An initial set of use cases;
- An initial business case;
- An initial risk assessment;
- An initial project plan;
- Prototypes.

The purpose of the elaboration phase is to analyze the problem domain, establish the overall product architecture, eliminate the highest risks, and refine the project plan. Evolutionary prototypes (as well as throwaway prototypes) are developed to mitigate risks and address technical issues and business concerns (such as investors or key customers). Some key deliverables this phase might include are:

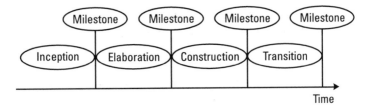

Figure 2.7 Rational Unified Process model.

- A relatively complete use case model supplemented with text as appropriate;
- Architecture description;
- Revised risk assessment;
- Revised project plan;
- Initial development plan;
- Initial user manual;

During the construction phase, the remaining components are developed, integrated, and thoroughly tested. Key deliverables from this phase include:

- Software product operating on target platform;
- Revised user manual;
- Complete description of current release.

The purpose of the transition phase is to transition the product from development to the user community. Activities that would typically be performed include:

- Beta testing by users;
- Conversion of existing information to new environment;
- Training of users;
- Product rollout.

In addition to these four phases, the RUP also incorporates the following six best practices:

1. Iterative software development;
2. Requirements management;
3. Component-based architectures;
4. Visual software modeling;
5. Software quality verification;
6. Change control.

Not surprisingly, several of these best practices are tightly coupled with tools developed by Rational.

Some of the advantages of this approach are:

- It incorporates an iterative development model.
- It incorporates requirements management and change control.
- It is based on industry-standard UML and component-based modeling.

Some of the disadvantages are:

- Training in risk assessment and mitigation techniques is required to reap the benefits of iterative development.
- To take full advantage of the model, Rational's software development tools must be used.

2.8   Summary

Choosing a software life-cycle model is a difficult task. The life-cycle model can have far-reaching implications that go well beyond the software development process and extend into the product support and maintenance phase. Recall that the lifetime of a typical software product can be from two to five times as long as the development time. The ability of your maintenance and support organization to provide cost-effective software updates and feature enhancements is directly related to the life-cycle model and the software development process used to develop the product.

References

[1]   Pressman, R. E., "What a Tangled Web We Weave," *IEEE Software*, January/February 2000, pp. 18–21.

[2]   ANSI/IEEE Standard 830-1998, IEEE Recommended Practice for Software Requirements Specifications.

[3]   ANSI/IEEE Standard 1016-1998, IEEE Recommended Practice for Software Design Descriptions.

[4]   ANSI/IEEE Standard 1012-1998, IEEE Standard for Software Verification and Validation Plans.

[5] Cusumano, M. A., and D. B. Yoffe, "Software Development on Internet Time," *IEEE Computer*, October 1999, pp. 60–69.

[6] Boehm, B., "A Spiral Model for Software Development and Enhancement," *IEEE Computer*, Vol. 21, 1988, pp. 61–72.

[7] Pressman, R., *Software Engineering: A Practitioner's Approach*, New York: McGraw-Hill, 3rd ed., 1992.

[8] Withey, J. V. "Implementing Model Based Software Engineering in your Organization: An Approach to Domain Engineering," *CMU/SEI-94-TR-01*, Carnegie-Mellon University, Pittsburgh, PA, Software Engineering Institute, 1994.

[9] Object-orientation FAQ, available on the World Wide Web at http://www.cyberdyne-object-sys.com/oofaq2/index.htm (accessed February 2001).

[10] "Rational Unified Process: Best Practices for Software Development Teams," Rational Software Corp. White Paper, available at http://www.rational.com/products/whitepapers (accessed February 2001).

Note: URLs cited were accurate as of April 2001.

3

Software Development Process

For a manufacturing company, the key to improving quality is controlling variation. Controlling variation is achieved by having well-defined processes and by collecting data on actual variation. An example of a manufacturing parameter that can vary is tolerance. To control tolerance to an acceptable level, limits are established. If the tolerance exceeds established limits, a root-cause analysis is performed to determine why the limits were exceeded. As a result of the root-cause analysis, corrective action is implemented which changes the process or adjusts the limits. The key points are: (1) the process is defined, (2) it is followed, and (3) products are constantly evaluated to ensure that they conform to established requirements.

Results of evaluations are used to drive process improvement. This concept is known as the Shewhart cycle, shown in Figure 3.1. It was developed by Walter Shewhart in the 1920s and put into practice as a result of the work of Dr. W. Edwards Deming [1, 2].

For software companies, the key to improving quality lies in applying the principles of the Shewhart cycle. Controlling variation—in the work performed by software engineers—is a challenge faced by most software development organizations. Software development organizations known for the high quality of their products (such as HP and Motorola) have learned how to measure and control variation. These organizations all have well-defined software development processes.

Issues regarding the software development process and its significance in improving software are presented in this chapter by way of a list of

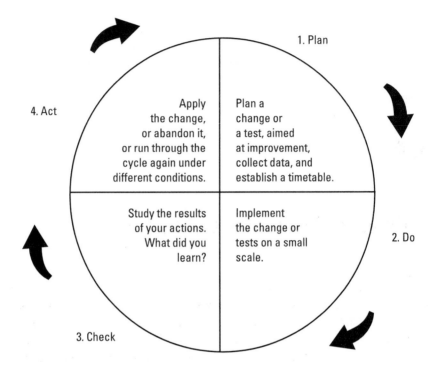

Figure 3.1 The Shewhart cycle.

frequently asked questions (FAQs). An example of a software development process based on the waterfall model is included in Appendix G. Outlines of some of the deliverables called out by this process are included in Appendix H.

3.1 Software Development Process FAQs

Why Must the Process Be Written?

A key attribute of a good process is that it is written. If the process is written, it can then be read, understood, questioned, communicated, and modified, and most importantly, improved. It is not possible to do all this when the process exists in someone's head. Writing down your process makes good business sense.

Much of the recent work in software quality and software process improvement has been focused on capability assessments (SEI CMM^{SM} [3]

and SPICE [4]), supplier capabilities (ISO [5], TickIT [6], and Trillium [7]), and software process improvement (ISO 12207 [8] and Bootstrap [9]). A written development process is a common thread that appears throughout all of these initiatives.

Won't a Written Process Stifle Creativity?

This concern is unfounded and stems from a lack of understanding of what a process is. A written process defines the mechanics of developing software. It does not define how software engineers do what they do. In fact, it can be argued that a good process allows software engineers more time to be creative, since they don't have to spend time thinking about the more mundane aspects of their job (like what information needs to be included in a software design description document).

In every other engineering discipline, processes and procedures have been developed based on good engineering practice and years of experience. These processes and procedures enable engineers to focus more of their time on developing creative and innovative products in a manner that ensures that the product can be successfully developed, manufactured, supported, and maintained. Written processes and procedures used in other engineering disciplines haven't stifled creativity.

As experience is gained from developing products, this experience can be factored into the process so that you can learn from past mistakes and achieve continuous process improvement. A written software development process provides a mechanism for building upon past experiences and avoiding making the same costly mistakes. A written process is a characteristic of mature software organizations and can have a significant effect on quality, development cost, schedule, and time to market.

Our Process Was Never Written Down, but It Seems to Work—Why Change It?

If you have an unwritten process that seems to work, then by all means—write it down! Putting a process on paper in no way changes your process. Writing the process down will make it easier to:

- Train new people in how your organization develops software;
- Improve product quality by making process improvements based on past mistakes and experience;
- Identify those areas where improvements are needed;
- Achieve predictable software development.

How Can the Software Engineering Manager Be Persuaded to Follow a Written Procedure?

Some managers like working in an environment where the process is undefined and undocumented. Unfortunately, this often leads to inefficiency and, many times, less than stellar product quality. So how do you convince someone that they should follow a written process? They can either come to this realization on their own or they can be directed to do this by their management. The latter case is discussed in detail in Part IV.

One way to help someone come to this realization is to build a case based on cost. Collect data from past projects that shows how much time and effort were spent developing, testing, and debugging the software. Some examples of metrics to collect are:

- Total lines of source code developed;

- Total software engineering person-hours spent;

- Number of bugs identified prerelease;

- Number of bugs identified postrelease;

- Total effort spent developing and executing tests;

- Find/fix time for bugs found prerelease;

- Find/fix time for bugs found postrelease.

Then propose that the software engineering manager and someone who represents software quality work together on developing a flexible process that could be used on the next project. The goal would be to make improvements based on the metrics you collected from past projects. The key is to work collaboratively and to remain flexible. Compromise is often the best solution.

How Can a Written Process Improve Software Quality?

By itself, a written software development process won't improve quality. The process must (1) be followed by everyone, (2) be flexible and changeable, (3) include metrics that measure process effectiveness and form the basis for changes to the process, and (4) be actively managed.

Once a software development process is in place, some of the intangible benefits that can be realized are:

1. It helps connect software engineering to other engineering disciplines within the R&D organization.

2. It helps establish a corporate memory on software development so that the organization can learn from past mistakes.

3. It helps improve the use of valuable resources by:

   a. Reinforcing the principles of predictable software development (discussed in Part IV);

   b. Providing a mechanism for learning from others;

   c. Allowing software engineers to spend more time solving problems requiring their creative energy;

   d. Reducing rework and allowing software engineers to move onto new projects sooner;

   e. Providing a training tool for new software engineers.

4. It can help increase the likelihood of successfully introducing new technology.

5. It provides consistency and lowers overall costs.

6. It provides a framework for continuous process improvement (the Shewhart cycle).

An extensive list of resources related to software process improvement can be found in the *Software Process Newsletter* [10] published by the IEEE Technical Council on Software Engineering, as well as the SEI's home page on the World Wide Web.

We Don't Have (or Don't Follow) a Written Procedure, and the Quality of Our Software Isn't Too Bad—Why Should We Change?

Customers will tolerate software that "isn't too bad" for just so long. Companies that develop leading-edge technology typically have a group of customers who are called early adopters. These customers are willing to accept lower quality software but only for a relatively short time. As the leading-edge technology becomes more widely accepted and integrated into competitors' products, the early adopters become mainstream customers. Product quality is a key factor in retaining the base of mainstream customers.

From experience, we as consumers know that we tend to tell many more people about an unhappy experience with a product than we tell about a happy one. The same holds for software.

What Is Software Quality Anyway?

Some of the many definitions of software quality that have been suggested are included in Section 13.1. Regardless of which definition you ascribe to, knowing your customers, what they need, and how they use your products are all part of the intangible attributes that collectively lead to software quality.

As we will see in Chapter 9, knowing your customers and how they use your products can play a key role in helping you test your software. Furthermore, tradeoffs between quality, features, and schedule represents one of the most important decisions that organizations typically make when developing software. This issue is discussed in detail in Chapter 13.

For a thorough discussion of software quality measures, refer to the SEI report on software quality measurement [11].

What Do We Do After We Write Down Our Current Process?

That depends on your organization. Are you satisfied with the quality (however you define quality) of the software you produce? More importantly, are your customers satisfied? If they aren't, how would you know? Do you typically have a large number of customer-reported bugs during the first few months following the release of a new software product or version? Are your products perceived to be significantly better than competitors' products? Based on the answers to these questions, you may need to look at ways you can improve the perceived quality of your product. Having a written process will help you do this. You can collect some process and product data that documents where you are now product-quality-wise, then make some process changes (for example, require that a software design description be written before coding begins, or institute code inspections), and see how the changes affect product quality.

How Can the Process Be Tailored to Suit the Needs of the Project Team?

Your software development process should be viewed as a framework. As part of each project, a software development project plan should be written. The purpose of this plan is to define in detail the specific tasks, activities, deliverables, and tools that will be required for the project. In this way, the software development process can be tailored to meet the specific needs of each project.

Deviations from the software development process need to be justified based on using good engineering judgment. Management, the product support organization, and the quality organization should be required to agree to all deviations from the software development process. In this way, you can provide flexibility in a manner that still retains appropriate checks and balances.

How Can Information Collected from Using the Process Be Used to Improve the Process?

By carefully selecting a set of appropriate process and product metrics (see Chapter 7), this data can be used to improve process and product quality. For example, data collected on the types of defects found during code inspections is an example of a process metric that could be used to improve your coding standards. Once common problems have been reflected back into the coding standards, they are much less likely to occur in the future. Similarly, data collected on the types of problems reported by customers is an example of a product metric that can be used to improve the software validation test suite to be more representative of actual customer use of the product. Including such tests in the test suite will increase the likelihood that similar types of problems will be caught and corrected before the product is released.

Who Is Responsible for Enforcing the Process?

Ideally, there should be no need for enforcement. Everyone should understand the value to the company derived by following the process. When the process is owned by the software development organization (meaning that software engineers were actively involved in developing the process), enforcement is not an issue. When software engineers are not involved in developing the process, enforcement is an issue.

Project managers should bear most of the responsibility of ensuring that the process is followed. The quality organization may have some oversight in this area, but viewing the quality organization as the enforcer diminishes its effectiveness in achieving the company's overall quality objectives.

Who Should Be the Keeper of the Process?

It is important that the mechanism for changing the software development process be clearly defined. Ideally, this responsibility should be shared by those who are bound to follow it in a manner that allows for input, discussion, assessment, and revision in a timely and controlled manner. Ownership is key.

3.2 Summary

A written software development process is essential to make significant improvements in software quality. The process needs to be written so that it can be read, understood, communicated, followed, and most importantly, improved. Having a written software development process enables software V&V activities to become woven into the fabric that defines a company's software development culture. A written software development process is a required element for predictable software development.

Ownership of the process by the software development organization is vitally important. Ownership will go a long way in ensuring that the process is followed. Measuring the effectiveness of the software development process should be standard practice. Use the data collected to drive improvements to the process. This approach is based on the principles of statistical process control, which have been successfully applied in many other engineering and manufacturing disciplines.

References

[1]   Shewhart, W., *Statistical Methods from the Viewpoint of Quality Control*, Washington, D.C.: U.S. Dept. of Agriculture, 1939; New York: Dover, 1968.

[2]   Deming, W. E., *Out of the Crisis*, Cambridge, MA: MIT Center for Advanced Engineering Study, 1982.

[3]   Paulk, M. C., et al., *The Capability Maturity Model: Guidelines for Improving the Software Process,* Reading, MA: Addison-Wesley, 1995.

[4]   Dorling, A., "SPICE: Software Process Improvement and Capability dEtermination," *Software Quality Journal,* Vol. 2, 1993, pp. 209–224.

[5]   ANSI/ISO/ASQ Q-9000-3-1997, Guidelines for the Application of ANSI/ISO/ASQ Q-9001-1994 to the Development, Supply, and Maintenance of Software, ASQC, 1997.

[6]   A Guide to Software Quality Management System Construction and Certification to ISO-9001 (TickIT Guide), Issue 4.0, January 1998, British Standards Institute, 1995.

[7]   Coallier, F., "TRILLIUM: A Model for the Assessment of Telecom Product Development and Support Capability," *IEEE TCSE Software Process Newsletter,* Winter 1995.

[8]   International Standard ISO/IEC 12207:1995, Information Technology—Software = lifecycle processes.

[9]   Haase, V., et al., "Bootstrap: Fine-Tuning Process Assessment," *IEEE Software,* July 1994, pp. 25–35.

[10] El Emam, K., ed., *Software Process Newsletter*, published by IEEE TCSE, No. 2, winter 1995.

[11] Florac, W., "Software Quality Measurement: A Framework for Counting Problems and Defects," CMU/SEI-TR-92-022, SEI, 1992.

4

Economic Justification

> Good Enough [quality] has nothing to do with mediocrity. It has to do
> with rational choices as opposed to compulsive behavior. [1]

In most organizations, the pressure to get products to market as quickly as possible is intense. Application development time frames that once took years are now compressed to months. In some markets, software products are refreshed every two to three months. For Web applications, the advent of Internet time has led to development cycles measured in days and weeks. As a result, many organizations are looking for ways to streamline the development process in order to meet increasing market pressures. And whether they recognize it or not, many organizations are making decisions related to product quality based on some notion that the product is good enough.

In today's highly competitive global economy, successful organizations have learned to make tradeoffs between time to market and time to profit. Time to market is a well-understood concept. Time to profit is not as well understood. This concept is illustrated by Figure 4.1.

Time to profit represents the time from when a product is released to the break-even point—the point at which the revenue stream generated by sales of the product exceeds the cost of maintaining and supporting the product.

When the software development organization is focused solely on time-to-market goals, the quality of the product frequently suffers. Releasing a low-quality product usually results in higher maintenance and support

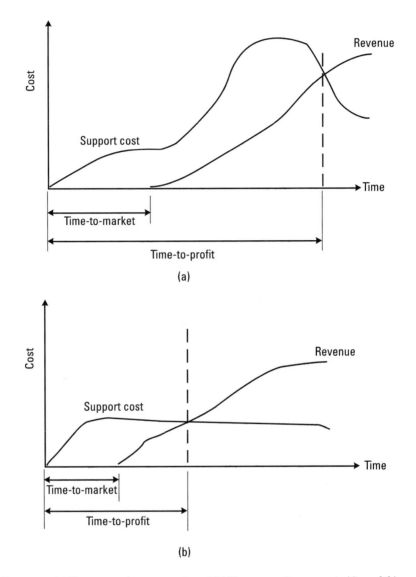

Figure 4.1 (a) Time-to-market approach and (b) Time-to-profit approach. (*From:* [2].)

costs and unhappy customers. The break-even point occurs much later (if at all).

Alternatively, if the software development organization is geared toward achieving time-to-profit goals, the quality of the product is usually much better, thus reducing overall maintenance and support costs. Lower maintenance and support costs means happier customers. The break-even point occurs much sooner, which means higher profits. In a highly competitive marketplace, organizations need to make informed decisions regarding the balance between achieving time-to-market and time-to-profit goals.

In this chapter, we discuss the economic justification for performing software V&V activities. Understanding the economics of software V&V is crucial to understanding how your organization can make these tradeoffs.

4.1 Economic Justification

Organizations perform specific tasks as part of the software development process because management believes such tasks are economically justified. For example, organizations may send software engineers to training courses to learn new programming techniques, such as object-oriented design (OOD), or to learn how to use tools that support OOD. These training costs (both the cost of the training and the time spent at training sessions) can be economically justified by management based on the return that it is likely to provide in terms of improved product design, lower development and maintenance costs, and so on.

Organizations may spend considerable amounts of time and money performing tasks that will (it is hoped) identify customer requirements with a high degree of certainty. Tasks such as rapid prototyping, conjoint analysis [3], and quality function deployment (QFD) [4–6] all have a measurable cost. For all of these tasks, management must be convinced that they will yield a positive return on investment. Software engineers learn new skills that help them produce better products in less time. Marketing people learn what the customer really wants. And customers get a higher quality product that meets their needs in the time frame that they require.

Like any other activity, there is a cost associated with performing software V&V tasks. Obviously, the benefits must be greater than the costs. However, with software V&V tasks, there is also a cost associated with not performing these activities. The question is which cost is greater.

Several studies have been performed to try to answer this question. A landmark study performed by Dr. Barry Boehm [7] reported that the cost to find and fix defects found during the software development process increased significantly the later the defect was found. As illustrated in Figure 4.2, the relative cost to find and fix a defect increases dramatically the longer the defect remains in the product. For example, the cost of finding and fixing a

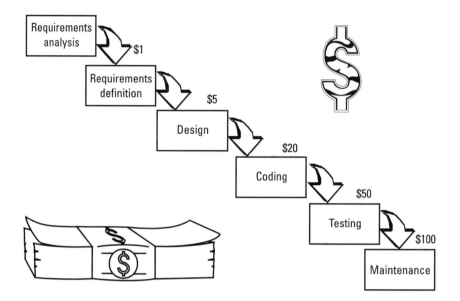

Figure 4.2 Relative cost factor to find and fix defects. (*Source*: [7].)

defect found during the requirements definition phase increases by a factor of 50 if the defect is not found until the testing phase and by a factor of 100 if the defect is not found until after the product is shipped. Other cost data summarized by Humphrey [8] are consistent with that reported by Boehm.

Costs associated with software quality are typically incurred as a result of software V&V activities that may include defect detection, removal, and prevention activities. The costs associated with performing these activities are relatively straightforward and easy to measure. For example, costs associated with performing requirements, design and code inspections, developing and executing software validation tests, and other similar software V&V tasks are relatively simple to determine by tracking person-hours.

Costs resulting from not performing these activities are a little more difficult to identify. For example, as a result of not doing inspections, the testing cycle extends longer than originally planned, thereby delaying product release by several weeks. As a result of not doing validation testing, the product is released with many defects that customers find. This creates a significant increase in call volume to your customer support center. A patch release may be required, diverting resources from other projects.

While it may be difficult to identify these costs, it is important to collect this information so that organizations can make informed decisions regarding specific software V&V activities to perform. Once these costs are identified and measured, they can be used to help drive process improvements, which can lead to lower development costs, shorter time to market, and higher customer satisfaction.

4.2 Software Defect Cost Models

Developing a software defect cost model can help identify the costs associated with software defects. The model should identify costs associated with such things as software development, documentation, and testing prior to release to customers (prerelease), as well as costs incurred after the software is released (postrelease). An example of such a model is illustrated in Figure 4.3. In this model, factors that affect the cost of software defects are identified. Note that the upper branch of the fishbone diagram shown in Figure 4.3 depicts an often-ignored component of the cost of software defects. This component is lost sales due to the product being late to market as a direct result of quality problems that are identified during product development.

Another way to look at costs associated with software defects is the defect removal cycle. This cycle represents the activities associated with finding and fixing defects both prerelease and postrelease. Typical defect removal cycles are shown in Figures 4.4 and 4.5. Activities are identified based on the tasks that are performed when a defect is found in the product, usually as a result of testing. Modeling the defect removal process and measuring the time it actually takes to perform the tasks identified is important for justifying software V&V activities.

Once you collect the data for your organization, you can compare it to that shown in Tables 4.1 and 4.2. Some of the assumptions made are:

- Empirical data supports a find-fix cycle time of 10–30 hours per defect prerelease [8, 10] and 20–60 hours per defect postrelease. These time estimates include all the activities shown in Figures 4.4 and 4.5.

- Cost of labor of $100 per hour is an average for software engineers and is fully loaded, meaning that the cost includes salary plus benefits and overhead. Substitute your actual labor cost.

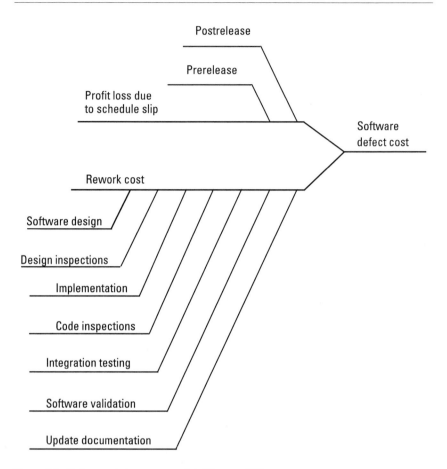

Figure 4.3 Software defect cost model. (*Source:* [9].)

- The number of defects to be removed varies from project to project and from company to company. Substitute actual numbers that you have observed from past projects.
- The postrelease find-fix cycle time is higher because of the additional tasks required (refer to Figure 4.5). These costs do not include the costs associated with scrapping inventory of a defective product and reissuing an updated software release to customers.

Pressman [11] suggests that the cost of performing software V&V activities can be economically justified if:

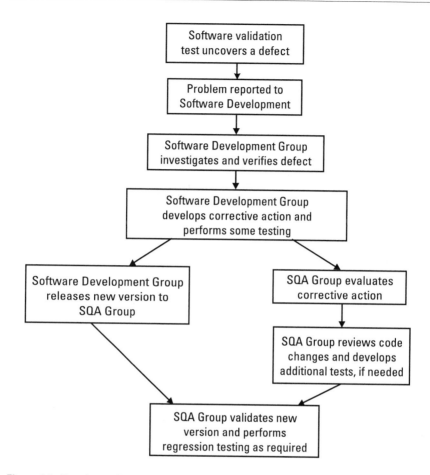

Figure 4.4 Prerelease find-fix cycle.

$$C_3 > C_1 + C_2 \qquad (4.1)$$

where:

C_3 = cost of defects without software V&V activity. Estimate C_3 using historical data from previous projects that didn't have software V&V.

C_1 = actual costs of software V&V activities. Estimate C_1 using the cost of people and equipment on similar projects that did have software V&V.

C_2 = cost of defects not found by software V&V. Estimate C_2 using the postrelease defect removal model and counting the number of defects found by customers.

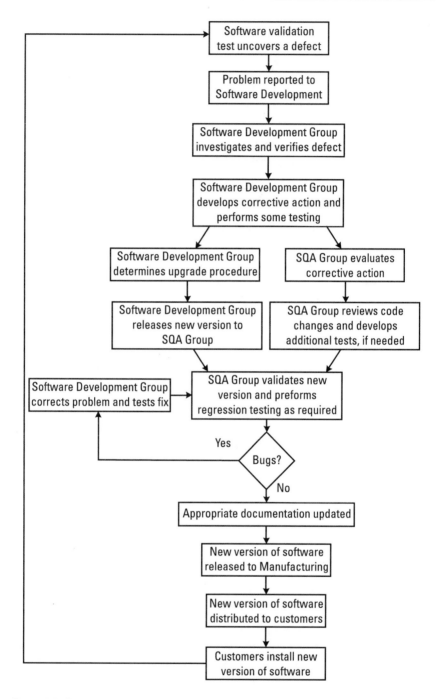

Figure 4.5 Postrelease find-fix cycle.

Table 4.1

Typical Prerelease Defect Removal Costs

Average find/fix time (hours/defect)	Average cost of labor, fully loaded ($/hr)	If the number of defects to be removed is...	Then the defect removal cost is...
10	$100	125	$125,000
30	$100	250	$750,000

Table 4.2

Typical Postrelease Defect Removal Costs

Average find/fix time (hours/defect)	Average cost of labor, fully loaded ($/hr)	If the number of defects to be removed is...	Then the defect removal cost is...
20	$100	25	$50,000
60	$100	100	$600,000

4.3 Measuring the Cost of Quality

Juran has described the cost-of-quality measure as a way to "quantify the size of the quality problem in language that will have impact on upper management" [12]. The cost-of-quality measurement is composed of the following three activities:

1. *Detection.* Detection activities are focused on tasks that help find defects.
2. *Prevention.* Prevention activities are centered on tasks that help prevent defects from occurring in the first place.
3. *Removal.* Removal activities include a variety of tasks related to isolating, correcting, and verifying bug fixes as well as costs associated with preparing distribution media and redistributing software.

Examples of prevention, detection, and removal tasks are shown in Table 4.3.

Table 4.3
Examples of Prevention, Detection, and Removal Tasks

Prevention	Detection	Removal
Training	Inspections	Fault Isolation
Planning	Testing	Fault Analysis
Simulation	Auditing	Root-Cause Analysis
Modeling	Monitoring	Software Modifications
Consulting	Measuring	Document Modifications
Qualifying	Verification	Test Modifications
Certifying	Validation	Regression Testing
Process Improvements	Requirements Tracing	Rework Inspections
Configuration Management		Problem Tracking
		Scrap and rework of media
		Duplication/Distribution

The motivation for measuring the cost of quality is to use this information to convince management that it is more cost-effective to spend time and effort on defect detection and prevention-related activities than on defect-removal activities.

4.4 Summary

The evidence overwhelmingly indicates that the sooner defects in requirements, design, and code are found, the easier and less expensive they are to fix. Software V&V activities are focused on helping to find defects as soon in the development process as possible. It is always cheaper to do it right the first time than to do it over and over again. The economic motivation for software V&V is discussed further in Chapter 12.

Additional references on software economics can be found in the SEI's Annotated Bibliography on the World Wide Web, at http://www.sei.cmu.edu. Several of these are included in the Selected Bibliography for this chapter.

References

[1]   Bach, J., "Good Enough Quality: Beyond the Buzzwords," *IEEE Computer*, August 1997, pp. 96–98.

[2]   Fujimura, A., "Software Engineering Needs a Zero Defect Culture," *Computer Design*, September 1993, pp. 78–79.

[3]   Cattin, P., and R. R. Wittink, "Commercial Use of Conjoint Analysis: A Survey," *Journal of Marketing*, Vol. 46, No. 3, 1982, pp. 44–53.

[4]   Hauser, J. R., and D. Clausing, "The House of Quality," *Harvard Business Review*, No. 3, May–June 1988, pp. 63–73.

[5]   Lamia, W. M., "Integrating QFD with Object Oriented Software Design Methodologies," *Transactions from the Seventh Symposium on Quality Function Deployment*, June 1995, pp. 417–434.

[6]   Zultner, R. E., "Quality Function Deployment (QFD) for Software: Structured Requirements Exploration," in G. G. Schulmeyer and J. I. McManus (eds.), *Total Quality Management for Software*, New York: Van Nostrand Reinhold, 1992.

[7]   Boehm, B. W., *Software Engineering Economics*, Englewood Cliffs, NJ: Prentice-Hall, 1981.

[8]   Humphrey, W. S., *A Discipline for Software Engineering*, Reading, MA: Addison-Wesley, 1995, pp. 275–277.

[9]   Ward, J., "Calculating the Real Cost of Software Defects," *Assoc. for the Advancement of Medical Instrumentation (AAMI) 27th Annual Conference Proceedings*, 1992, p. 90.

[10] Humphrey, W. S., *Managing the Software Process*, Reading, MA: Addison-Wesley, 1989, p. 12.

[11] Pressman, R., *Software Engineering: A Practitioner's Approach*, 3rd ed., New York: McGraw-Hill, 1992, pp. 587–588.

[12] Juran, J. M., and F. M. Gryna, *Juran's Quality Control Handbook*, 4th ed., New York: McGraw-Hill, 1988.

Selected Bibliography

Boehm, B., and P. Papaccio, "Understanding and Controlling Software Costs," *IEEE Transactions on Software Engineering*, Vol. 14, No. 10, October 1988, pp. 1462–1477.

Geringer, P., and W. Hutzler, *Analytical Methods in Software Engineering Economics*, New York: Springer-Verlag, 1994.

Wellman, F., *Software Costing*, Englewood Cliffs, NJ: Prentice-Hall, 1992.

Part II
Overview of Software Verification Activities

"Verification" and "validation" refer to two distinctly different sets of activities, yet the terms are often used interchangeably. Let us clarify what is meant by these terms.

"Verification" is "[t]he process of evaluating a system or component to determine whether the products of a given development phase satisfy conditions imposed at the start of that phase" [1]. Verification activities are in-process activities performed concurrently with software development. Another way to view verification activities is that verification helps answer the question "Are we building the product right?"

Verification activities are discussed in detail in Chapters 5–8.

"Validation" is "[t]he process of evaluating a system or component during or at the end of the development process to determine whether it satisfies specified requirements" [1]. Validation activities are performed after the software is developed to determine if the software correctly implements the requirements. Another way to view validation activities is that validation helps answer the question "Did we build the right product?"

Validation activities are discussed in detail in Part III, Chapters 9–11.

Verification activities are defined around three basic processes: inspection, measurement, and configuration management. In Chapters 5 and 6, we introduce the inspection process and describe how it can be applied to perform requirements, design, code, and test inspections. An extensive collection of supporting materials for the inspection process is included in Appendixes A–F.

In Chapter 7, the measurement process is introduced. The process of implementing a software measurement program is discussed, along with examples of specific metrics that support software V&V activities.

In Chapter 8, the configuration management process is covered. Tasks related to identification, baseline management, and auditing and reporting are discussed.

Reference

[1]   IEEE Standard 610.12-1990, IEEE Standard Glossary of Software Engineering Terminology, © 1990.

5

The Inspection Process

An inspection is a powerful tool that can help achieve significant improvements in software quality.

Defect-removal efficiency is a measure of the relative number of defects found by customers as compared with the number found by the company that developed the software. Capers Jones [1] identified several companies that have managed to achieve defect-removal efficiencies that exceed 99%. Defect-removal efficiency is calculated as:

$$\left[\frac{\text{Number of defects found prior to releasing a product}}{\begin{array}{c}\text{Number found prior to release, plus the number reported by}\\\text{customers during the first } n \text{ months of actual use}\end{array}}\right] \times 100\%$$

In these companies, formal inspections are an important factor contributing to high defect-removal efficiencies. In fact, in his continuing study of software development practices at hundreds of companies, Jones has found that formal inspection is one of the common practices performed by those companies considered to be "Best in Class" [2]. (See Chapter 15 for more information on common practices performed by best-in-class companies.)

To understand why formal inspections are such an important part of the software development process, consider the following:

- Requirements are the most common source of problems in the software development process.

- Requirements are written in English, by people who typically have little or no training in writing requirements for software.

- The English language is imprecise, ambiguous, and nondeterministic, whereas software is precise, unambiguous, and deterministic.

Make a photocopy of the page containing the text in Figure 5.1 and give it to 10 of your colleagues. Ask them to follow the directions and answer the question. No further information should be provided and people should complete this task by themselves.

In practice, if 10 people try this exercise, you will likely get 10 different answers to what seems to be a very simple question. However, the ambiguity of English becomes apparent when you ask people how they arrived at their answers. Some say, "I counted all the *e*'s on the page, even the ones outside the box." Some say, "I interpreted the instructions to mean only count the *e*'s in the box." Still others say, "I only counted the *e*'s within the quoted text." Imagine the confusion and misinterpretation when you are talking about complex technical requirements for software.

This chapter introduces the inspection process. Chapter 6 includes a discussion of how the inspection process can be applied to the different deliverables produced during the software development process.

Directions: Count the number of occurrences of the letter *e* on this page and write your answer in the space provided.

While inspections will not solve all problems, they are enormously effective. [Inspections] have been demonstrated to improve both quality and productivity by impressive factors. Inspections are not magic and they should not be considered a replacement for testing, but all software organizations should use inspections or similar technical review methods in all major aspects of their work. This includes requirements, design, implementation, test, maintenance, and documentation. [3]

Answer: The letter *e* appears _____ times.

Figure 5.1 Inspection exercise.

The inspection process is presented by using a collection of FAQs. To supplement the answers to the FAQs, an extensive collection of reference material is included in the Appendices.

5.1 Inspection Process FAQs

What Is an Inspection?

An inspection is a formal, rigorous, in-depth technical review designed to identify problems as close to their point of origin as possible. Michael Fagan [4] developed the inspection process while he was at IBM in the 1970s. Inspections have not changed much since first described by Fagan. What has changed is the realization that this process can make a significant impact on software quality. There have been numerous studies [5–7] done over the past 20 years to document the economic benefit of inspections on quality.

The objectives of the inspection process are to:

- Find problems at the earliest possible point in the software development process;
- Ensure that agreement is reached on rework that may need to be done;
- Verify that any rework done meets predefined criteria.

In addition to these objectives, inspections:

- Provide data on product quality and process effectiveness;
- Build technical knowledge among team members;
- Increase the effectiveness of software validation testing;
- Raise the standard of excellence for software engineers.

Why Is an Inspection Considered Formal?

Inspections are called formal because there are defined roles and responsibilities for each of the participants. There is also a defined process that is followed in the weeks leading up to the inspection meeting, during the inspection meeting, and in follow-up activities after the meeting. Having a formal process ensures that the objectives of the inspection will be met. However, at most inspections, black tie is optional!

Who Participates in an Inspection?

An inspection typically requires five to seven people. Each person is assigned a specific role and each role has specific responsibilities associated with it. The roles are:

Moderator: Coordinates the inspection and leads the discussion

Producer: Responsible for the work being inspected

Reader: Paraphrases the work inspected at the inspection meeting

Inspector: Inspects the product

Recorder: Records problems discussed at the inspection meeting

Manager: Supervises the producer

What Are the Roles and Responsibilities of the Participants?

Well-defined roles and responsibilities are a key attribute of the inspection process. The roles and responsibilities of the moderator, producer, reader, inspector, recorder, and manager are defined in Appendix A.

Throughout the software development process for a given project, people may be asked to fill several different roles. You may play the role of an inspector at one inspection and be the producer for another. As the producer, you receive the benefits of having a talented group of people help you improve the quality of your work. They, in return, will expect the same of you.

Do Managers Attend the Inspection Meeting?

Equally important as who participates in inspections is who does not participate. The manager participates in the inspection process but does not attend the inspection meeting. Experience has shown that the inclusion of managers at the inspection meeting changes the inspection. Regardless of the manager's behavior at the meeting, the focus consciously or unconsciously shifts from the product to the producer. It is for this reason that managers do not attend inspection meetings.

Why Is the Producer Present?

The producer's responsibilities at the inspection meeting are to clarify, not justify. The producer answers questions, but does not attempt to explain why—only what and how. The moderator ensures that comments and criticisms are directed at the product and not the producer.

How Are Inspections Different from Walk-throughs?

Inspections are different from walk-throughs in several key areas, as shown in Table 5.1.

What Are the Key Attributes of the Inspection Process?

The first attribute of the inspection process is the well-defined roles and responsibilities of the inspection team members. These are listed in Appendix A.

Table 5.1
Inspections Versus Walk-Throughs

Attribute	Inspection	Walk-through
Objectives	Find problems.	Find problems.
	Verify rework that is done.	Discuss alternative solutions.
	Focus is on whether the product as written meets all requirements.	Focus is on demonstrating how the product meets all requirements.
Decision making	Inspection team makes all decisions based on consensus.	Producer makes all decisions.
Leadership	Trained moderator.	Usually the producer.
Attendance	Peers with documented attendance.	Peers and technical managers. Attendance not documented.
Presentation of material	Material presented by reader.	Material presented by producer.
Metrics	Formally required.	Optional.
Procedures	Formally documented.	Informal.
Training	Required for all participants.	No training required.

The second attribute is documentation. An example of a documented inspection process is included in Appendix B. The information in Appendices A through D can be used to develop an inspection process for your organization.

The third attribute is the collection of product and process metrics. Product and process metrics are collected in order to improve both the software development process and the inspection process. One example of how you could use product metrics to improve your product is to perform a Pareto analysis of the defect data collected from several code inspections. The purpose of Pareto analysis is to "separate the vital few from the trivial many." It has been said that 80% of the defects come from 20% of the causes. This data-analysis method helps to direct your work where the most improvement can be made.

A Pareto analysis would indicate the most common coding errors that software engineers have made. This information can then be used to revise the coding standards so that this type of defect is less likely to occur in the future. Similarly, an analysis of process metrics (such as how many errors are found versus how many defects are found) can be used to improve the inspection process.

The Inspection Problem Report Form and the Inspection Summary Form shown in Appendix C illustrate the types of metrics to collect.

The fourth attribute of the inspection process is inspecting against "that which came before." A basic principle of the inspection process is that you inspect a document or code against previous documentation. In addition, there may be company or project standards (such as coding conventions) that are relevant for use during the inspection.

The fifth attribute is supporting infrastructure. The success of the inspection process depends on the support of management. To be effective, inspection training is required for all people who are to be involved. This training can be completed in a few hours and can be based on the information contained in the Appendices. Training is required to ensure that each participant is aware of the roles and responsibilities that they may be asked to fulfill.

Because inspections are very different from the types of meetings software engineers usually participate in, training in how to behave at an inspection is essential. Participants need to learn how to direct their criticism at the product and not the producer. They need to learn the types of questions to ask (such as, "What does this section of code do?") and more importantly, what questions to not ask ("Why did you do it that way?"). For many software engineers, the temptation to roll up their sleeves and get into problem solving is very great. This behavior needs to be changed during an inspection. A good idea for a company implementing inspections is to have a few practice inspections to allow people to become familiar with the process and the group dynamics.

In addition to the commitment to training, project managers need to plan for inspections by including them on project schedules. If inspections are not part of the schedule, they are less likely to occur, even with the best of intentions.

Lastly, to be successful, inspections require the support of managers and supervisors. Managers and supervisors need to allow people to participate on inspection teams. This requires a time commitment that sometimes will conflict with other priorities.

Who Decides What Is to Be Inspected?

Deciding what to inspect is not easy. Inspections require a considerable time commitment and therefore selecting what to inspect needs to be done judiciously. Usually, a producer and the producer's manager decide on the need for an inspection. It is important to note that the producer's manager is involved only in the decision to conduct the inspection, and not in the inspection itself. Potential producers should view inspections as a positive step taken to improve product quality and reduce rework.

Developing criteria such as the following, used for selecting code modules for inspection, is a useful way to help make the decision.

- A module performs functions that are critical to the correct operation of the product.
- A module is determined to be relatively more complex than other modules based on objective evaluation with industry standard complexity metrics such as McCabe Cyclomatic Complexity [8] and Halstead Software Science [9]. (See Sections 7.3.1.1 and 7.3.1.2 for an overview of these metrics.)
- In the past, there have been a relatively high number of errors found in modules that perform similar functions.
- A relatively new or inexperienced software engineer wrote the module.

Similar criteria should be developed for each type of product that is inspected.

How Do You Know If You're Ready to Perform an Inspection?

Being ready to perform an inspection means that the necessary documentation is prepared and in order. It also means that the required inspection training has been performed and that there is support from management. Table 5.2 illustrates the required documentation needed for an inspection.

What Material Is Required to Conduct an Inspection?

The materials needed to conduct the inspection are shown in Table 5.2.

Many companies have developed their own internal coding standards and conventions. For consistency, improved readability, and maintainability, it is important that such documents be included in code inspections.

Prompting checklists can be used for all types of inspections. These checklists should address common problems observed in the information being inspected and should be updated frequently based on the product and process data collected during inspections. Examples of checklists are included in Appendix D.

How Is This Material Disseminated?

The producer is responsible for providing the required materials to the moderator in a timely manner. The moderator is responsible for distributing the materials to the inspection team. This can be done at the overview meeting (if one is scheduled). The moderator ensures that the inspection team receives the material at least five working days prior to the inspection meeting.

What If the Inspection Team Does Not Have Five Working Days to Review Materials?

Remember the Boy Scouts' motto, "Be Prepared!"? Well, that is the motto of the inspection team also. Experience has shown that five working days are the minimum required to adequately prepare for an inspection. The moderator is responsible for ensuring that the team has adequate time to prepare. There is no point conducting the inspection if the team is not prepared. If the team is not prepared, the moderator postpones the inspection meeting.

Table 5.2
Ready for Inspection?

Type of Inspection	Item Being Inspected	Ready to Inspect If...	Materials Required for Inspection Team
Requirements	SRS	Inspection training performed. Product Concept (or the document that precedes the SRS) has been reviewed and approved.	SRS and product concept specification (or the document that precedes the SRS). Requirements checklist.*
Design	SDD	Inspection training performed. The SRS has been inspected and all outstanding issues have been resolved.	SRS and the SDD design checklist.*
Code	Source code modules	Inspection training performed. The SDD has been inspected and all outstanding issues have been resolved. Modules selected for inspection based on defined criteria.* The source code has been compiled with no errors.	Line-numbered source code listing, the SDD, and company coding standards. Coding checklist.*
Validation Tests	Test Procedures	Inspection training performed. The SRS has been inspected and all outstanding issues have been resolved.	Test procedures and the SRS. Test checklist.*

* Examples of these items are included in Appendix D.

We're Having Our First Inspection and I Am One of the Inspectors. What Should I Do to Prepare?

First, know your role and responsibilities (see Appendix A). Next, based on the information you received, familiarize yourself with the document you are inspecting. Review this document against the "document that came before," using the prompting checklists and standards as reminders of things to check. Now go back to the document you are inspecting and look for potential problems—places where the requirements defined in the earlier document are not being met; or places where the standards and conventions are not being followed.

Each time you find a potential problem, record it on an Inspection Problem Report Form. Continue until you've gone through the entire document being inspected. If, during your preparation, you have questions that deal with understanding what is being done (not why it is being done), ask the moderator or producer for clarification before the inspection meeting.

Remember that your objective is to find problems—not solve them. Last, keep track of your preparation time.

Who Decides What Is a Problem?

The inspection team reaches consensus on each issue raised and decides what issues are to be recorded as errors or defects.

What Is an Error?

An error is a problem in which the software or its documentation does not meet defined requirements and is found at the point of origin. For example, a coding problem found during a code inspection is an example of an error.

What Is a Defect?

A defect is a problem in which the software or its documentation does not meet defined requirements and is found beyond the point of origin. For example, a requirements problem found during a code inspection is an example of a defect.

What if the Producer Does Not Agree?

The producer doesn't get a vote! The inspection team decides which problems are recorded as errors or defects. The producer does not participate in making this decision.

I'm an Inspector and I've Completed My Preparation. It's Time for the Inspection Meeting. What Happens Now?

The moderator calls the meeting to order and determines if the inspectors are prepared. If the moderator is satisfied that the team is adequately prepared, the inspection begins. The reader starts by paraphrasing the first chunk of information from the work product. (Note that a reader is usually required only for code inspection.)

The moderator then goes around the table and solicits any potential errors or defects from the team. Each potential error or defect is discussed and the team reaches consensus as to whether a potential problem should be recorded as an error or defect. The producer is asked to clarify issues as needed.

Each potential problem is recorded on an Inspection Problem Report form. The recorder ensures that the information entered on the problem report forms is complete and accurate and reflects any team discussions and clarifications.

After the reader has completed paraphrasing the whole work product, the moderator asks the recorder to read back all of the problem reports to ensure that they were recorded correctly. The team decides if the severity of the problems found warrants another inspection or if the moderator can review the corrective action without another inspection meeting. The recorder records the meeting duration information on the Inspection Summary Form.

If another meeting is required, the moderator schedules the next meeting. The moderator then adjourns the meeting.

How Does the Moderator Know If the Inspectors Are Prepared?

One way of determining if the team is prepared is to ask each inspector to write down how much time he or she spent preparing for the meeting. If, in the moderator's opinion, the team is not adequately prepared, the moderator postpones the meeting. Alternatively, the moderator can meet with the inspectors before the meeting to see if they are prepared.

How Does the Moderator Keep the Meeting Focused?

It isn't always easy. Selection of an effective moderator is crucial to the success of the inspection. An ineffective moderator can be detrimental to the inspection process. The person selected must have the ability and skills to keep the meeting focused and deflect criticism from the producer and onto the product being inspected. A good moderator intervenes as little as possible but as much as necessary. Training and practice are key.

What Happens If the Producer Becomes Defensive?

The moderator needs to take control and reassure the producer that the comments are directed at the product and not at him or her. The moderator needs to reinforce the objectives of the inspection, which is to find problems, not fix them—and remind everyone to stay focused on this objective.

How Do You Justify the Preparation Time Required?

The preparation time is justified by the following:

- Have a large group of inspectors to select from, and limit each person's preparation time during any given year.

- Be very selective in what you choose to inspect.

- Document the problems found by the team and compare the effort required to find these problems with the effort required to find the same problems other ways (i.e., by testing).

- Document the amount of time actually spent in an inspection.

Why Are Inspection Meetings Limited to Two Hours, and What Happens If the Meeting Runs Over?

Inspection meetings require intense concentration and focus. Experience has shown that after two hours, most people's ability to concentrate and remain focused decreases. If the meeting runs over, the moderator schedules a continuation meeting on another day.

What Information (If Any) Should Be Made Public Regarding Inspections?

This is very controversial, because most people are averse to having what is perceived as their competence (or incompetence, as the case may be) posted for all to see. Rather than posting results of individual inspections, consider posting only summary results after completing half a dozen or so inspections. In that way, people will see that there is management support and quality improvement but without personalizing it.

When Is the Inspection Officially Completed?

The inspection is officially completed when the moderator closes out the rework section on the Inspection Problem Report Form for all problems identified.

5.2 Summary

All the best-in-class companies that are pushing or exceeding 99% [defect-removal] efficiency levels use formal inspections, quality assurance groups, and trained testing specialists. Of course, high defect-removal efficiency does not guarantee success. A company can have unhappy or dissatisfied customers for other reasons. However, high levels of customer satisfaction strongly correlate with high levels of defect-removal efficiency. Conversely, software firms whose defect-removal efficiency levels sag below 85% almost never have really happy clients because their software is too unreliable. [1]

References

[1] Jones, C., "Software Defect-Removal Efficiency," *IEEE Computer*, Vol. 29, No. 4, April 1996, pp. 94–95.

[2] Jones, C., *Software Quality: Analysis and Guidelines for Success*, Boston, MA: International Thomson Computer Press, 1997.

[3] Humphrey, W. S., *Managing the Software Process*, Reading, MA: Addison-Wesley, 1989, p. 172.

[4] Fagan, M., "Design and Code Inspections to Reduce Errors and Improve Program Development," *IBM Systems Journal*, No. 3, 1976, pp. 182–210.

[5] Humphrey, W. S., *Managing the Software Process*, Reading, MA: Addison-Wesley, 1989, pp. 186–187.

[6] Grady, R. B., and T. Van Slack, "Key Lessons in Achieving Widespread Inspection Use," *IEEE Software*, July 1994, pp. 46–57.

[7] Banard, J., and A. Price, "Managing Code Inspection Information," *IEEE Software*, March 1994, pp. 59–69.

[8] McCabe, T. J., "A Software Complexity Measure," *IEEE Transactions on Software Engineering*, Vol. 2, 1976.

[9] Halstead, H. M., *Elements of Software Science*, New York: North-Holland, 1977.

Selected Bibliography

Fagan, M. E., "Advances in Software Inspections," *IEEE Transactions on Software Engineering*, Vol. SE-12, 1986, pp. 774–751.

Friedman, D. P., and G. M. Weinberg, *Walkthroughs, Inspections, and Technical Reviews,* 3rd ed., New York: Dorset House, 1990.

Gilb, T., and D. Graham, *Software Inspection,* Reading, MA: Addison-Wesley, 1993.

Hatton, L., "Static Inspection: Tapping the Wheels of Software," *IEEE Software,* Vol. 12, 1995, pp. 85–87.

Wheeler, D., B. Brykczynski, and R. Meeson, Jr., (eds.), *Software Inspection: An Industry Best Practice,* Los Alamitos, CA: IEEE Computer Society Press, 1996.

Web Resources

The Software Inspection and Review Organization (SIRO) home page is available at: http://www.ics.hawaii.edu/~siro/. SIRO is a voluntary organization devoted to the exchange of information about group-based examination of software work products. The scope of SIRO includes, but is not restricted to:

- Promoting exchange of ideas and information on the state of practice;
- Facilitating emerging inspection and review techniques;
- Providing a clearinghouse for support resources;
- Surveying and reporting on industry use of techniques and metrics.

SIRO maintains an extensive bibliography of materials related to inspections, formal technical reviews, and walk-throughs.

Note: URLs cited were accurate as of April 2001.

6

Applying the Inspection Process

To be most effective, inspections must be an integral part of the software development process. The inspection process can be easily adapted and applied to a variety of deliverables associated with the software development process, including the software requirements specification (SRS), the software design description (SDD), the source code, and the test scripts.

Before discussing how to adapt and apply the inspection process, we need to review issues related to integrating inspections into the software development process and, more importantly, into a company's culture. The goal is for inspections to become institutionalized.

6.1   Attributes of a Good Process

The SEI has done an extensive amount of research into issues that affect an organization's ability to consistently develop high-quality software. As you would expect, the software development process is a key element in delivering high-quality software. The SEI has identified the following key attributes of a good process:

- The process is written.
- The process is flexible and can be changed.
- Everyone agrees to follow the process.

- The process includes metrics, which are used to measure process effectiveness.
- Metrics are the basis for changing the process.
- The process is actively managed.

These attributes, while applicable to almost any process, are particularly relevant for software-related processes and are indicators of process maturity. In a highly competitive global economy, those organizations that exhibit higher levels of process maturity will produce higher quality products and will be more productive, efficient, and profitable.

To help introduce inspections into your organization, an example of an inspection process is included in Appendixes A through E. This material can be used to document your inspection process and form the basis for inspection training materials.

6.1.1   Institutionalizing Inspections

Making inspections part of your company's culture can be a difficult task. Management may question the cost savings that can be realized by judicious use of inspections and may ask for an economic justification. You should be prepared to provide such a justification. As discussed earlier, there is considerable economic data available to justify the use of inspections.

Surprisingly, some software engineers and project managers may be reluctant to accept inspections. Some software engineers fear peer reviews and have legitimate concerns regarding the use of such reviews as part of performance reviews. Some project managers may be reluctant to incorporate inspections into project schedules because of a lack of understanding of the benefits and a focus on short-term objectives (e.g., meeting a schedule) at the expense of long-term goals (e.g., increasing customer satisfaction). Understanding the root causes of this reluctance is essential to overcoming resistance to institutionalizing inspections. Some of the key issues that need to be addressed are:

1. Management

    a. Does management understand and support the objectives of the inspection process?
    b. Is management willing to commit the resources necessary to train inspectors?
    c. Is management willing to include inspections in project schedules?

2. Software development process

a. Is there a written software development process? If not, could one be developed?

b. Is there management support for preparing a software development process?

c. If one exists, can it be modified to include inspections at appropriate points in the process?

d. Is the software development process being actively managed?

e. Does the software engineering organization support the inspection process?

f. Can you identify potential obstacles (such as those mentioned above)?

g. Are resources available to train people in the inspection process and is there a commitment to provide this training over time as new employees are hired?

3. Inspection Metrics

a. Is there a definition of what product and process metrics will be collected from inspections and how this data will be used?

b. Is a continuous improvement process in place that identifies improvements to the inspection process based on collected data?

6.1.2 Real-Life Experiences

Many companies have successfully institutionalized inspections. Hewlett-Packard (HP) has used inspections successfully for over 15 years. The results of widespread adoption of the inspection process at HP have been reported [1]. Based on this experience, HP has standardized the use of inspections across the company. Key parts of the plan are:

- Proactively support inspection champions and sponsors.

- Reinforce management awareness with economic justification for inspections.

- Build an infrastructure strong enough to achieve and hold software core competence.

- Measure the extent to which the process is used.

HP's standardization plan is not an attempt to regulate the inspection process, but rather to ensure that the process is applied in a manner that is most effective for the organizations using it.

Lucent Technologies (formerly Bell Labs) has been measuring the effectiveness of its formal inspections since 1986 [2]. By applying a set of metrics to over two dozen software projects, the cost of removing defects with code inspections was reduced by 300% when compared with testing alone.

Further information regarding experiences with the inspection process can be found on the World Wide Web at the Software Inspection and Review Organization (SIRO) home page.

6.2   Requirements Inspections

If you can only afford to do one inspection on a project, you will get the biggest return on investment from a requirements inspection. A requirements inspection should be the one inspection that is never skipped.

As we saw earlier, requirements are frequently subject to misinterpretation. Misinterpretation is usually the result of poorly written, incomplete, inconsistent, and ambiguous requirements. An obvious question is: "Why can't we write better requirements?" Unfortunately, there's no simple solution for this problem. Many people with different backgrounds and skill sets are typically involved in the requirements-writing process and most of these people are not aware of the impact that poorly written requirements can have on a software development project. There are a couple of things you can do, however, to teach people how to write good requirements.

First, you can provide an example of a well-written requirements document. If you can't find one, you can define some attributes for good requirements documents. Examples of such attributes are included in Appendix E. Second, you can develop a Requirements Inspection Checklist, similar to the one included in Appendix D, that is specific to your products and organization. The key to making checklists effective is to update them frequently with new information gleaned from inspections performed at your company. By doing this, you'll avoid making the same mistakes twice.

Once you have identified an example of a well-written requirements document, attributes for good requirements, and a Requirements Inspection Checklist, call a meeting with the folks who usually write requirements and review this material with them. Let them know that the requirements they write will be measured against these standards. Stress the importance of writing good requirements in terms of the economic impact to the company. Recall that studies have shown that an error that cost $350 to find and fix in the requirements definition phase of a project can cost more than $12,000 (more than 34 times as much) to find and fix if is not found until the validation testing phase [3].

6.2.1 Objectives and Prerequisites

The objectives and prerequisites for a requirements inspection are summarized in Table 6.1.

6.2.2 Requirements Inspection Process

6.2.2.1 Planning Phase

During the planning phase, the moderator and the inspection team are selected. For a requirements inspection, the moderator should select inspectors from a wide range of disciplines in the organization. For example, the inspection team should include representatives from software engineering, software QA, marketing, customer support, technical publications, manufacturing, and other relevant groups within your organization. Selecting inspectors from several disciplines and functions will result in a much better inspection of the SRS because the product will be inspected from many different points of view.

Table 6.1
Requirements Inspection Objectives and Prerequisites

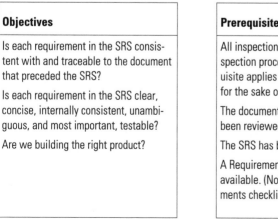

Objectives	Prerequisites
Is each requirement in the SRS consistent with and traceable to the document that preceded the SRS?	All inspection team members received inspection process training. (Note: This prerequisite applies to all types of inspections and for the sake of brevity, will not be repeated.)
Is each requirement in the SRS clear, concise, internally consistent, unambiguous, and most important, testable?	The document that preceded the SRS has been reviewed and approved.
Are we building the right product?	The SRS has been internally reviewed.
	A Requirements Inspection Checklist is available. (Note: An example of a requirements checklist is included in Appendix D.)

The moderator and the producer identify relevant inspection materials, including:

- SRS to be inspected;

- Document that preceded the SRS;

- Requirements Inspection Checklist (refer to Appendix D);

- Attributes of Good Requirements Specifications (refer to Appendix E).

Each member of the inspection team must make a commitment to devote the necessary time to the inspection process. In the case of a requirements inspection, preparation time will vary based on familiarity with the product and the product's complexity. As a rule of thumb, preparation time can be estimated at about 10 pages per hour. Of course, this estimate can vary significantly based on many factors. The duration of the inspection meeting should be based on an inspection rate of about 10 to 20 pages per hour. As your organization gains experience with the inspection process, you can revise these estimates accordingly.

The moderator sets the date, time, and location for the inspection meeting and distributes the inspection materials at least five working days prior to the meeting. The moderator should record the total planning time on the Inspection Summary Form.

6.2.2.2   Preparation Phase

During the preparation phase, each member of the inspection team prepares for the inspection meeting by reviewing the inspection materials and noting potential discrepancies in the SRS. The Requirements Checklist should be used to focus attention on specific areas that there have been problems with previously. Inspectors should record each potential discrepancy on an Inspection Problem Report Form (see Appendix C) so that page numbers, questions, and other references can be recorded ahead of time. This will save time during the inspection meeting.

Inspectors are encouraged to ask questions of the producer during the preparation phase. Such questions should be aimed at providing understanding and clarification, and not justification.

Members of the inspection team keep track of their preparation time. The moderator records the total preparation time of the whole team on the Inspection Summary Form.

6.2.2.3 Inspection Meeting Phase

At the inspection meeting, the moderator must first determine if the inspection team is adequately prepared. One way to do this is to ask each member of the team to write down how much time they spent preparing. Another way to judge preparedness is to ask to see the Inspection Problem Report Forms. A third way is for the moderator to meet with the inspectors individually before the meeting to assess preparedness. The moderator uses his or her best judgment to decide if the team is prepared. Remember that the moderator has to be willing (and able) to postpone the inspection meeting if, in the moderator's judgment, the team is not adequately prepared. By taking this action, the moderator reinforces the need for preparation.

If the team is prepared, the moderator begins the inspection by reviewing the ground rules (outlined in Appendix B). The moderator then goes around the table and asks for potential discrepancies on the SRS on a paragraph-by-paragraph basis. Each potential discrepancy is discussed. As the team reaches consensus on each potential discrepancy, it is so noted on the Inspection Problem Report Form. After all potential discrepancies have been discussed, the moderator will recap and ask the team if they feel a follow-up inspection is warranted. If not, the moderator will work with the producer to ensure corrective action is completed.

The moderator records the duration of the meeting and completes the Inspection Summary Form (refer to Appendix C). Two working days after the meeting, the moderator distributes meeting minutes.

6.2.2.4 Follow-up Phase

The moderator works with the producer to resolve discrepancies raised at the meeting. Upon successful completion, the moderator will complete the Corrective Action portion of the Inspection Summary Form to indicate that the inspection has been completed.

6.3 Design Inspection

> Finally, there are those systems in which the design errors prove so gross that no system test is ever reached—the system collapses of its own developmental weight before integration is achieved. How many of these does it take to justify the institution of design reviews? [4]

Most every software engineer can relate to the above observation made by Friedman. Unfortunately, we continue to deceive ourselves into believing that we are capable of designing very complex systems without the benefit of design inspections. More often than not, these projects are not successful and organizations spend enormous sums of money correcting problems that should have never occurred in the first place. In a business climate that is constantly looking for cost savings and improved productivity, this is one activity that could result in significant savings, if only it was applied.

6.3.1   Objectives and Prerequisites

The objectives and prerequisites are shown in Table 6.2

6.3.2   Design Inspection Process

Design inspections should be performed on those aspects of the product design that warrant an inspection. How do you decide what warrants an inspection? You need to use good engineering judgment. Every aspect of the design cannot be inspected, so you need to be selective in what you inspect.

Table 6.2
Design Inspection Objectives and Prerequisites

Objectives	Prerequisites
Does the design, as expressed in the SDD, address all of the requirements of the SRS?	The SRS has been inspected and all follow-up actions completed.
Are all design elements traceable to specific requirements contained in the SRS?	The SDD has been internally reviewed. A Design Inspection Checklist is available. (Note: An example of a high-level design and a detailed design checklist are included in Appendix D.)
Does the design conform to project and company standards?	If the design is done using CASE tools, relevant reports and diagrams (such as data dictionaries, data flow diagrams, and entity-relationship diagrams) from such tools should be made available.
Are we building the product correctly?	

Those aspects of the design that are new, that have been troublesome in the past, and that are crucial to the proper functioning of the product are all appropriate criteria to use in deciding what to inspect.

In addition, software design is sometimes done in two stages: high-level design and detailed design. If this is the case in your company, planning the design inspection should take this into account.

6.3.2.1 Planning Phase

During the planning phase, the moderator and producer select the inspection team. Given the nature of the SDD, inspection team members should be selected from software engineering, software QA, and other functions as appropriate. For example, if the design being inspected is for software that interfaces to some hardware your company develops, include an engineer from the hardware group on the inspection team.

Again, the moderator needs to get commitments from the inspection team members that they can take the time needed to prepare for the inspection meeting. A design inspection may require more preparation time than a requirements inspection because the information is more complex and abstract. As a rule of thumb, preparation time should be based on about five pages per hour. The inspection meeting should be based on an inspection rate of about 5–10 pages per hour.

The moderator and the producer together decide if an optional overview meeting is needed, based on (1) the inspection team's familiarity with the product, (2) the complexity of the SDD, and (3) the amount and complexity of the inspection materials.

If an overview meeting is needed, the moderator and producer determine what material to present at the overview meeting. The producer is responsible for presenting this information. The moderator arranges to distribute the inspection materials at the overview meeting.

The moderator sets the date, time, and location for the overview meeting (if needed) and the inspection meeting and distributes the inspection materials at least five working days prior to the inspection meeting. If an overview meeting is held, the moderator distributes the inspection materials at that time.

The moderator records the total planning time and time spent on an overview meeting on the Inspection Summary Form.

6.3.2.2 Overview Meeting Phase

The purpose of the overview meeting is to familiarize the inspection team with the product and the inspection materials in order to facilitate understanding. At the meeting, the producer will present an overview of the product, in an attempt to show how this piece fits into the big picture. The producer should also review the organization and content of the inspection materials so that the team becomes familiar with what is included.

Inspection team members are free to ask questions at the overview meeting as long as the questions are aimed at gaining an understanding of the material being presented. The moderator ensures that questions from the team are along these lines. The moderator will record the time spent preparing for the overview meeting, as well as the total time spent by the team at the meeting, on the Inspection Summary Form.

6.3.2.3 Preparation Phase

During the preparation phase for a design inspection, team members should become very familiar with the inspection materials, the SDD, and the appropriate Design Checklist (high-level design or detailed design). The Design Checklist (examples included in Appendix D) is used to focus the inspectors' attention on those areas that are known problem areas.

Each inspector should record any discrepancies on an Inspection Problem Report Form and should keep track of their preparation time. The moderator records the total preparation time on the Inspection Summary Form.

6.3.2.4 Inspection Meeting Phase

At the inspection meeting, the moderator must first determine if the inspection team is adequately prepared and reviews the ground rules described in Appendix B.

The moderator begins the inspection by asking the team for potential discrepancies on each paragraph in the SDD. Comments on other parts of the SDD are held until the team gets to that part.

The team must reach consensus on each potential discrepancy and also decide how to categorize each discrepancy they do agree on. This information is recorded on the Inspection Problem Report Form and is used later on as the basis for making improvements to the Design Checklist.

After all of the sections have been discussed, the moderator will recap the discrepancies the team has agreed on and ask if the team wants to schedule a follow-up inspection. If not, the moderator is responsible for working with the producer and reviewing the corrective actions. If the team wants a follow-up inspection, the moderator schedules it.

The moderator records the duration of the inspection meeting on the Inspection Summary Form and adjourns the meeting. The moderator distributes meeting minutes within two working days of the meeting.

6.3.2.5 Follow-Up Phase

As requested by the team, the moderator works with the producer to resolve discrepancies raised at the meeting. Upon successful completion, the moderator will complete the Corrective Action portion of the Inspection Summary Form to indicate that the inspection has been completed.

6.4 Code Inspection

> We didn't mean to, but in software we have created the first artifact that exhibits the human duality of body and soul. The soul of software is invisible, intangible, silent, weightless, deaf, mute, blind, paralyzed. Like a soul, too, it is complex and hard to understand. It is a structure of logical symbols organized in a framework according to someone's model of some aspect of the world. How do you visualize the invisible? How do you grasp the intangible? How do you hear the silent? [5]

Most software engineers have at least one story of a bug that they introduced into some product that probably could have been caught if the code was inspected. The cost of finding and fixing that one bug can range from 10 to 100 times the cost of finding and fixing the bug at a code inspection. This is why code inspections should become part of the software development process.

6.4.1 Objectives and Prerequisites

The objectives and prerequisites are shown in Table 6.3.

6.4.2 Code Inspection Process

Code inspections are the most frequently used type of inspection. This is probably due to the fact that we tend to focus a lot of attention on the coding phase of the software development process, to the detriment of the earlier phases. A key aspect of code inspections is deciding what to inspect. Code inspections require much more preparation and concentration than do requirements inspections and even design inspections. Therefore, judiciously choosing what to inspect is important to maximize the benefit. You should develop criteria similar to that shown in Appendix F to help make this decision.

Table 6.3
Code Inspection Objectives and Prerequisites

Objectives	Prerequisites
Is the code consistent with the design as expressed in the SDD?	The SDD has been inspected and all follow-up actions completed.
Is the code traceable to specific requirements identified in the SDD?	The code has been compiled with no errors. A tool such as Lint can be used to identify other potential coding errors.\
Does the code conform to project and company coding standards?	A Code Inspection Checklist is available.
Are we building the product correctly?	(Note: Examples of checklists for C and C++ are included in Appendix D.)

6.4.2.1   Planning Phase

The moderator and the producer should jointly identify the members of the inspection team. Team members should be selected based on their expertise in software engineering, their familiarity with the product, and their involvement with the project. People from groups other than software engineering (i.e., user interface, software QA, hardware engineering) should be considered if they are able to understand and evaluate the material being inspected (that is, that they have at least a reading knowledge of the language the software is written in).

Again, the moderator needs to get a commitment from inspection team members that they can take the time needed to prepare for the inspection. A code inspection will require more preparation time than a design inspection because the information is more complex and abstract. As a rule of thumb, preparation time should be based on about 50 lines of C source code per hour. The inspection meeting should be based on an inspection rate of about 100–200 lines of C source code per hour. (Note: A line of C source code is not well defined.)

The moderator and the producer together decide if an optional overview meeting is needed based on (1) the inspection team's familiarity with the product, (2) the complexity of the module being inspected, and (3) the complexity of the inspection materials.

If an overview meeting is needed, the moderator and producer determine what material to present at the overview meeting. The producer is responsible for presenting this information. The moderator sets the date, time, and location for the overview meeting (if needed) and the inspection meeting and distributes the inspection materials at least five working days prior to the inspection meeting.

The inspection materials should include the SDD (the document that precedes the code), a line-numbered source listing of the code (to facilitate references to specific lines of code), and the Coding Checklist (similar to that included in Appendix D).

The moderator records the total planning time and time spent on an overview meeting on the Inspection Summary Form.

6.4.2.2 Overview Meeting Phase

The purpose of the overview meeting is to familiarize the inspection team with the product and the inspection materials in order to facilitate understanding. At the meeting, the producer will present an overview of the product and explain how this module fits into the big picture. The producer should also review the organization and content of the inspection materials so that the team becomes familiar with what is included.

Inspection team members are free to ask questions at the overview meeting as long as the questions are aimed at gaining an understanding of the material being presented. The moderator ensures that questions from the team are along these lines.

6.4.2.3 Preparation Phase

To prepare for the inspection meeting, each inspector becomes very familiar with the module being inspected, the SDD, and the Coding Checklist. Each inspector reviews the module's source listing and looks for potential discrepancies between the code and the SDD. The Coding Checklist helps focus attention on areas known to be problems. Each discrepancy is noted on an Inspection Problem Report Form, identifying the relevant line numbers in the source listing and SDD paragraph references.

In addition to preparing as described above, the reader must also be able to paraphrase sections or chunks of the source code so that the moderator can focus the team's attention on one chunk at a time.

6.4.2.4 Inspection Meeting Phase

At the inspection meeting, the moderator must first determine if the inspection team is adequately prepared and reviews the ground rules as described in Appendix B.

The moderator begins the inspection by asking the reader to paraphrase the first chunk from the module source listing. The reader does this, and the moderator then asks the team for potential discrepancies on that chunk.

Comments on other parts of the code are held until the reader gets to the appropriate chunk.

The team must reach consensus on each potential discrepancy and also decide how to categorize each discrepancy that they do agree on. This information is recorded on the Inspection Problem Report Form and is used later on as the basis for making improvements to the Coding Checklist.

After all of the chunks have been discussed, the moderator will recap the discrepancies the team has agreed on and ask if the team wants to schedule a follow-up inspection. If not, the moderator is responsible for working with the producer and reviewing the corrective actions. If the team wants a follow-up inspection, the moderator schedules it.

The moderator records the duration of the inspection meeting on the Inspection Summary Form and adjourns the meeting. The moderator distributes meeting minutes within two working days of the meeting.

6.4.2.5   Follow-Up Phase

As requested by the team, the moderator works with the producer to resolve discrepancies raised at the meeting. Upon successful completion, the moderator will complete the Corrective Action portion of the Inspection Summary Form to indicate that the inspection has been completed.

6.5   Test Script Inspection

Like all other deliverables produced during the software development process, tests are subject to misunderstanding and can benefit from selective inspection. The primary benefit to be gained by applying the inspection process to test procedures is that it can help identify potential misunderstandings between the software engineers and the software validation test engineers. Identifying and correcting such misunderstandings before the validation testing phase begins results in a more effective and efficient testing process.

6.5.1   Objectives and Prerequisites

The objectives and prerequisites are shown in Table 6.4.

6.5.2   Test Procedure Inspection Process

6.5.2.1   Planning Phase

The moderator and the producer should jointly identify the members of the inspection team. Team members should be selected based on their expertise

Table 6.4

Test Script Inspection Objectives and Prerequisites

Objectives	Prerequisites
Do the validation tests accurately reflect requirements defined in the SRS?	The tests have been reviewed internally and executed at least once.
Have validation tests taken advantage of knowledge of the design where appropriate?	A Test Procedure Inspection Checklist is available. (Note: An example is included in Appendix D.)
Is the project ready to enter the validation testing phase?	Every test has an expected result.

in software engineering, their familiarity with product requirements, and their involvement with the features that are being tested. In most cases, an overview meeting is not required.

The moderator and the producer identify relevant inspection materials, including (1) SRS, (2) test procedures to be inspected, and (3) Test Procedure Inspection Checklist (refer to Appendix D). As for all inspections, commitment from the team members is essential.

The moderator sets the date, time, and location for the inspection meeting and distributes the inspection materials at least five working days prior to the meeting. The moderator should record the total planning time on the Inspection Summary Form.

6.5.2.2 Preparation Phase

To prepare for the inspection meeting, each inspector becomes very familiar with the test procedures being inspected, the SRS, and the Test Procedure Inspection Checklist. Each inspector reviews the test procedures and looks for potential discrepancies between the test and the SRS. The checklist helps focus attention on areas known to be problems. Each discrepancy is noted on an Inspection Problem Report Form, identifying the relevant locations in the Test Procedure and SRS paragraph references.

6.5.2.3 Inspection Meeting Phase

At the inspection meeting, the moderator must first determine if the inspection team is adequately prepared and reviews the ground rules as described in Appendix B.

The moderator begins the inspection by asking the team for potential discrepancies on the first test.

The team must reach consensus on each potential discrepancy and also decide how to categorize each discrepancy that they do agree on. This information is recorded on the Inspection Problem Report Form and is used later on as the basis for making improvements to the Test Procedure Inspection Checklist.

After all of the tests have been discussed, the moderator will recap the discrepancies the team has agreed on and ask if the team wants to schedule a follow-up inspection. If not, the moderator is responsible for working with the producer and reviewing the corrective actions. If the team wants a follow-up inspection, the moderator schedules it.

The moderator records the duration of the inspection meeting on the Inspection Summary Form and adjourns the meeting. The moderator distributes meeting minutes within two working days of the meeting.

6.5.2.4   Follow-Up Phase

As requested by the team, the moderator works with the producer to resolve discrepancies raised at the meeting. Upon successful completion, the moderator will complete the Corrective Action portion of the Inspection Summary Form to indicate that the inspection has been completed.

6.6   Summary

In this chapter, we have discussed how to apply the same inspection process to several different deliverables produced as part of the software development process. By applying the inspection process and by collecting data resulting from performing inspections, you can expect to achieve significant improvements both in the product and in your process.

References

[1]   Grady, R. B., and T. VanSlack, "Key Lessons in Achieving Widespread Inspection Use," *IEEE Software*, July 1994, pp. 46–57.

[2]   Banard, J., and A. Price, "Managing Code Inspection Information," *IEEE Software*, Vol. 11, March 1994, pp. 59–69.

[3]   Good, D. L., "Cost-Effectiveness," *ACM Software Engineering Notes*, April 1986, p. 82.

[4]   Friedman, D. P., and G. M. Weinberg, *Walkthroughs, Inspections, and Technical Reviews,* 3rd ed., New York: Dorset House, 1990, p. 310.

[5]   Weiner, L. R., *Digital Woes: Why We Should Not Depend on Software,* Reading, MA: Addison-Wesley, 1993, p. 38.

7

Software Quality Metrics

Lord Kelvin observed, "When you can measure what you are speaking about, and express it in numbers, you know something about it; but when you cannot measure it, when you cannot express it in numbers, your knowledge is of a meager and unsatisfactory kind; it may be the beginning of knowledge, but you have scarcely in your thoughts advanced to the stage of science" [1]. We might loosely translate this as, "To measure is to know."

Recall the last product that your organization released. See if you can answer the following questions about that product:

- How large was the product (as measured by lines of source code or megabytes of memory)?
- What was the overall productivity of the software engineering group on the product (as measured per thousand lines of code or KLOC per person-hour)?
- How many bugs were found in the product before it was released?
- How many bugs did customers find in the first three months after release?
- Was the overall quality of this product better or worse than the previously released product?

For many software organizations, this type of basic information is not known. In other industries, such information is routinely collected and used by management to make decisions that drive process improvement. In the software industry, however, relatively few organizations routinely collect and use this type of information to improve the software development process.

Size, productivity, number of defects, and relative quality are key indicators that are extremely important for any organization that is serious about quality improvement.

In this chapter, a process for identifying and collecting software metrics that support software quality and software V&V activities is discussed. Identifying and collecting software process and product metrics allows you to:

- Make objective assessments as software is being developed as to whether the software quality requirements are being met;
- Provide a quantitative assessment of software quality that can provide the basis for decisions regarding the software's fitness for use;
- Make objective assessments of the effectiveness of the software development process.

There are excellent books and articles written on software metrics. One of the best is the book by Grady and Caswell [1]. Their book describes their experience in implementing a company-wide software metrics program at HP. Another excellent resource for helping to establish a software metrics program is the IEEE standard for a software quality metrics methodology, IEEE-Standard 1061-1998 [2]. In addition to defining a framework for identifying and collecting software quality metrics, the standard provides numerous examples and an exhaustive annotated bibliography.

These two sources will be used for presenting a process for implementing a software metrics program. The purpose of the software metrics program is to identify both process and product metrics. Additionally, specific metrics related to software V&V activities are identified here and in Chapter 10.

7.1   Strategy for Implementing a Software Metrics Program

The motivation for a software metrics program comes from the fact that the more attributes of software we can measure, the more control we can exert over changing those attributes in a way that will result in process improvement.

Grady and Caswell's experience in implementing a software metrics program at HP has resulted in valuable information that can be used to help start a software metrics program in your organization. Grady and Caswell [1] have identified 10 steps that will lead to implementation of a software metrics program:

1. Define the objectives for the software metrics program.
2. Assign responsibility.
3. Do research.
4. Define initial metrics to collect.
5. Sell the initial collection of these metrics.
6. Get tools for automatic data collection and analysis.
7. Establish training in software metrics.
8. Publicize success stories.
9. Create a metrics database.
10. Establish a way for improving the process in an orderly way.

Defining clear objectives is crucial for success. These objectives should address the expected costs and cost savings that are possible, as well as expected improvements in quality. Remember that quality improvements have both a cost and cost savings. The costs are associated with identifying and collecting metrics. The cost savings derive from lower support costs after product release, fewer maintenance releases, higher customer satisfaction, and as a result, increased sales.

Another key lesson we should learn from Grady and Caswell is that the metrics program should be "only a part of an overall strategy for software development process improvement" [1]. Without an overall program for process improvement, metrics are of little value.

7.2 Software Quality Metrics Framework

IEEE Standard 1061-1998 [2] addresses steps 3, 4, and 6 of HP's 10-step process and provides a process for answering the two most difficult questions to answer when considering a software metrics program: "What to measure?" and "How to measure it?"

Grady and Caswell suggest starting with three simple metrics: size, defects, and effort. While these three metrics are a good starting place, IEEE Standard 1061-1998 [2] defines an approach, in the form of a plan, for identifying and collecting those metrics that relate to quality requirements.

7.2.1   Definitions

IEEE Standard 1061-1998 [2] defines a methodology for establishing a software quality metrics framework. The standard includes many definitions, a few of which are repeated in Table 7.1.

7.2.2   The Framework

The software quality metrics framework is shown in Figure 7.1. The framework is a hierarchy that consists of four levels. At the topmost level are quality requirements that the software product must meet. These requirements are usually expressed in the customer's terms. For example:

- The product will work on the platforms and operating systems currently used in our organization.

- The product will be reliable and will provide mechanisms to prevent loss of data.

- The product will provide the necessary functionality required for accomplishing some task.

- The product will be easy to use.

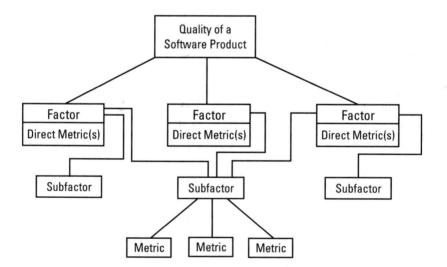

Figure 7.1   Software quality metrics framework. (*Source:* [2] © 1998, IEEE. Reprinted with permission.)

Table 7.1
Definitions from IEEE Standard 1061-1998

metrics framework	A decision aid used for organizing, selecting, communicating, and evaluating the required quality attributes for a software system. A hierarchical breakdown of factors, subfactors, and metrics for a software system.
quality factor	A management-oriented attribute of software that contributes to its quality.
quality subfactor	A decomposition of a quality factor to its technical components.
direct metric	A metric that does not depend upon the measure of any other attribute.
predictive metric	A metric applied during development and used to predict the values of a software quality factor.
software quality metric	A function whose inputs are software data and whose output is a single numerical value that can be interpreted as the degree to which software possesses a given attribute that affects its quality.
process metric	A metric used to measure characteristics of the methods, techniques, and tools employed in developing, implementing, and maintaining the software system.
product metric	A metric used to measure that characteristic of any intermediate or final product of the software development process.

From: IEEE Standard 1061-1998 [2]. © 1998, IEEE. Reprinted with permission.

The second level of the framework represents specific quality factors that relate to the overall quality requirements. Quality factors are an interpretation of the customer's quality requirements and are shown in Table 7.2.

The third level of the framework represents quality subfactors that are obtained by decomposing each quality factor into measurable attributes. Quality subfactors are expressed in terms meaningful to software engineers and are independent of any one quality factor. Quality subfactors associated with the quality factors listed in Table 7.2 are shown in Table 7.3.

At the fourth level are direct metrics. At least one direct metric is associated with each quality factor. Direct metrics serve as the quantitative representation of a quality factor. Examples of direct metrics are shown in Table 7.4.

If we put all the information on quality requirements, quality factors, subfactors, and direct metrics together, we have the information shown in Table 7.5.

7.2.3 Applying the Software Quality Metrics Methodology

This part of the IEEE Software Metrics Methodology answers the "What to measure?" question and can be implemented using a five-step process [2]:

Table 7.2
Quality Factors Associated with Quality Requirements

Quality Requirement	Quality Factor	Description
The product will work on multiple platforms and operating systems currently being used in our organization.	Portability	An attribute that bears on the ability of software to be transferred from one environment to another.
The product will be reliable and will provide mechanisms to prevent loss of data.	Reliability	An attribute that bears on the capability of software to maintain its level of performance under stated conditions for a stated period of time.
The product will provide the necessary functionality required to accomplish some task.	Functionality	An attribute that bears on the existence of certain properties and functions that satisfy stated or implied needs of users.
The product will be easy to use.	Usability	An attribute that bears on the effort needed for use (including preparation for use and evaluation of results) and on the individual assessment of such use by users.

From: IEEE Standard 1061-1992. © 1992, IEEE. Reprinted with permission.

1. Establish software quality requirements.
2. Identify software quality metrics.
3. Implement the software quality metrics.
4. Analyze the software metrics results.
5. Validate the software quality metrics.

7.2.3.1   Establish Software Quality Requirements

By far, the most difficult part of this process is establishing quality requirements. There are some hurdles that need to be overcome before the process of identifying quality requirements can begin in earnest. Typically, these hurdles are related to the following questions:

- What group is empowered to define software quality requirements?
- How should customers provide input?
- How are requirements conflicts resolved?

Table 7.3
Quality Subfactors Associated with Quality Factors

Quality Factor	Quality Subfactors	Description
Portability	Hardware independence	The degree to which software does not depend on specific hardware environments.
	Software independence	The degree to which software does not depend on specific software environments.
	Installability	The effort required for adjusting software to a new environment.
	Reusability	The degree to which software can be reused in applications other than the original application.
Reliability	Nondeficiency	The degree to which software does not contain undetected errors.
	Error tolerance	The degree to which software will continue to work without a system failure that would cause damage to users. Also, the degree to which software includes degraded operation and recovery functions.
	Availability	The degree to which software remains operable in the presence of system failures.
Functionality	Completeness	The degree to which software possesses necessary and sufficient functions to satisfy user needs.
	Correctness	The degree to which all software functions are specified.
	Security	The degree to which software can detect and prevent information leak, information loss, illegal use, and system resource destruction.
	Compatibility	The degree to which new software can be installed without changing environments and conditions that were prepared for the replaced software.
	Interoperability	The degree to which software can be connected easily with other systems and operated.
Usability	Understandability	The amount of effort required to understand software.
	Ease of learning	The degree to which user effort required to understand software is minimized.
	Operability	The degree to which the operation of software matches the purpose, environment, and physiological characteristics of users, including ergonomic factors such as color, shape, and sound.
	Communicativeness	The degree to which software is designed in accordance with the psychological characteristics of users.

From: IEEE Standard 1061-1992. © 1992, IEEE. Reprinted with permission.

Table 7.4
Examples of Direct Metrics

Quality Subfactors	Direct Metrics	Description
Hardware independence	Hardware dependencies	Count hardware dependencies
Software independence	Software dependencies	Count software dependencies
Installability	Installation time	Measure installation time
Reusability	Other applications software can be used in	Count number of other applications software can be or has been used in
Nondeficiency	Test coverage	Measure test coverage
	Inspection coverage	Count modules that have had code inspection
Error tolerance	Data integrity	Count situations where user data becomes corrupted
	Data recovery	Measure ability to recover corrupted data
Availability	Percentage of time software is available for use	Time software available for use divided by total time software could be available for use (expressed as a percentage)
Completeness	Test coverage	Call pair measure or branch coverage measure
Correctness	Defect density	Count defects discovered in each version of software prior to release
Security	Data integrity	Count situations where user data becomes corrupted
	User security	Number of illegal users who are not prevented from using software
Compatibility	Environmental changes	Number of environmental variables that must be changed after software is installed
Interoperability	Operability in mixed application environments	Number of mixed application environments the software can work in correctly
Understandability	Learning time	Time for new user to learn software features

Table 7.4 (continued)

Quality Subfactors	Direct Metrics	Description
Ease of learning	Learning time	Time for new user to learn how to perform basic functions of software
Operability	Human factors	Number of negative comments from new users regarding ergonomics, human factors, etc.
Communicativeness	Human factors	Number of negative comments from new users regarding ergonomics, human factors, etc.

From: IEEE Standard 1061-1992. © 1992, IEEE. Reprinted with permission.

The first hurdle requires that a team be empowered to define software quality requirements. Forming a team that represents all points of view and is acknowledged to be the group that will define software quality requirements is essential for success.

Getting customer input can also be tricky. Customers more often tell you what they don't want rather than what they do want. For example, customers might make statements such as, "I don't want the software to cause my system to lockup as frequently as the current system does" or, "I don't like they way the user interface works on this application" or, "I don't mind if the system crashes once in a while, as long as I don't lose any data." Customers are sophisticated when it comes to software products. Customers realize that they can't afford defect-free software, nor are they willing to wait for it.

So how do you define software quality requirements that are representative of what customers expect? First, talk to your customers. Conduct a quality survey or a focus group. Gather information about the quality of your current products. Find out how good the competitor's products are relative to yours. Do some side-by-side comparisons. And try to put yourself in your customer's shoes. Ask what you would expect if you were buying your products. Survey people in functional groups within the organization that typically deal with customers (such as technical support personnel, application engineers, and sales reps) and get input on what customers tell them about your products.

Next you need to associate each of the software quality requirements with a quality factor. This step requires an understanding of what the software quality requirements are and what the quality factors represent.

Table 7.5
Quality Requirements, Quality Factors, Subfactors, and Direct Metrics

Quality Requirement	Quality Factor	Quality Subfactors	Direct Metrics
The product will work on multiple platforms and operating systems currently being used in our organization.	Portability	Hardware independence	Hardware dependencies
		Software independence	Software dependencies
		Installability	Installation time
		Reusability	Other applications software can be used in
The product will be reliable and will provide mechanisms to prevent loss of data.	Reliability	Nondeficiency	Test coverage
			Inspection coverage
		Error tolerance	Data integrity
			Data recovery
		Availability	Percentage of time software is available for use
The product will provide the necessary functionality required to accomplish [some task description].	Functionality	Completeness	Test coverage
		Correctness	Defect density
		Security	Data integrity
			User security
		Compatibility	Environmental changes
		Interoperability	Operability in mixed application environments
The product will be easy to use.	Usability	Understandability	Learning time
		Ease of learning	Learning time
		Operability	Human factors
		Communicativeness	Human factors

From: IEEE Standard 1061-1992. © 1992, IEEE. Reprinted with permission.

Once the association is completed, the quality factors must be ranked in order of importance. It is at this time that the team must assess technical feasibility, resolve requirements conflicts, and establish priorities. This may take a bit of negotiating and compromising, as some software quality requirements will impact cost, schedule, and functionality. Once you have identified the set of quality factors, you need to get buy-in from the rest of the organization.

7.2.3.2 Identify Direct Metrics

One or more direct metric is associated with each quality factor. Remember that the direct metrics are quantitative measures that reflect the quality factors they are associated with. Each direct metric is assigned target value. In this way, you can measure the degree to which the product possesses the attributes associated with the quality factors.

For example, if one of the quality factors selected was usability, a direct metric that could be associated with that factor might be the time it takes for an untrained user to learn how to the use the software and perform some specific task. The target value for this metric might be 10 minutes. The set of direct metrics and their target values should be reviewed and approved as well.

Each direct metric selected should be documented. IEEE Standard-1061-1998 [2] suggests a format similar to that summarized in Table 7.6.

Table 7.7 shows an example of how a direct metric might be documented.

Table 7.6
Documenting Direct Metrics

Item	Description
Name	Name of the metric
Costs	Costs associated with using this metric
Target Value	Numerical value to be achieved to meet quality requirement
Tools	Software/hardware tools required to help compute metric value
Application	Description of how metric result is to be used
Data Items	Data required as input to compute metric value
Computation	Steps required to compute metric

From: IEEE Standard 1061-1998 [2]. ©1998, IEEE. Reprinted with permission.

Table 7.7
Documenting a Direct Metric

Item	Description
Name	Number of defects detected in selected modules
Costs	Minimal; data can be obtained from bug-tracking tool
Target Value	5
Tools	Spreadsheet
Application	Metric is used for relative comparison to values obtained for other modules
Data Items	Count defects detected at code inspections
Computation	Sum number of defects reported against specific modules

From: IEEE Standard 1061-1998 [2]. © 1998, IEEE. Reprinted with permission.

7.2.3.3   Implement the Direct Metrics

The third step of the five-step process is to implement the direct metrics by defining the data collection procedures and associated tools to collect the data needed for the metrics. Each data item required to compute a direct metric should be documented. The IEEE Standard 1061-1998 [2] suggests a format for documenting data items, which is summarized in Table 7.8.

Table 7.8
Documenting Data Items Required for Direct Metrics

Item	Description
Name	Name given to a data item
Metrics	Metrics associated with the data item
Definition	Straightforward description of the data item
Source	Location of where the data originates
Procedures	Procedures (manual or automated) for collecting the data
Representation	Manner in which data is represented; for example, precision, format, units, etc.
Storage	Location of where the data is stored

From: IEEE Standard 1061-1998 [2]. ©1998, IEEE. Reprinted with permission.

7.2.3.4   Analyze Software Quality Metric Results

Once the data collection is underway, the results need to be analyzed within the context of the project's overall software quality requirements. Any metrics that fall outside of their respective targets should be identified for further analysis. Depending on the results of the analysis, some redesign, or recoding, may be required. Some additional documentation may be required, or some additional testing may be needed. In some cases, no changes at all may be the outcome where metrics only slightly exceed their target ranges and are deemed not critical.

It is important to understand what the metrics represent and not just accept them at face value. Understanding, insight, and confidence in the results can be achieved by delving into the conditions and circumstances that lead to the results reflected by metrics.

7.2.3.5   Validate the Software Quality Metrics

The purpose of validating the metrics is to gain confidence that the numbers reflect reality and eventually to begin to use certain metrics as predictors of those quality attributes (such as reliability) that cannot be measured during software development.

Validation of metric values is based on assessing the statistical significance of the metrics to the quality factors it represents. The details of this process are beyond the scope of this book. The reader is encouraged to refer to IEEE Standard 1061-1998 [2] (as well as the earlier edition IEEE Standard 1061-1992), which contain a thorough description of this process.

7.3   Metrics That Support Software Verification Activities

There are a number of metrics that support the software verification activities described in this book. A few examples are discussed here. Metrics that support software validation activities are discussed in Chapter 10.

7.3.1   Complexity

Through experience, we have learned that the more complex code is, the more difficult it is to maintain, understand, document, test, and support [3–5]. Complexity is a direct metric that can be associated with the quality subfactor correctability and the quality factor maintainability, as shown in Table 7.9.

By applying a complexity measure to a wide sample of the code produced by your organization, you can establish a complexity baseline. This

Table 7.9
Complexity as a Direct Metric

Quality Factor	Quality Subfactor	Direct Metric
Maintainability	*Correctability*	*Complexity*
An attribute that bears on the effort needed for specific modifications.	The degree of effort required to correct errors in software and cope with user complaints.	

From: IEEE Standard 1061-1998 [2]. © 1998, IEEE. Reprinted with permission.

baseline represents the norm for your organization. The norm for your organization may be very different from the norm for other organizations. Once established, this norm can then be used to identify:

- Candidate modules for code inspections;
- Areas where redesign may be appropriate;
- Areas where additional documentation is required;
- Areas where additional testing may be required.

Complexity measures can also be used for a product baseline, which will be discussed in Chapter 8. In this way, you can see how the complexity of the entire product changes as the product evolves throughout the software development process.

Now that we have discussed ways in which complexity measures can be used, let's look at how complexity can be measured.

7.3.1.1   McCabe Cyclomatic Complexity Metric

The McCabe Cyclomatic Complexity metric [6] uses the control flow structure of a program as a relative measure of its complexity. The Cyclomatic complexity is computed as:

$$\text{Cyclomatic complexity} = E - N + 2P$$

where:

$$E = \text{number of edges (or transfers of control)}$$
$$P = \text{number of control paths into the program}$$

N number of nodes (sequential groups of statements containing only one transfer of control)

Use this metric to establish a complexity baseline by measuring complexity on as much of your organization's code as possible. Once you have
established a baseline, look for individual modules whose Cyclomatic complexity falls outside your baseline.

There are several commercially available tools that compute Cyclomatic complexity. (Refer to the References section at the end of this chapter.)

7.3.1.2 Halstead's Software Science

Rather than use a program's structure to compute complexity, Halstead [7]
developed an algorithm for measuring complexity based on a program's size
expressed in terms of the number of unique operators and operands used.

Given the following parameters about a program:

η_1 number of distinct operators

η_2 number of distinct operands

N_1 number of occurrences of operators

N_2 number of occurrences of operands

The results produced include:

η program vocabulary η_1 η_2

There are several commercially available tools that compute Halstead's
Software Science complexity metric.

7.3.2 Defect Metrics

Defect metrics are collected from Inspection Summary Reports. Categoriz-
ing these metrics by defect type (i.e., logic, interface, data definition, documentation), origin, and severity will identify areas of the software
development process that need improvement.

Defect metrics support software V&V activities by allowing for the
tracking of defects by module. This can identify modules that may be candidates for redesign or require additional testing. This can also potentially
identify software engineers who may need additional training in good software engineering practices.

7.3.3 Product Metrics

Product metrics are measures that represent the product your organization has developed. These measurements are essential for software V&V activities and adjusting some of these activities accordingly.

Examples of some key product metrics to collect during the development phase include:

- Number and type of defects found during requirements, design, code, and test inspections;
- Number of pages of documentation delivered;
- Number of new source lines of code created;
- Number of source lines modified;
- Total number of source lines of code delivered;
- Average complexity of all modules delivered;
- Average size of modules;
- Total number of modules;
- Total number of bugs found as a result of unit testing;
- Total number of bugs found as a result of integration testing;
- Total number of bugs found as a result of validation testing;
- Productivity, as measured by KLOC per person-hour.

For example, you may want to adjust the nature and type of regression testing performed based on the number of source lines modified. You may need to add additional tests based on the average complexity of the code.

Tying these measures to product baselines (discussed in Chapter 8) can provide insights into the nature of your product and your software development process. This information can be used to help drive further process improvements.

7.3.4 Process Metrics

Process metrics are intended to reflect the effectiveness of your processes. By collecting these measures and analyzing the results over several projects, you can identify trends that should lead to process improvements.

Examples of some key process metrics to collect include:

- Average find-fix cycle time;

- Number of person-hours per inspection;

- Number of person-hours per KLOC;

- Average number of defects found per inspection;

- Number of defects found during inspections in each defect category;

- Average amount of rework time;

- Percentage of modules that were inspected.

For example, by analyzing the defects found during code inspections, you may find that the same type of defect occurs frequently. To remedy this problem, you can develop a new coding standard that would help prevent this defect from occurring on future projects. The defect-correction time can be used as leverage to institute more effective defect-detection and prevention techniques on future projects.

7.4 Summary

When instituting a measurement program, the following set of attributes, suggested by Humphrey [8], should be considered:

- The measures should be robust.

- The measures should suggest a norm.

- The measures should relate to specific product and process properties.

- The measures should suggest an improvement strategy.

- The measures should be a natural result of the software development process.

- The measures should be simple.

- The measures should be predictable and trackable.

- The measures should not be used as part of a person's performance evaluation.

Measurements support basic software quality improvement principles. Measurements can provide the leverage to drive software process improvements. However, unless you establish aggressive quality improvement plans and goals, nothing will change. Most importantly, these goals must be quantitative.

It is very important to recognize the difference between changing and improving. Improving is based on measurement, while changing is based on perception. The way you know that a change is an improvement is through measurement.

References

[1]   Grady, R. B., and D. L. Caswell, *Software Metrics: Establishing a Company-wide Program*, Englewood Cliffs, NJ: Prentice-Hall, 1987.

[2]   IEEE Standard 1061-1998, IEEE Standard for a Software Quality Metrics Methodology, © 1998 by IEEE, Inc.

[3]   McCabe, T. J., and C. W. Butler, "Design Complexity Measurement and Testing," *Communications of the ACM*, Vol. 32, No. 12, 1989, pp. 1415–1425.

[4]   Walsh, T. I., "Software Readability Study Using a Complexity Measure," *Proc. National Computer Conference*, New York: AFIPS, 1979.

[5]   Ward, W. T., "Software Defect Prevention Using McCabe's Cyclomatic Complexity Metric," *Hewlett Packard Journal*, April 1989, pp. 64–69.

[6]   McCabe, T. J., "Complexity Measure," *IEEE Transactions on Software Engineering*, Vol. SE-2, No. 4, 1976, pp. 308–320.

[7]   Halstead, H. M., *Elements of Software Science*, New York: North-Holland, 1977.

[8]   Humphrey, W. S., *Managing the Software Process*, Reading, MA: Addison-Wesley, 1989, pp. 308.

Web References

Information on commercially available tools for measuring complexity can be found on the World Wide Web at:

- McCabe & Associates home page at http://www.mccabe.com;
- Setlabs, Inc. home page at http://www.molalla.net/~setlabs.

See also Brian Marick's list published periodically in the Usenet discussion group: comp.software.testing.

It is not the intention of the author to recommend or endorse the tools listed here.

Note: URLs cited were accurate as of April 2001.

8

Configuration Management

> The most frustrating software problems are often caused by poor configuration management. The problems are frustrating because they take time to fix, they often happen at the worst time, and they are totally unnecessary. [1]

The Verazanno Narrows Bridge, connecting Staten Island to Brooklyn, New York, is the longest suspension bridge in the world, with a center span of 4,260 feet. The $325 million project was started in 1959 and scheduled for completion in 1965. The project was actually completed in November 1964—under budget and ahead of schedule.

Why is it that over 35 years ago we were able to complete such an incredible engineering feat on time and under budget, but today we have difficulty delivering software to customers on time and with features customers want?

What can we learn from building bridges that can be applied to building software? We know that:

- Software is conceptual and intangible, whereas bridges are physical and very tangible.

- In order to build a bridge, you need a well-defined and documented process.

- The process identifies all of the parts needed, usually in the form of a bill of materials and also includes a detailed assembly procedure.

The assembly procedure usually includes an exploded parts diagram. This diagram shows how all the parts fit together.

Many people have a hard time understanding why software is so difficult to build. This lack of understanding often leads to:

- Lack of control;
- Lack of monitoring;
- Lack of traceability;
- Uncontrolled changes.

When more than two people work on the same software project, there is a real potential their work will conflict. These conflicts can be in one or more of the following areas [2]:

- *Simultaneous update.* How can you prevent one person from inadvertently undoing the changes of another?
- *Shared and common code.* How do you ensure that when a bug is fixed in code shared by several people, all of them are notified? How do you notify everyone that bugs found in common code have been fixed?
- *Versions.* On large projects, there may be several versions of the product in existence at the same time. When a bug is found and fixed in one version, how do you determine if the same bug exists in other versions? How do you ensure that the fix is made to all affected versions?

To prevent these conflicts, some form of process control is required. Configuration management can best be described this way:

Applying configuration management to a project is similar to buying insurance. The amount of money and effort to be spent on configuration management should be based on the value of the product, the perceived risks, and the impact on the product if one of the perceived risks should actually materialize. The question to be answered for each project is then: What is required to obtain a reasonable degree of assurance that the integrity of the product will be maintained? [3]

And lastly, it is important to keep in mind that "[n]o matter where you are in the system lifecycle, the system will change and the desire to change it will persist throughout the lifecycle" [4].

Because of its importance to project success, configuration management is a key software verification activity.

8.1   Software Configuration Managment Basics

Software configuration management (SCM) is a set of management disciplines performed within the context of the software development process. Critical SCM functions include:

- *Identification.* The identification functions address a wide range of issues related to identifying the software configuration items included in a baseline as well as identifying baselines themselves. Refer to Section 8.2.

- *Baseline management.* As software configuration items are built to form baselines, these baselines must be managed and controlled. Criteria for defining, building, and managing baselines are all part of the baseline management function. Refer to Section 8.3

- *Auditing and reporting.* The auditing and reporting functions address issues related to ensuring that what we think is included in a baseline actually is included, as well as providing a level of assurance that SCM procedures are being followed throughout the project. Refer to Section 8.4.

SCM provides a common point of integration for all planning, oversight, and implementation activities for a product—which usually includes software, user documentation (both printed and on-line), and various forms of media including CD-ROM, flash memory, diskette, tape, Electrically Programmable Read-Only Memory (EPROMs), and printed materials.

There are several excellent references on the subject [1–5]. There are two ANSI/IEEE standards that address SCM. ANSI/IEEE Standard 828-1998 [6] provides an outline for an SCM Plan. ANSI/IEEE Standard 1042-1987 [7] includes a very thorough overview of SCM as well as examples of SCM plans that would be appropriate for embedded software applications, a small experimental software project, and a software maintenance activity.

As with any other activity worth doing, SCM activities must be planned. The two ANSI/IEEE standards mentioned above provide excellent resources for developing an SCM plan for a given project.

8.1.1   Definitions

Some key SCM terms that are defined in ANSI/IEEE Standard 1042-1987 [7] are presented in Table 8.1.

8.1.2   Example of a Manufacturing Process

In order to manufacture a product, you need a manufacturing process that includes (1) a bill of material (BOM), (2) a detailed assembly procedure, and (3) an exploded parts diagram. Examples of a real BOM and an exploded parts diagram for something we are familiar with (a lawnmower) are shown in Figures 8.1 and 8.2.

Table 8.1
Definitions from IEEE Standard 1042-1987

Baseline	A baseline is a milestone in the software development process marked by the delivery of one or more software configuration items. A baseline consists of software configuration item(s) that have been formally reviewed and agreed upon, and that thereafter serves as the basis for further development. A baseline can be changed only through formal change control procedures.
Software Configuration Item	A software configuration item is a collection of software elements treated as a unit for the purposes of configuration management.
Configuration	A configuration is defined as consisting of a parts list and an exploded parts diagram which defines all of the elements of a baseline and how they fit together.
Configuration Control Board	The configuration control board (CCB) has responsibility for reviewing and approving changes to baselines. The CCB usually consists of representatives of the project team.
Software	Software, in the context of configuration management, is defined as information that is structured with logical and functional properties. It is created and maintained in many forms and representations over the course of its development
Version	A version is a specific instance of a baseline or a software configuration item.

From: IEEE Standard 1042-1987 [7] © 1988, IEEE. Reprinted with permission.

REF. NO.	PART NO.	CODE	DESCRIPTION	REF. NO.	PART NO.	CODE	DESCRIPTION
1	747-0824		Control Handle Ass'y. (Std.)	34	736-0452		Bell-Wash. .39" I.D.
	647-0004		Control Handle Ass'y. (Deluxe)	35	710-1055		Hex Bolt 3/8-24 x 1" Lg.
2	710-1205		Rope Guide	36	742-0621		21" Blade
3	720-0279		Handle Knob 1/4-20 Thd.		742-0721		21" Mulching Blade (Optional)
4	710-1174		Curved Hd. Bolt 5/16-18 x	37	736-0169		L-Wash. 3/8" I.D.*
			2" Lg.	38	712-0241		Hex Nut 3/8-24 Thd.
6	720-0276		Hand Knob	39	736-0356		Bell-Wash. .39" I.D. x 1.38"
7	710-0605		Oval C-Sunk Mach. Scr.	40	712-0798		Hex Nut 3/8-16 Thd.*
8	736-0501		Spr. Wash. .66" I.D.	41	15261A		Height Adj. Plate
9	712-0324		Hex L-Nut 1/4-20 Thd.	42	15262B		Pivot Bar
10	746-0876		Throttle Lever	43	14832		Spring Lever Ass'y. w/Knob
11	749-0538C		Upper Handle	44	738-0507B		Shld. Bolt .5" Dia. x .357"
12	720-0226		Foam Grip (Optional)	45	736-0105		Bell-Wash. .38" I.D. x .88" O.D.
13	749-0928		Lower Handle	46	738-0102		Axle Bolt
14	726-0240		Cable Tie	47	720-0190		Spring Lever Knob
15	764-0310		Rear Catcher Frame†	48	732-0417A		Spring Lever
16	746-0550		Control Cable—39" (410, 412, 414, 424)	49	14578		Height Adj. Ass'y. Comp.—R.H.
					14579		Height Adj. Ass'y. Comp.—L.H.
	746-0737		Control Cable—51" (411, 413, 423, 425)				(Not Shown)
				50	14765		Pivot Bar
	746-0553		Control Cable—36" (416, 418, 426, 428)	51	782-5002		Front Baffle
17	746-0842		Throttle Control Wire—51" (410, 412, 414, 424)	52	710-0654		Hex L-Wash. Hd. Scr. 3/8-16 x 1" Lg.
	746-0847		Throttle Control Wire—42" (411, 413, 423, 425)	53	782-5003		Rear Baffle
				54	710-1017		Torx Mach. AB-Tap Scr. 1/4 x .62" Lg.
	746-0843		Throttle Control Wire—55" (416, 418, 426, 428)	55	710-0892		Hex L-Wash. Hd. AB-Tap Scr. 1/4 x .62" Lg.
18	764-0311		Front Catcher Frame†	56	682-0516		Handle Brkt. Ass'y.—R.H.
19	764-0309		Grass Bag†	57	682-0515		Handle Brkt. Ass'y.—L.H.
	764-0457		Grass Bag w/Logo†	58	782-0310		21" R.D. Deck
20	714-0104		Int. Cotter Pin 5/16" Dia.	59	**		Wheel Ass'y. Comp.
21	732-0678		Door Spring—R.H.	60	**		Hub Cap
22	732-0677		Door Spring—L.H.	61	764-0433		Grass Bag††
23	782-7000		Rear Discharge Door	62	731-1322		Hard Top Cover††
24	751B213146		Cable Clamp	63	710-0286		Pan Hd. Mach. Scr. 1/4-20 x .5" Lg.††
	7510007755		Casing Clamp (Tec.)	64	712-0324		Hex Nylon L-Nut 1/4-20 Thd.††
25	646-0875		Throttle Body	65	782-9011		Mounting Bracket††
26	811-00185		Throttle Box Comp. (Incl. Ref. 7, 8, 9, 10, 25)	66	782-5007		Mulching Baffle Plug (Optional)
27	—		Engine	67	782-5004		Mulching Baffle—R.R. (Optional)
28	710-1237		Hex Wash. Hd. Scr. #10-32 x .62" Lg.	68	731-1405		Deflector (Optional)
				69	711-0996		Rod (Optional)
	710-0871		Hex Sems Scr. #10-32 x .3" Lg. (Tec.)	70	726-0201		Push Speed Nut (Optional)
				71	710-0192		Truss Scr. #10-24 x .38" Lg.
29	735-0639		Spark Plug Boot (Optional)	72	720-0275		Knob
30	732-0700		Wire Rod	73	731-1506		Deck Shroud (Optional)†
31	731-1236		Rear Flap	76	748-0376		Blade Adapter (416 Only)
32	753-0484		Blade Adapter Kit	77	736-0524		Blade Bell Support (416 Only)
33	710-1044		Hex Bolt 3/8-24 x 1.5" Lg.				

Figure 8.1 Parts list for a lawnmower.

Look closely at the information that is included here. The BOM in Figure 8.1 identifies each part with a part number. The exploded parts diagram in Figure 8.2 graphically illustrates how all the parts fit together. With these facts and a detailed assembly procedure, you have enough information to assemble the parts and build a lawnmower.

If we apply a manufacturing process to building software, we'll need a parts list that represents all of the software parts needed to build the product. We'll need an exploded parts diagram that shows where the parts are and how they fit together. Figures 8.3 and 8.4 illustrate an example of a software parts list and exploded parts diagram. In addition, we need to create a build

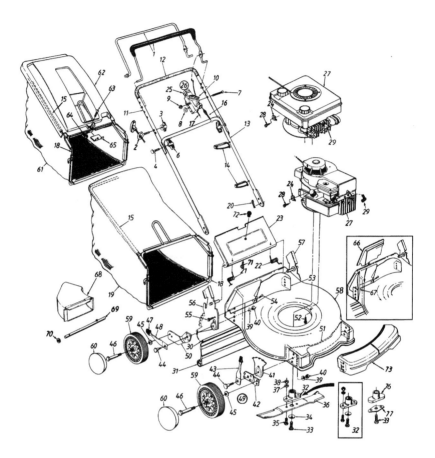

Figure 8.2 Exploded parts diagram for a lawnmower.

procedure that can be used to make the product. A build procedure may be as simple as a make script or as complicated as a document that describes the steps required to make the product.

8.2   Identification

Identification includes the functions associated with naming, labeling, and version control.

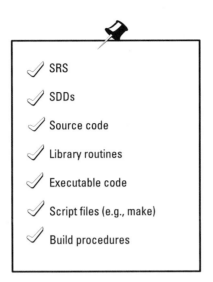

Figure 8.3 A software parts list.

8.2.1   Naming and Labeling

Identification determines how all of the parts of the product are identified and how baselines, which are built from the parts, are identified. The following are key points to consider regarding identification:

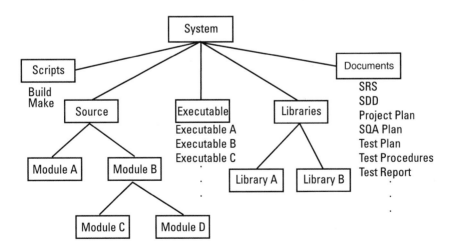

Figure 8.4 A software exploded parts diagram.

- Each software configuration item must be identified and uniquely labeled.

- The identification and labeling scheme should reflect the structure of the product.

- Criteria for identifying and labeling software configuration items need to be established.

- Criteria for identifying and labeling all forms of tests and test data need to be established.

- Criteria for identifying support tools used to build baselines need to be established. It is important to include the compilers, linkers, assemblers, make files, and other tools used to translate the software and build baselines. This ensures that you can always recreate the exact information produced by those tools long after they have been changed, replaced, or updated.

- Special attention may be needed for third party or purchased software that is incorporated into your company's product, especially if there are copyright or royalty issues involved. Criteria for how third party or purchased software will be integrated into your product in a manner that will allow this software to be easily removed, replaced, or updated should be established.

- Special attention may be needed for software that is being reused from other products or software that is intended to be reused.

- Special attention may be needed for prototype software that is intended to be replaced.

8.2.2   Version Control

Version control provides support for parallel development by enabling branching and merging. Parallel development is important because it:

- Allows different projects to use the same source files at the same time;

- Isolates work that is not ready to be shared by the rest of the project;

- Isolates work that should never be shared (i.e., fixing a bug that exists only in an older release);

- Allows software engineers to continue development along a branch even when a line of development is frozen (e.g., during software validation testing).

To support parallel development, SCM tools must support branching, file comparison, and merging functions. Branching is an SCM function in which a configuration item (usually code) evolves simultaneously along two or more branches, with new versions added independently to each branch. This concept is illustrated in Figure 8.5.

File comparison is a facility that compares files with the same name in two or more different branches or baselines and identifies those files that are different.

Merging is the process of selectively applying changes made to source files in branches or other baselines to the corresponding source files in the

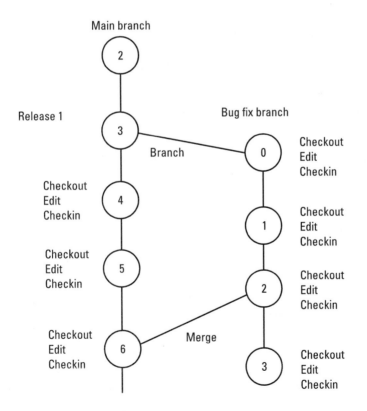

Figure 8.5 Branching and merging.

main branch. Branching, file comparison, and merging are key functions for supporting SCM, especially for larger projects.

A version control procedure that provides a mechanism for making changes to a known baseline in a controlled manner. Key requirements of this procedure are as follows:

- Proposed changes to baselines must have some level of review.
- The impact (to cost, schedule, software development, and manufacturing) of proposed changes must be identified and understood.
- Where appropriate, approval of the CCB, key managers, and project team members must be obtained;
- Approved changes must be properly implemented.
- Once changes are approved, all affected parties are notified of the changes.

8.2.3   Software Configuration Items

Examples of software configuration items are shown in Table 8.2.

8.3   Baseline Management

Baseline management applies to the many different types of baselines. It includes managing the workspace of individual developers, assessing changes to baselines, managing incomplete versions of software during development, and managing versions of the product once they are released to customers (this is also referred to as release engineering). Each of these types of baselines is discussed below.

Creating and managing baselines is an effective way to allow many people to work concurrently. Baseline management basics are discussed below in the form of FAQs.

What Baselines Are Required to Be Defined and Managed?

Baselines are typically aligned with major milestones on projects. It is important to apply the baseline concept to documents as well as to code. For example, there may be a requirements baseline that represents the approved SRS, a design baseline, which represents the approved SDD, and several code baselines. Each version of software produced by the software engineering group constitutes a baseline. During the software validation phase, the ability to

Table 8.2
Examples of Software Configuration Items

Items	Related Information
Product concept specification	
Software project plans	Software development plan
	Software quality assurance plan
	SCM plan
	Software V&V plan
Software requirements specification (SRS)	
Software design descriptions (SDDs)	
Source code	Source listings
	Executable files
	Make files
	Libraries
Database descriptions	Schema and file description
	Initial content
SCM procedures	Source tree structure
	Daily build procedures
	Backup procedures
	Software problem reports
Software release process	Internal release process
	External release process
	Release documentation
Software test documents	Test plans
	Test procedures
	Test scripts
	Test data
	Test reports
User documentation	User manuals
	On-line help
	System administration documentation
	Service documents
Maintenance documentation	Software maintenance plan
	Software problem reports
	Change requests

control changes to code, and thus manage baselines, is extremely important, as we will see in Chapter 9.

How Is the Current Software Configuration Defined?

The current software configuration can be thought of as a snapshot of everything the project has produced at some point in time. It can include documents, software (source, object, executables), tests, and user information. Specifically for software, a configuration is defined in terms of the functionality it embodies at the time the snapshot is taken. This functionality changes over time and should be measured against the requirements defined in the SRS.

Who Must Approve Changes to Baselines?

In many organizations, a CCB has responsibility and authority for approving changes to baselines. The CCB consists of people representing a cross-section of the project and typically include software engineering, software QA, project management, technical publications, manufacturing, and other functions as appropriate. This board is empowered to review and approve changes to the various baselines defined in the project plan. The CCB also has responsibility for communicating approved changes to the rest of the organization, thus helping to make software development more visible and tangible.

How and Where Are Baselines Created and Physically Controlled?

Document baselines are created and controlled by using a document control system. Such a system consists of procedures that define how documents are reviewed, approved, and changed in a controlled manner. Software tools to control document baselines may be used if appropriate.

Code baselines are always created using a configuration control tool. There are many commercially available tools for creating and controlling changes to code. In addition to tools, procedures are required to reinforce the tools. Once a baseline is created, software engineers must be prevented from making unapproved changes.

How Are People Informed of Changes?

Communicating changes is very often a difficult problem. Not everyone is interested or needs to know details of every change made to the product. One of the functions of the CCB should be to disseminate approved changes to the project in an appropriate manner.

How Are Baselines Verified?

Baselines are verified by examination (in the case of document baselines) or by inspection and testing (in the case of code baselines). If the features that a baseline is supposed to implement are known, the task of verifying the baseline against known features is conceptually straightforward.

Are Baselines Tied to Project Milestones?

Many baselines are tied to project milestones. Document baselines are usually tied to project milestones such as requirements defined or design completed. But there are also many baselines that may not be tied to a specific milestone. During the coding phase, there may be many baselines created. A few may be tied to a specific milestone such as code freeze, but most are not. As we will see in Chapter 9, during software validation testing, there can be several baselines created as bugs are fixed and verified.

Baselines that are tied to project milestones should be identified in the project plan.

What Information Is Required to Process a Change to a Baseline?

The information required to approve a change to a baseline should be defined by the CCB. For a document baseline, typically the information required might include a list of all the pages that have changed, a summary of the changes, and the changed pages, showing the actual changes to the text.

During the course of a software development project, many baselines are created. One of the most important tasks associated with creating new baselines is assessing the differences between them. Knowing what has changed from one baseline is essential. If problems are encountered in a new baseline, the first question that is asked is what has changed from the previous baseline.

For software baselines, there are two reasons to make changes to code: adding functionality and fixing bugs. When adding functionality, identifying the specific features being added is important when processing a change to the baseline. When fixing bugs, the specific bugs fixed and the modules that are affected by the fix should be provided when processing a change to the baseline.

This becomes especially crucial during the software validation testing phase of the project. It is during this stage that there must be tight control over changes to software. Many projects have a code freeze milestone. After code freeze, the only changes that should be made to the software are changes in response to bugs reported from testing activities. With this level of control, you can associate code changes to bug fixes for purposes of conducting mini inspections to ensure that bug fixes have not inadvertently introduced new bugs. You can also identify changes to source code by module from one baseline to the next. By doing this and by then comparing the list of changed modules to the bug reports that were supposed to have been fixed, you can determine if there were any unapproved changes made to the code.

What Tools, Resources, and Training Are Required to Perform Baseline Change Assessments?

Tools required to perform a baseline change assessment for code baselines are relatively simple. As mentioned earlier, a file comparison tool that can identify changes to source code across baselines and provide a list of changed modules is required. There are many commercially available tools that can provide this information. Resources and training required to do this assessment will of course vary based on project size and complexity. The group that is managing baselines should be the group that provides the baseline change assessment information. It makes sense for the software QA group to perform the analysis of this information and report the results to the project team or the CCB.

What Metrics Should Be Used to Assess Changes to a Baseline?

In trying to determine if changes to a software baseline should be accepted, it is helpful to apply a basic set of metrics to the baseline in order to provide the CCB or project management team with additional information. Examples of the kinds of metrics that are useful include:

- Complexity;
- Average module size;
- Number of modules changed;
- Number of bugs fixed and verified;
- Code coverage.

Additional information on these metrics is included in Chapters 7 and 10.

How Are Unauthorized Changes to Source Code Prevented, Detected, and Corrected?

It is not possible to prevent unauthorized changes to source code. Software engineers love nothing more than a technical challenge. Advertising that your system can prevent unwanted changes presents such a challenge. A far better approach is to provide software engineers with training and an understanding of why unapproved changes are not good for the project. Using a commercially available SCM tool will provide an adequate degree of security.

The baseline change assessment procedure described above can be used to detect unauthorized changes to code baselines. These changes should be presented to the project team and the CCB for resolution.

What Tools, Resources, and Training Are Required To Perform Baseline Management?

A fully featured software CM tool is an absolute requirement for most every software development project. There are several commercially available SCM tools that can provide the level of control required for many types of projects.

The scope and size of a project will determine the resources required for SCM functions. In some organizations, the software engineering group performs SCM responsibilities. This approach may work well for small projects, but quickly falls apart on larger projects where communication and timeliness of information are key. SCM functions can be effectively performed as part of an SQA group. On larger projects, there may be justification for a separate SCM group.

Everyone involved with producing documents and software will require some SCM training. This can range from basic SCM principles to details of using SCM tools.

8.3.1 Workspace Management

Software engineers need to have a consistent and reproducible workspace area that they can use for development activity. This workspace area (commonly called a play area, or a sandbox) allows developers to develop and debug their code while sharing those files that need to be shared and shielding the rest of the project from the inherent instability of evolving code. SCM tools used on most projects need to support this capability.

8.3.2   Baseline Change Assessment

Another baseline management function that should be supported by the SCM tools is baseline change assessment. This assessment provides an effective way to manage changes to software and can be used throughout the development phase, and especially during the software validation testing phase.

During development, new modules that are integrated into a baseline will frequently have undesirable effects. A baseline change assessment helps identify those modules most recently integrated in order to determine where the problems are.

During software validation testing, the baseline change assessment is used to ensure that the only changes that are made to the code are changes associated with bug fixes. By comparing the source files of the current version with the previous version, you can identify the modules that have changed. If you then match the changed modules with the affected modules indicated on your bug reports, you can determine if only those modules that should have changed, did change.

8.3.3   Version Management

An essential SCM function is reliably building and re-creating versions of the product as it evolves and after it is released. During development, incomplete versions of the product are built and tested on a regular basis. The SCM tools need to be able to re-create previous versions exactly, since frequently it may be desired to retreat to a previous version. Once development is completed, the SCM tools need to manage the versions of software that are released to customers. All necessary information (including the specific compilers, linkers, and other tools used) must be maintained in order to ensure that each released version of the product can be recreated.

8.4   Auditing and Reporting

Auditing and reporting procedures are intended to provide assurance that the software product matches the software configuration items (software and documents). This typically can include such activities as ensuring that the source code and the software documentation match and that the software and the user documentation match.

Auditing and reporting helps answer the following questions:

- Are mechanisms in place to provide an audit trail such as change histories?

- Does there need to be more than one type of audit performed for each baseline?

- How are subcontractors involved in an audit?

- How are third party software configuration items managed, controlled, and audited?

- Is there a separate audit trail for each baseline; for each component; for each functional group?

- What are the audit trail requirements imposed by other organizations, such as customers, regulatory agencies, and corporate policies?

- What tools, resources, and training are required to perform each type of audit?

- What type of information needs to be maintained after product development is completed and for how long?

- How is software (in its physical media form) retained?

- Are secure storage facilities required?

- Is media protected from disaster? How?

Auditing and reporting includes tasks associated with auditing, reporting, and records collection and retention.

8.4.1 Auditing

Audits are one way an organization can ensure that the project team has done all of the required work in a way that satisfies customer requirements and external obligations. During the course of a software development project, several different types of audits may be performed. These include in-process audits, functional audits, physical audits, and quality system audits. Several attributes of each of these different types of audits are illustrated in Table 8.3.

8.4.2 Configuration Status Accounting

A configuration status accounting procedure consists of mechanisms for capturing status information regarding each configuration item and for reporting this status in a timely manner. Configuration status accounting becomes a critical task as the size and complexity of a project increases. The reports that are produced are most frequently used by project management to assess the current status of a project.

Key requirements of this procedure include:

- Identifying the types of information that project managers need;
- Identifying the degree of control needed by project management;
- Identifying the reports required and the different audiences for each report;
- Identifying the information required to produce each report.

8.4.3 Reports, Record Collection, and Retention

As each audit is performed, the results are reported and distributed to the project team. Record-collection procedures identify the specific information that needs to be collected and retention procedures define how long the information should be kept.

8.5 Summary

Some of the key points regarding SCM are:

- Change is inevitable.
- Defined procedures are required to manage change effectively without preventing change from occurring.
- Software, since it exists in many different forms, presents many challenges from a control, management, and tracking perspective.
- Knowing what you have and how you got there is very important.
- Being able to re-create exactly what is delivered to customers is essential.

Maintaining project deliverables throughout the product life cycle (which can be many years) is a key benefit of SCM. This benefit means that when (not if) you decide to make changes to your product, you will have the benefit of all available knowledge of the requirements, design, implementation, and test.

Table 8.3

Types of Audits

Attribute	In-Process Audit	Functional Audit (FA)	Physical Audit (PA)	Quality Systems Audit
Objectives	Verify the consistency of the design as it evolves through the development process.	Verify that functionality and performance are consistent with requirements defined in the SRS.	Verify that the as-built version of software and documentation are internally consistent and ready for delivery.	Independent assessment of the compliance to the software QA plan (SQAP).
Materials Required	SRS; SDDs; Source code waivers; Approved changes; Software verification & validation plan (SVVP); Test results	SRS; Executable code waivers; Test programs; Software V&V reports; In-process audit reports; Test documentation; Completed tests; Planned tests.	Waivers; Architecture; SRS and SDDs; Approved changes; Acceptance; Test documentation; Customer documentation; Approve product labeling; Software version; FA reports.	SQAP; All documents associated with software development activities.
Activities	Hardware and Software interfaces consistent with SRS and SDDs. Code fully tested to SVVP. Evolving design matches SRS. Code consistent with SDDs.	Audit test documentation against test data. Audit SV&V report. Ensure results of reviews have been incorporated.	Audit SRS. FA reports for actions taken. Sample SDDs for completeness. Audit customer. Manuals for completeness and consistency. Software delivery media and controls.	Examine quality program documents. Selective compliance testing. Interview staff. Perform in-process audits. Examine FA and PA reports.
Results	In-process audit reports noting all discrepancies.	FA report recommending approval, contingent approval, or disapproval.	PA report recommending approval, contingent approval, or disapproval.	Overall evaluation of compliance with the software quality program.

References

[1]   Humphrey, W. S., *Managing the Software Process*, Reading, MA: Addison-Wesley, 1989.

[2]   Babich, W. A., *Software Configuration Management: Coordination for Team Productivity*, Reading, MA: Addison-Wesley, 1986.

[3]   Buckley, F., *Implementing Configuration Management*, 2nd ed., Los Alamitos, CA: IEEE Computer Society Press, 1996.

[4]   Bersoff, E. H., et al., *Software Configuration Management*, Englewood Cliffs, NJ: Prentice-Hall, 1980.

[5]   Bryan, W., et al., *Software Configuration Management*, Los Alamitos, CA: IEEE Computer Society Press, 1980.

[6]   ANSI/IEEE Standard 828-1998, IEEE Standard for Software Configuration Management Plans, © 1983 by IEEE, Inc.

[7]   ANSI/IEEE Standard 1042-1987, IEEE Guide to Software Configuration Management, © 1988 by IEEE, Inc.

Part III
Overview of Software Validation Activities

Recall the definitions of "verification" and "validation": verification is "[t]he process of evaluating a system or component to determine whether the products of a given development phase satisfy conditions imposed at the start of that phase" [1]. In other words, "Are we building the product right?" Validation is "[t]he process of evaluating a system or component during or at the end of the development process to determine whether it satisfies specified requirements" [1]. In other words, "Did we build the right product?"

Validation activities are defined around three basic processes: testing, measurement, and software reliability growth. In Chapter 9 we discuss testing as a validation activity. Different levels of testing and the objectives of each are discussed. As with any activity, the testing process must be planned. An outline for a software validation test plan is discussed. References to several ANSI/IEEE standards are provided.

In Chapter 10, several measures that enable the planning, scheduling, and managing of the testing process are discussed. In Chapter 11, the concept of software reliability growth is presented in the context of information that can be used by management in deciding when to stop testing and release the product.

Reference

[1]   ANSI/IEEE Standard 610.12-1990, IEEE Standard Glossary for Software Engineering Terminology, © 1990 by IEEE, Inc.

9

Testing

Testing is the process of executing programs with the intention of finding errors. [1]

Testing can show the presence of bugs but never their absence. [2]

The above observations by Myers and Dijkstra illustrate common misconceptions about testing. Unfortunately, many people still think that testing can be used to demonstrate that their software doesn't have any bugs. Confusion regarding what testing can and cannot do is rampant throughout the industry. In fact, many people do not understand just how difficult testing is. Myers offers the following example to illustrate how problematic it can be:

A program accepts as input three integer values. The three values represent the three sides of a triangle. Based on the three values, the program is to determine whether the triangle is isosceles, scalene, or equilateral. [1]

As an exercise, try writing down the set of test cases that you think would adequately test this simple program. For example, you would want a test in which all three integers were zero (an invalid triangle). Myers identifies a set of test cases that would adequately test the program, most of which were based on actual errors that were detected in various versions of programs written for this exercise. After you've written down the tests that you think are needed, take a look at Appendix I. Compare your set with the set presented there. How did you do?

On average, even experienced programmers can think of only slightly more than half of the test cases needed. The point of this exercise is to illustrate just how difficult it is to develop a set of thorough test cases for even a trivial program. Imagine how many tests would be required for a complex application.

Consider another trivial program from Humphrey [3] that analyzes strings of alphabetic characters, 10 at a time. There are 26^{10} possible combinations of inputs this program could expect to see. Would it be feasible to test all possible combinations of inputs?

To test all possible inputs, a minimum of 26^{10} (~141 trillion) tests would be required. Assume it takes very little time to write these tests. If it took only one microsecond to execute each test, it would take about 4.5 years to execute all of the 141 trillion tests once.

Clearly, for most software products where the size of the input space is many orders of magnitude larger than this trivial example, the time required to develop and execute such large numbers of tests cannot be economically justified, even if it were feasible.

If we cannot test all possible combinations of inputs, our objective then becomes to select a relatively small number of tests that have a high probability of finding defects. An obvious question: How do you write tests that can do this?

There is no magic formula for writing tests that have a high probability of finding defects. There are, however, some good testing practices that should be followed to help maximize the benefit gained from the testing activity. These good testing practices (based on Myers [1]) are summarized as follows:

- A good test case is one that has a high probability of detecting an undiscovered defect, not one that shows that the program works correctly.

- It is impossible to test your own program.

- A necessary part of every test case is a description of the expected result.

- Avoid nonreproducible or on-the-fly testing.

- Write test cases for valid as well as invalid input conditions.

- Thoroughly inspect the results of each test.

- As the number of detected defects in a piece of software increases, the probability of the existence of more undetected defects also increases.
- Assign your best people to testing.
- Ensure that testability is a key objective in your software design.
- Never alter the program to make testing easier.
- Testing, like almost every other activity, must start with objectives.

In this chapter, we will review levels of testing, test methods that are appropriate for each level, and types of tests. We will also discuss a concurrent development/testing model that is more effective than commonly used testing approaches. Lastly, we discuss the process of planning a testing activity.

There are several excellent books written on software testing [4–7]. These books provide much more depth and insight into the complexities of testing. This chapter is intended as an overview for practitioners who have not been exposed to any formal training in testing. After reviewing the material in this chapter, I strongly urge those who are so inclined to do further study in this area.

9.1 Levels, Methods, and Types of Tests

Testing can be viewed as a hierarchy composed of different levels, methods, and types, as shown in Figure 9.1.

9.1.1 Test Levels

Each level of testing has specific objectives and limitations. The lowest, most basic testing level is called *unit* or *module testing*. The objectives of unit testing are to find defects in logic, data, and algorithms by testing modules individually. The next testing level is called *integration testing*. The objectives of integration testing are to find defects in interfaces between units by testing selected units as a group. The next level is called *validation* or *system testing*. Recall once again the definition of validation: "The process of evaluating a system or component during or at the end of the development process to determine whether it satisfies specified requirements" [8]. The objectives of validation testing are to determine if the software meets all of its

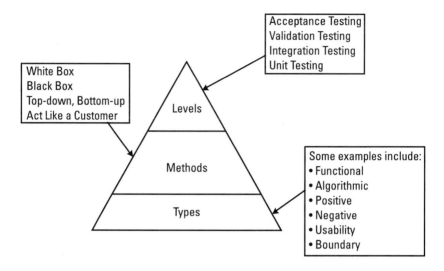

Figure 9.1 Testing hierarchy.

requirements as defined in the SRS. *Regression testing* entails selectively rerunning validation tests to ensure that bug fixes have not introduced new bugs.

Some organizations actively involve customers in testing by providing prerelease software for customer evaluation through what is commonly called *alpha and beta testing.* Customers are frequently reluctant to participate in such activities because (1) there is no guarantee that problems found by customers will be fixed, and (2) such testing requires time and resources that customers may not have.

Beta testing can be a useful activity for customers and developers if it is planned and scripted so that customers are expected to follow a defined sequence of activities and developers commit to fixing problems reported by customers.

Another level of testing is referred to as *acceptance testing.* Acceptance testing is similar to validation testing, with one difference—the customer is actively involved.

Note that within the software industry, terms such as "unit testing," "integration testing," "validation testing," and "alpha and beta testing" are not used consistently. Therefore, within your organization, it is important that the objectives of these testing activities be precisely defined to minimize confusion and maximize return on investment.

Now let us look at each of these levels in more detail.

9.1.1.1 Unit Testing

The objective of unit testing is to find bugs in individual modules by testing them in an isolated environment. Unit testing is usually considered part of the coding process and typically requires a significant investment in "scaffolding," as illustrated in Figure 9.2. Unfortunately, unit testing is often viewed more as a debugging activity than as a testing activity. Understanding the difference between debugging and testing is very important.

Debugging is defined as the process of detecting, locating, and correcting faults in a computer program [8]. Testing is defined as the process of operating a system or component under specified conditions, observing or recording the results, and making an evaluation of some aspect of the system or component [8].

In many organizations, unit testing is an informal activity performed by software engineers on their own modules with little or no test documentation. To increase the return on investment in unit testing, the use of a buddy system can help. In such a system, each software engineer is assigned a peer who is responsible for unit testing their partner's code. That way, software engineers are not testing their own code. Why is this important? From experience we know that when software engineers test their own code, they

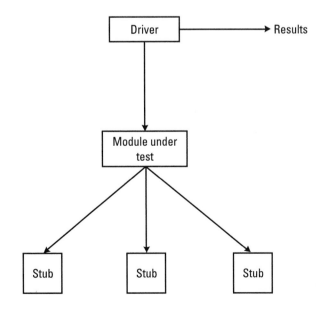

Figure 9.2 Unit testing environment.

subconsciously write tests that show that the code works, rather than writing tests that will find places where the code does not work.

In addition, the following questions can be used as a checklist when developing unit test cases:

- *Algorithms and logic.* Have algorithms and logic been correctly implemented?

- *Data structures (global and local).* Are global data structures used? If so, what assumptions are made regarding global data? Are these assumptions valid? Is local data used? Is the integrity of local data maintained during all steps of an algorithm's execution?

- *Interfaces.* Does data from calling modules match what this module expects to receive? Does data from called modules match what this module provides?

- *Independent paths.* Are all independent paths through the module identified and exercised?

- *Boundary conditions.* Are the boundary conditions known and tested to ensure that the module operates properly at its boundaries?

- *Error handling.* Are all error-handling paths exercised?

IEEE-Standard 1008-1987 [9] provides additional information on unit testing.

9.1.1.2   Integration Testing

The objective of integration testing is to find bugs related to interfaces between modules as they are integrated together. One question frequently asked is, "If all modules are unit tested, why is integration testing necessary?" Here are some answers.

- One module can have an adverse effect on another.

- Subfunctions, when combined, may not produce the desired major function.

- Individually acceptable imprecision in calculations may be magnified to unacceptable levels.

- Interfacing errors not detected in unit testing may appear.

- Timing problems (in real-time systems) are not detectable by unit testing.

- Resource contention problems are not detectable by unit testing.

Integration testing covers a broad range of activities, beginning with the testing of a few modules and culminating with the testing of the complete system. Let us look briefly at the different approaches that can be used.

Incremental integration is a systematic approach to integration whereby the product is constructed and tested in small chunks so that errors are easy to observe, isolate, and correct. Incremental integration can be performed top-down or bottom-up. In top-down integration, modules are integrated by moving downward through the program hierarchy starting with the topmost or main module, as illustrated in Figure 9.3.

Top-down integration, as defined by Pressman [10] is performed as follows:

1. The main control module is used as a driver, and stubs are substituted for all modules directly subordinate to the main module.

2. Depending on the integration approach selected (depth or breadth first), subordinate stubs are replaced by modules one at a time.

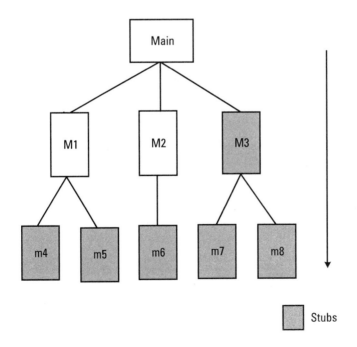

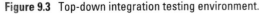

Figure 9.3 Top-down integration testing environment.

3. Tests are run as each individual module is integrated.
4. On the successful completion of a set of tests, another stub is replaced with a real module.
5. Regression testing is performed to ensure that errors have not developed as a result of integrating new modules.

The process is repeated from step 2 until the whole program is integrated. There are some inherent problems with top-down integration, as described by Pressman [10]:

- Many times, calculations are performed in the modules at the bottom of the hierarchy.
- Stubs typically do not pass data up to the higher modules.
- Delaying testing until lower-level modules are ready usually results in integrating many modules at the same time rather than one at a time.
- Developing stubs that can pass data up is almost as much work as developing the actual module.

This leads to another integration approach called bottom-up integration. Pressman [10] defines the bottom-up integration procedure as follows:

- Integration begins with the lowest-level modules, which are combined into clusters, or builds, that perform a specific software subfunction.
- Drivers (control programs developed as stubs) are written to coordinate test case input and output.
- The cluster is tested.
- Drivers are removed and clusters are combined moving upward in the program structure.

As with the top-down approach, the bottom-up method has drawbacks, including (1) the whole program does not exist until the last module is integrated, and (2) timing and resource contention problems are not found until late in the process.

In many organizations, software developers are responsible for performing some form of integration testing. Unfortunately, many organizations pay little attention to intergration testing, and as a result, developers frequently use the Big Bang approach: They integrate all of the product's modules together in one fell swoop and start testing. What usually happens is that there are a lot of problems. Since all the pieces have been integrated, it is usually more difficult to find the offending modules.

Further, the distinction between unit testing and integration testing is often fuzzy. Often, unit tests are repeated as modules are integrated together. Clearly, to maximize return on investment, integration tests need to be written that help determine if the interfaces between modules are working as defined in the design specifications. If unit tests can be used for this purpose, that's good. If they can't, then additional tests need to be written.

Refer to ANSI/IEEE Standard 829-1998 [11] for more information on documenting the testing process.

9.1.1.3 Validation Testing

The objective of validation testing is to determine if the software meets all of its requirements as defined in the SRS.

Frequently, organizations perform what is referred to as validation testing without the benefit of written requirements. A question to ask then, is, Can validation testing be effective without written requirements?

When you perform validation testing without written requirements, what you are actually doing is demonstrating that the software "does what it does." Is "what it does" what it is supposed to do? Without written requirements, how would you know? My advice to those organizations that perform validation testing without written requirements is as follows.

First and foremost, write the requirements down before the tests are developed. This is so important, it is recommended that anyone on the project team who has the ability to do it be assigned the task. We will discuss this topic further in Chapter 15 and Appendix L.

If for some reason the requirements cannot be written down, then the people who write tests will need to have domain knowledge, that is, knowledge of the product and how customers use the product in their environment. Domain knowledge is not easy to come by. And testers with domain knowledge are scarcer than hen's teeth. Based on their domain knowledge, testers can develop tests based on how they expect the software to work and their knowledge of how customers would use the software in their environment. Clearly, this is not always possible.

If you can't get the requirements written down and don't have testers with domain knowledge, whatever testing you do will likely be superficial and of little value to you or your customers.

As part of validation testing, regression testing is performed to determine if the software still meets all of its requirements in light of changes and modifications made to the software. Regression testing involves selectively repeating existing validation tests, not developing new tests.

9.1.1.4   Alpha and Beta Testing

The objectives of alpha and beta testing are often vague. If you are going to invest time and resources in this activity, there should be clear objectives to maximize return on investment. If you choose to perform alpha and beta testing by providing prerelease versions of software to some subset of your customers, be aware of the following:

1. For alpha and beta testing to be most effective, you should provide your customers with an outline of the things that you would like them to focus on and specific test scenarios for them to execute. In this way, you can get very specific and valuable feedback from key customers.

2. Provide customers who are actively involved in your alpha and beta testing program with a commitment to fix defects that they find when they perform the test scenarios you identify for them. This provides the motivation customers need to commit resources to alpha and beta testing your software.

9.1.1.5   Acceptance Testing

Acceptance testing is similar to validation testing, except that customers are present or directly involved. Acceptance testing can be a repeat of (or subset of) the same tests used for validation testing or can employ tests developed entirely by customers. In the latter case, it would be prudent to ask your customer for those tests in advance so that you can run as many of them as possible as part of your validation testing activity.

9.1.2   Test Methods

Just as there are levels of testing, there are several different testing methods. For example:

- *White box* or *glass box* testing is a method of testing in which knowledge of the software's internal design is used to develop tests.

- In *functional* or *black box* testing, no knowledge of software design is used and tests are strictly based on requirements and functionality.

- *Top-down* and *bottom-up* are examples of methods for performing incremental integration testing, whereby modules are integrated and tested based on their position in the module hierarchy.

- *Act-like-a-customer* (ALAC) testing is a test method in which tests are developed based on knowledge of how customers use your software. ALAC tests are based on the principle illustrated in Figure 9.4. From experience we know that complex software products have many bugs and that customers typically find only a small percentage of these bugs. To maximize benefit to your customers, focus testing and bug-fixing activities on those bugs that your customers are likely to find.

Table 9.1 summarizes the levels of testing and test methods that are most appropriate for each level.

9.1.3 Test Types

In addition to different levels of tests and different methods, there are also many different types of tests that can be used. Table 9.2 lists examples of test types.

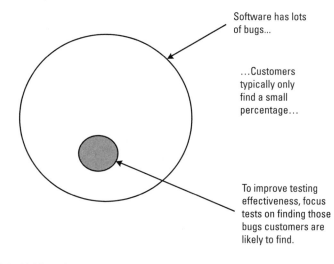

Software has lots of bugs...

...Customers typically only find a small percentage...

To improve testing effectiveness, focus tests on finding those bugs customers are likely to find.

Figure 9.4 ALAC testing.

Table 9.1
Testing Levels and Test Methods

Test Level	Objectives	Performed by	Test Environment	Test Methods
Unit	Find bugs in logic, data, and algorithms in individual modules.	Software engineers	Isolated. Stubs and scaffolding may be required.	White box
Integration	Find bugs in interfaces between modules.	Software engineers	Isolated or simulated. Stubs and scaffolding required.	White box Top-down and bottom-up
Validation	Determine if software meets SRS.	QA	Actual	Functional and ALAC
Regression	Determine if software still meets SRS in light of changes.	QA	Actual	Functional and ALAC
Acceptance	Determine if software meets customer requirements.	Customer, QA, or project team	Actual (usually at customer site)	Functional and ALAC

Table 9.2
Test Types

Functional	Load/Stress
Algorithmic	Security
Positive	Performance
Safety-related tests	Documentation
Compatibility	Timing
Life	Error checking
Negative	Power failure
Usability	Out of resources/space
Boundary	Installation
Startup and shutdown	Upgrade
Configuration	Volume scalability tests
Platform	Throughput/performance tests

Some of the more common test types are:

- *Functional.* Tests designed to determine if specific functions/features work as specified.

- *Algorithmic.* Tests designed to determine if specific algorithms have been implemented correctly.

- *Positive tests.* Tests designed to determine if a feature produces results that are consistent with the stated requirements when the software is used properly.

- *Negative tests.* Tests designed to determine if the software behaves reasonably when faced with invalid inputs or unexpected operator actions.

- *Usability tests.* Tests that exercise specific user interface features in order to determine if the software behaves as would be expected by trained/untrained users.

- *Boundary tests.* Tests that exercise specific limitations of the product, such as minimum and maximum values, to determine if the software behaves reasonably.

- *Startup/shutdown tests.* Tests designed to determine if startup and shutdown functions have been implemented correctly.

- *Configuration tests.* Tests designed to determine if a feature produces results that are consistent with the stated requirements when the software is used properly.

- *Platform tests.* Tests designed to determine if the software works properly on all supported platforms/operating systems.

- *Load/stress tests.* Tests that exercise the product under stated or expected load conditions.

When planning a testing effort, it is critically important that an appropriate mix of the many test types be included in the overall suite of tests developed. Using a broad mix of test types increases the likelihood that defects will be uncovered and therefore increases the return on investment.

9.2   Concurrent Development/Validation Testing Model

Given an understanding of the different levels of testing and what they can achieve, the different testing methods, and the many test types, we now need to understand the relationship between development and testing. In organizations where this relationship is not understood, validation testing often happens as illustrated in Figure 9.5.

In these organizations, software development begins with only a vague statement of requirements. Developers must fill in the blanks where requirements are missing. When they do this, they frequently don't update the requirements document. As they get closer to being done (however they define "done"), they throw the software over the proverbial wall to QA. As QA is not usually aware of how the developers chose to fill in the blanks, they can do only a cursory test at best. Since there are no criteria defined to determine when to stop testing, most organizations use the calendar. When testing is done this way, product quality is lower and the return on investment is much less than it could be.

To increase the return on investment from your testing effort, you need a good understanding of testing levels, methods, and types. Ideally, you should plan to perform a mix of testing activities, commensurate with risk and business objectives. In this way, you will be more likely to find problems before your customers do.

How can you do this? First, get QA involved as early as possible. Second, use a concurrent development/validation testing model similar to that shown in Figure 9.6.

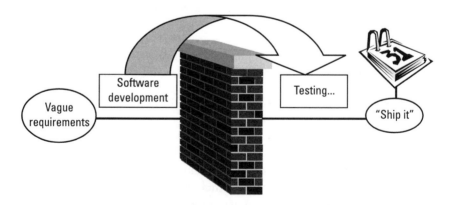

Figure 9.5 Typical validation testing process.

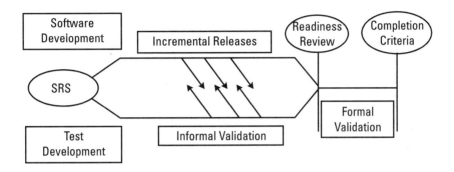

Figure 9.6 Concurrent development/validation testing model.

In this model, software development and validation testing activities are based on a complete and updated SRS. Once the SRS is available, software development activities like design and coding begin. Similarly, validation activities, such as test planning (discussed in Section 9.3) and test development, also begin in parallel with development activities. The key to the concurrent development/testing model is that development and testing are both based on the SRS.

As developers complete coding, unit testing, and integration testing, pieces of the product are made available to QA. In the meantime, QA has been planning the testing effort and developing tests based on the SRS. QA can now begin to test these incremental pieces. This approach enables QA to ensure that its tests are correct and provides immediate feedback to developers.

9.2.1 Informal Validation

As development continues, incremental releases are provided to QA, which develops its tests in the same order as the incremental features are being developed. By the time coding is completed, all of the validation tests that need to be run should have been written and run at least once. Thus, the majority of problems should have been found, reported, and corrected by this time. This activity is referred to as *informal validation* because tests are run informally; some features are expected to be missing and some tests are expected to fail as a result. Informal validation:

- Provides an opportunity for validation tests to be developed and debugged early in the software development process;
- Provides early feedback to software engineers;
- Results in formal validation being less eventful, since most of the problems have already been found and fixed.

Once coding is completed and most all of the validation tests have been run at least once, the project team is ready for the validation readiness review.

9.2.2   Validation Readiness Review

The purpose of this review is to ensure that everything is in place before beginning formal validation. The main differences between informal validation and formal validation are as follows:

- During informal validation developers can make any changes needed in order to comply with the SRS.
- During informal validation QA runs tests and makes changes as necessary in order for the tests to comply with the SRS.
- During formal validation the only changes that can be made to the code are bug fixes in response to bugs reported during formal validation testing. No new features can be added at this time.
- During formal validation the same set of tests run during informal validation is run again. No new tests are added.

The purpose of this review is to ensure that formal validation begins only when the project is ready. Starting formal validation prematurely results in wasted effort, increased frustration, and pressure to release products with far too many defects.

Configuration management (discussed in Chapter 8) is essential for increasing the effectiveness of validation testing. CM tools provide a controlled environment and a mechanism for analyzing changes between baselines. Having CM tools in place and the code under version control is an essential criterion for starting validation testing.

The test plan (discussed in Section 9.3) should define the criteria that should be met before formal validation can begin. Example criteria include the following:

- Software development is completed (a precise definition of "completed" is required—refer to "Binary quality gates at the inch-pebble level" in Appendix L, Section L.2).
- The test plan has been reviewed, approved, and is under document control.
- A requirements inspection has been performed on the SRS.
- Design inspections have been performed on the SDDs.
- Code inspections have been performed on all "critical modules."
- All test scripts are completed and the software validation test procedure document has been reviewed, approved, and placed under document control.
- Selected test scripts have been reviewed.
- All test scripts have been executed at least once.
- CM tools are in place and all source code is under configuration control.
- Software problem reporting procedures are in place.
- Validation testing completion criteria have been developed, reviewed, and approved.

9.2.3 Formal Validation

After the validation readiness review is held and the project determines that the criteria have been met, formal validation begins. At this point in the project, software changes are restricted to changes required to fix bugs. *No new functionality can be added.*

During the formal validation phase, the following activities are performed.

1. The same tests that were run during informal validation are executed again and results recorded.
2. Software Problem Reports (SPRs) are submitted for each test that fails (i.e., the software does not meet requirements).
3. SPR tracking is performed and includes the status of all SPRs (i.e., open, fixed, verified, deferred, not a bug).

4. For each bug that is fixed, the SPR identifies the modules that were changed to fix the bug.

5. Baseline change assessment (discussed in Chapter 8) is used to ensure that only those modules that should have changed actually have changed and that no new features have slipped in.

6. Informal code reviews (not formal inspections) are selectively conducted on changed modules to ensure that new bugs are not being introduced.

7. Time required to find and fix bugs (find-fix cycle time) is tracked.

8. Regression testing is performed using the following guidelines:

   a. Use complexity measures discussed in Chapter 7 to help determine which modules may need additional testing.
   b. Use judgment in deciding which tests need to be rerun.
   c. Base decision on knowledge of software design and past history.

9. Track test status (i.e., passed, failed, or not run).

10. Record cumulative test time (cumulative hours of actual testing) for software reliability growth tracking (described in Chapter 11).

A key element of an effective testing effort is knowing when to stop testing. It is very important to have objective, measurable completion criteria defined, reviewed, and approved early in the development process. Some examples of completion criteria include the following:

- All test scripts have been executed.

- All SPRs have been satisfactorily resolved. (Resolution could include bugs being fixed, deferred to a later release, determined not to be bugs, and so on.) All parties must agree to the resolution. This criterion could be further defined to state that all high-priority bugs must be fixed, while lower-priority bugs can be handled on a case-by-case basis.

- All changes made as a result of SPRs have been tested.

- All documentation associated with the software (such as SRS, SDD, test documents) have been updated to reflect changes made during validation testing.

- The test report (discussed in Section 9.3) has been reviewed and approved.

Now that we have discussed the overall concurrent development/testing model, we will look at how to prepare a test plan to utilize it.

9.3 Test Planning

In order to make the most effective use of testing resources, we need to plan how those resources are to be used. The best way to do this is to write a test plan. Organizations need to plan a testing activity in the same way that they plan a development activity. I have long advocated the use of the following three documents for planning a testing effort:

1. *The test plan.* The test plan is a plan that defines the scope of the work to be performed. The test plan defines what must be done and who must do it. It is analogous to a software development plan in that it contains information that allows project managers to more accurately plan and schedule the testing activity.

2. *The test procedure.* The test procedure is a container document that holds all of the individual tests (referred to as *test scripts*) that are to be executed. It is important that tests be developed to be reused as many times as possible, again to increase return on investment. For that reason, the test procedure should contain a clean copy of all the unexecuted test scripts.

3. *The test report.* The test report documents what occurred when the test scripts contained in the test procedure were run. It is a good idea to include bugs found and fixed during the testing effort, as well as other relevant data, some of which is discussed in Chapter 10.

Example outlines of a test plan, test procedure, and test report are included in Appendix H. Let us now look at each of these documents in more detail.

9.3.1 Test Plan

The test plan is normally written by QA. In writing this document, it is important to describe all of the testing activities that are planned for the project. For example, if software engineers will be performing unit and integration testing, that should be so stated in the test plan.

The major focus of the test plan is to scope out the work that QA will be required to perform by answering the following three questions:

1. How many tests do we need?
2. How long will it take to develop those tests?
3. How long will it take to execute those tests?

QA is most often involved in performing validation or functional testing. In planning the effort to perform validation testing, the following topics need to be addressed in the test plan:

- Test estimation;

- Test development and informal validation;

- Validation readiness review and formal validation;

- Test completion criteria.

Let us look at each of these more closely.

9.3.1.1   Test Estimation

As the test plan starts to take shape, one of the first tasks that must be performed is test estimation. This task consists of the three following components, which correspond to the three questions posed above: (1) estimating the number of tests that need to be developed, (2) estimating the test development time, and (3) estimating the test execution time.

Estimating the number of tests that need to be developed is based on the requirements in the SRS. Humphrey observed that "[w]hile there is no magic way to select a sufficient set of practical tests, the objective is to test reasonably completely all valid classes for normal operation and to exhaustively test unusual behavior and illegal conditions" [3]. This determination needs to be made early on so that adequate resources (people and equipment) can be planned for, and accurate and realistic schedules can be developed.

The test estimate reflects the number of tests needed based on factors such as:

- Testing all features and functions defined in the SRS and related documents;

- Including an appropriate number of ALAC tests;

- Achieving some test coverage goal (see Chapter 10);

- Achieving a software reliability goal (see Chapter 11).

Test estimates should be based on and tied to specific sections of the SRS and other related documents. To do this, start with the SRS, review each requirement and, based on past experience, estimate the number of tests required to determine if the software has met the requirement. For an efficient way to estimate tests required, create a table similar to that shown in Table 9.3 within the test plan. In addition to tests that are tied directly to the SRS, you should also develop a reasonable number of ALAC tests that are representative of customer use of the product.

Acting like a customer also means developing tests that [12]:

- Do it wrong;

- Use wrong or illegal combinations of inputs;

- Don't do enough;

- Do nothing;

- Do too much.

The test estimate should also reflect the complexity of tests as well as whether they are manual or automated tests. Manual tests are tests that require a person to execute the test. Automated tests are developed like manual tests but can be executed repeatedly under computer control. Automated tests are particularly well suited for testing user interfaces. Several excellent automated test tools (generally referred to as capture/playback tools) are available. Refer to the References Section for Web sites devoted to software testing tools.

Developing tests should be viewed as an investment. The time and effort required to identify, write, and debug a test can be more than recouped based on the costs required to find and fix bugs once the product is released. Building up a large suite of good regression tests is like having money in the bank.

Like most estimating tasks, the first time you try it, you may find that your estimate and the actual number of tests developed are very different. At the end of a project, do a postmortem (see Appendix N) and determine why there was a discrepancy. Learn from past experience. Use estimates from past projects to help develop new estimates. If you do, your estimates will continually get better.

Remember, when estimating the number of tests required for each feature or function, take into account issues such as:

Table 9.3
Estimating Tests Required

SRS Reference	Estimated Number of Tests Required	Notes
4.1.1	3	2 positive and 1 negative test
4.1.2	2	2 automated tests
4.1.3	4	4 manual tests
4.1.4	5	1 boundary condition, 2 error conditions, 2 usability tests
...		
Total	165	

- *Test complexity.* It is better to have many small tests than a few large ones.

- *Different platforms.* Does testing need to be modified for different platforms, operating systems, and so on?

- *Automated or manual tests.* Will automated tests be developed? Automated tests typically take more time to create but do not require human intervention to run.

Once you have estimated the number of tests required, the next task is to estimate how much effort will be required to develop these tests. Again, rely on past experience to develop an accurate estimate for test development time. An average time (person-hours/test) can be used. This average time should include the time required to (1) write the first draft of the test script, (2) run the test once, and (3) find any errors in the test and revise the test script accordingly

Based on past experience, an average test development time is determined. If you have no idea what this number should be, write a few tests and measure the time it takes to write them, run them, and correct any errors. Use this time as the average and make adjustments down the road if necessary. Once an average is determined, you can arrive at the estimated test development time, as shown in Table 9.4.

Table 9.4
Estimated Test Development Time

Estimated Number of Tests	Average Test Development Time (person-hours/test)	Estimated Test Development Time (person-hours)
165	3.5	577.5

In a similar manner, we now need to estimate the test execution time. This time includes the time required to get systems set up for tests, execute tests, and report problems. Again, use past experience to arrive at an average here. Once an average is determined, you can arrive at the estimated test execution time, as shown in Table 9.5.

Plan on adding an additional 25% to 50% to the estimated test execution time to allow for regression testing. The amount will vary depending on factors such as how many inspections were held, integrity of the bug-fixing process, amount of new code versus reused/modified code, amount of unit and integration testing performed, and experience of the developers.

Based on these three measures (number of tests required, test development time, and test execution time) and the available resources, you can now develop a realistic validation testing schedule.

9.3.1.2 Test Development and Informal Validation

The test development task includes the work required to write the tests identified in the test plan. Different test methods as well as a wide variety of test types should be used. For example:

- *White box.* Use your knowledge of how the software is designed to maximize testing effectiveness by eliminating tests that test the same code repeatedly.

Table 9.5
Estimated Test Execution Time

Estimated Number of Tests	Average Test Execution Time (person-hours/test)	Estimated Test Execution Time (person-hours)	Estimated Regression Testing (50%) (person-hours)	Total Estimated Test Execution Time (person-hours)
165	1.5	247.5	123.75	371.25

- *Black box.* Use black box tests to test features without any knowledge of how the features are implemented.
- *ALAC.* Use your knowledge of how customers use your product to develop tests.

The test plan should describe how the test development work will be partitioned among the QA people on the project team. This task should also be synchronized with the software development plan so that tests are developed in the same order as features are implemented.

Informal validation, as we have already seen, involves developing and executing tests concurrently with feature development. This section of the test plan should describe how this will be performed, how problems found during informal validation will be reported to developers, and how QA will track problems and verify resolution.

9.3.1.3   Validation Readiness Review and Formal Validation

The validation readiness review criteria that must be met in order to start formal validation should be specified in this section of the test plan. Example criteria are listed in Section 9.2.2.

The formal validation testing process should also be described in the test plan. This would include activities such as bug tracking, baseline change assessments, and other tasks listed in Section 9.2.3.

9.3.1.4   Test Completion Criteria

The test plan needs to include the criteria that must be met to complete the testing activity. The criteria should be objective, easily measurable, and agreed to by project management early on in the project. Example completion criteria are listed in Section 9.2.3.

9.3.2   Test Procedure

As mentioned earlier, the test procedure is nothing more than a container document for the collection of test scripts that are to be run. Test scripts define the detailed steps that determine if the software meets a specific requirement. An integral part of each test script is the expected results. The test procedure document should contain an unexecuted, clean copy of every test so that the tests may be more easily reused.

Outlines for a test procedure and test script are included in Appendix H.

9.3.3 Test Report

The test report documents the results of the formal software validation testing process. An outline for a test report is included in Appendix H. Information typically found in a test report includes:

- Completed copy of each test script with evidence that this script was executed (i.e., dated with signature of person who ran the test);
- Copy of each SPR showing resolution;
- List of open or unresolved SPRs;
- Identification of SPRs found in each baseline along with total number of SPRs in each baseline (bar charts like those shown in Appendix L can help illustrate the trend);
- Regression tests executed for each software baseline.

The test report contains valuable information about what was found during the formal validation testing activity. This information will be extremely important for a project postmortem (see Appendix N) as well as any root-cause analysis (see Appendix O) that may be performed.

9.4 Summary

To recap some of the main points from this chapter:

- There are several levels of testing, each with its own objectives and goals.
- There are several methods of testing that can be used within each level.
- There are many types of tests that can be written.
- To increase the return on investment, testing should be planned based on a variety of testing levels, methods, and types.
- To increase the return on investment, the SRS needs to be the basis for developing validation tests.
- Validation testing is a complex activity that needs to be planned and managed.
- A concurrent development/testing model looks like that shown in Figure 9.6.

- Criteria that must be met to start formal validation testing should be included in the test plan.
- Criteria that must be met to complete formal validation testing should be included in the test plan.

Testing, to be effective, must be planned and performed rigorously in a controlled environment. Configuration management plays a key role in helping to increase the effectiveness of the testing activity.

References

[1] Myers, G. J., *The Art of Software Testing*, New York: Wiley, 1976.

[2] Dijkstra, E. W., "Structured Programming," in J. N. Buxton and B. Randell (eds.), *Software Engineering Techniques*, Brussels, Belgium: NATO Science Committee, 1970.

[3] Humphrey, W. S., *Managing the Software Process*, Reading, MA: Addison-Wesley, 1989.

[4] Kit, E., *Software Testing in the Real World*, Reading, MA: Addison-Wesley, 1995.

[5] Marick, B., *The Craft of Software Testing*, Upper Saddle River, NJ: Prentice-Hall PTR, 1995.

[6] Kaner, C., et al., *Testing Computer Software*, 2nd ed., Boston, MA: International Thomson Computer Press, 1993.

[7] Humphrey, W., *A Discipline for Software Engineering*, Reading, MA: Addison-Wesley, 1995.

[8] IEEE Standard 610.12-1990, IEEE Standard Glossary of Software Engineering Terminology, © 1990 by IEEE, Inc.

[9] ANSI/IEEE Standard 1008-1987, IEEE Standard for Software Unit Testing, IEEE, © 1987 by IEEE, Inc.

[10] Pressman, R., *Software Engineering: A Practitioner's Approach*, 3rd ed., New York: McGraw-Hill, 1992.

[11] ANSI/IEEE Standard 829-1998, IEEE Standard for Software Test Documentation, © 1998 by IEEE, Inc.

[12] Beizer, B., *Software Testing Techniques*, New York: Van Nostrand Rheinhold, 1983.

Web Resources

For lists of software testing tools, visit the following URLs:

- http://www.cigital.com/hotlist/comm-test.html
- http://www.testingfaqs.org

Note: URLs cited were accurate as of April 2001.

10

Validation Metrics

Effective validation activities are critical to the successful launch of new products. An effective software validation effort can lead to lower support costs, more satisfied customers, and more efficient use of scarce software engineering resources. As a result of fewer bugs, less time is required for bug fixing and therefore more time is available to work on the next product.

On the other hand, an unsuccessful validation effort can result in releasing a product that has a significant number of bugs. Customers will become dissatisfied with the product (especially if a competitor's product has significantly fewer bugs), and the organization's scarce software engineering and customer support personnel will spend most of their time fixing bugs and dealing with irate customers instead of generating revenue.

To help ensure that software validation activities are as effective as possible, a predictable development process (the focus of Part IV) is essential. To maximize the return on investment, the validation process must be carefully planned and closely managed. On any given software development project, you should be able to answer the following questions:

- How much time is required to find bugs, fix them, and verify that they are fixed?
- How much time has been spent actually testing the product?
- How much of the code is being exercised?
- Are all of the product's features being tested?

- How many defects have been detected in each software baseline?

- What percentage of known defects is fixed at release?

- How good a job of ALAC testing are we doing?

In this chapter we will discuss each of these questions and describe how the information can be used to improve the effectiveness of validation activities.

10.1　Time Measures

10.1.1　Find-Fix Cycle Time

The find-fix cycle time metric answers the question, "How much time is required to find bugs, fix them, and verify that they are fixed?" As illustrated in Figure 4.4, this measure includes the time required to:

- Find a potential bug by executing a test;

- Submit a problem report to the software engineering group;

- Investigate the problem report;

- Determine corrective action;

- Perform root-cause analysis (see Appendix O);

- Test the correction locally;

- Conduct a mini code inspection on changed modules;

- Incorporate corrective action into new baseline;

- Release new baseline to QA;

- Perform regression testing to verify that the reported problem is fixed and the fix hasn't introduced new problems.

The units of the find-fix cycle time metric are person-hours/defect. You can use this measure to help justify increasing the amount of effort spent on prevention and detection activities and to compute the cost of quality. This measure represents activities that fall into the nonconformance category.

10.1.2 Cumulative Test Time

This metric answers the question, "How much time has been spent actually testing the product?" This measure represents the cumulative testing time for all validation testing activities. It is important for the following reason: Often, during the final weeks prior to release, many defects are fixed and many changes are made to the software. Sometimes the version that is finally released has seen very little in the way of actual test time, since most of the regression testing performed may be very focused and very limited. Unfortunately, when changes are made, there is a good chance that new defects will be introduced. Unless the regression testing is comprehensive, these new defects will not be caught. So, measuring cumulative test time provides an indicator of how much testing this version has been exposed to. The higher the measure, the more confidence the organization should have in the release.

Cumulative test time is measured in test hours. This measure can be used to compute software reliability growth. (See Chapter 11.)

10.2 Test Coverage Metrics

10.2.1 Code Coverage

The code coverage metric answers the question, "How much of the code is being exercised?" There are two types of code coverage measures:

1. *Segment coverage.* Units are % of segments hit.
2. *Call-pair coverage.* Units are % of call pairs hit.

The code coverage measures are useful during all phases of testing. They help drive the development of additional tests to ensure that as much of the code is exercised as is possible.

10.2.1.1 Segment Coverage

A segment is a set of program statements that are executed unconditionally or executed conditionally based on the value of some logical expression or predicate in the program.

- Every (executable) statement is in some segment.
- A segment corresponds to an edge in a program's directed graph, as illustrated in Figure 10.1.

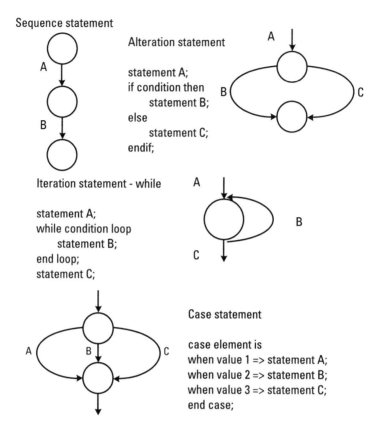

Figure 10.1 Directed graphs.

- Segment coverage is especially useful during unit and integration testing.
- Segment coverage is cumulative.
- A goal of 85% is a practical coverage value.

10.2.1.2 Call Pairs

A call pair is an interface whereby one module invokes another. Call-pair coverage is especially useful during integration testing to ensure that all module interfaces are exercised. A goal of 100% is a practical coverage value.

Note that because call-pair coverage is less detailed than segment coverage, it is more suitable for large systems.

10.2.2 Requirements Coverage

The requirements coverage metric answers the question, "Are all of the product's features being tested?" A requirements traceability matrix, similar to that shown in Table 10.1, is used to trace requirements (SRS) to tests.

The units for the requirements coverage metric are the percentage of requirements covered by at least one test. The metric is used to ensure that all features are covered by at least one test. The requirements traceability matrix is also useful for test estimates and for identifying tests that need to be changed when requirements change.

10.3 Quality Metrics

Organizations should be tracking the three following important quality metrics on a regular basis:

1. Defect removal percentage;
2. Defects reported in each baseline;
3. Defect detection efficiency.

Appendix L shows examples of bar charts representing these measures.

Table 10.1
Example of a Requirements Traceability Matrix

Requirement (SRS)	Design (SDD)	Code (Modules)	Tests (Test Procedure)	Notes
4.1.2 User interface	8.2.2 Entering data	userin.c	Test scripts #102, 103, 104	Range checking of user-entered data
4.1.4 Calculation accuracy and precision	5.6.3 Calculations	calc.c	Test scripts #405, 506, 660	Calculation accuracy and precision
4.1.5 Performance	4.2.3 Performance	all	Test scripts #221, 210-220	Performance measured with typical system loading
4.1.6 Data storage	4.4.1 Database	datab.c	Test scripts #321, 332, 333–336	Empty and full conditions checked

10.3.1   Defect Removal Percentage

The defect removal percentage answers the question, "what percentage of known defects is fixed at release?" This metric measures the percentage of defects that have been removed as compared with the number of defects known. It is computed by:

$$\left[\frac{\text{Number of bugs fixed prior to release}}{\text{Number of known bugs prior to release}} \right] \times 100$$

This measure can be used to help make decisions regarding process improvements, additional regression testing, and the ultimate release of the software. (See Figure L.4 in Appendix L.)

10.3.2   Defects Reported in Each Baseline

This measures the number of defects that were found in each baseline prior to release. This measure can be used to help make decisions regarding process improvements, additional regression testing, and ultimate release of the software. (See Figure L.3 in Appendix L.)

10.3.3   Defect Detection Efficiency

Defect-detection efficiency [1] answers the question, "how well are we performing ALAC testing?" This metric measures how successfully we are finding those defects our customers are likely to find. It is computed by means of the following equation:

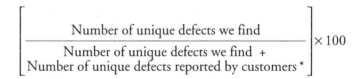

$$\left[\frac{\text{Number of unique defects we find}}{\substack{\text{Number of unique defects we find } + \\ \text{Number of unique defects reported by customers} ^{*}}} \right] \times 100$$

This measure can be used to help make decisions regarding release of the product and the degree to which your testing is similar to actual customer use. (See Figure L.5 in Appendix L.)

---

* The number of unique defects reported by customers is based on at least three to six months of actual customer use.

10.4 Summary

Measures related to the validation testing activity are essential for improving the effectiveness of this activity. These measures should be used to help define process improvements that will help increase the return on investment in validation testing.

References

[1] Jones, C., "Software Defect-Removal Efficiency," *IEEE Computer*, Vol. 29, No. 4, April 1996, pp. 94–95.

11

Software Reliability Growth

More often than not, software is delivered later than planned. When it is finally delivered, it typically has less functionality than the customer expected and the functionality that it does have is typically buggy.

This problem can frequently be traced to the fact that management and customers often have a different perspective on software quality. When asked about the quality of its product, management may say, "The software should be defect-free." While this statement expresses a noble goal, it is one that is not reachable. Customers, on the other hand, often have a very different perspective, as illustrated by the statement, "I expect the software to operate for x hours/week without any downtime." Clearly, customers realize that it is unreasonable to expect software to be defect-free. What the customer is expressing is a requirement for an expected level of reliability, "which is probably the most important of the characteristics inherent in the concept of 'software quality'" [1].

There are three key questions that are frequently asked during the last few weeks prior to software being released. These are:

1. Is this version of software ready for release (however "ready" is being defined)?
2. How much additional effort is required to release it?
3. When will it be ready for release?

The purpose of this chapter is to help provide answers for these questions by introducing a software reliability growth model. Such a model enables organizations to develop a reliability goal and to track progress toward that goal by collecting data during software validation testing, and as a result, providing answers to the three questions above. The information in this chapter provides only an overview. See References [1] and [5] for more in-depth discussions of this complex topic.

11.1 Definitions

Before we begin the discussion of software reliability growth modeling, we need to establish definitions of a few key terms. These are shown in Table 11.1.

11.2 The Test-Analyze-Fix Process

Software reliability can only change as a result of the test-analyze-fix process illustrated in Figure 11.1.

Testing stimulates the occurrence of failures. As each failure is detected, a root-cause analysis is performed (see Appendix O). Corrective action is applied, which corrects the immediate problem. Preventive action, based on

Table 11.1
Software Reliability Definitions

Software Reliability	The probability of failure-free operation of a computer program for a specified period of time operating in a specified environment [1].
Reliability Growth	The improvement in software reliability that results from correcting faults in the software [2].
Software Availability	The expected fraction of time during which the software functions acceptably [1].
Fault	A defect (or bug) in the software that causes a software failure.
Failure	A departure of the software's operation from user requirements.
Failure Intensity	The number of failures occurring in a given time period.
MTTF	The average value of the next failure interval.

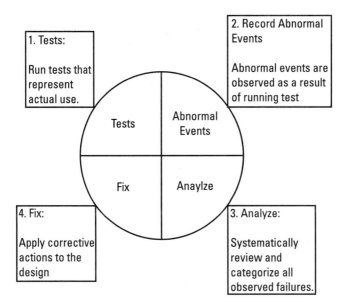

Figure 11.1 Test-analyze-fix process.

the root-cause analysis, prevents the same failure mode from occurring again and reduces the rate of failure mode occurrence.

Thus, one way to achieve growth in software reliability is by using testing to identify defects, changing the software to fix the defect, and then performing root-cause analysis, which should result in a reduction in the occurrence of a specific failure mode.

11.3 Reliability Growth Modeling

Modeling software reliability growth can help answer all three of the questions listed above. By having a robust model of how the reliability of the software changes over time, management can make decisions regarding testing, release, and expected level of support required after release. As observed by Musa:

> To model software reliability one must first consider the principal factors that affect it: fault introduction, fault removal, and the environment. Fault introduction depends primarily on the characteristics of the developed code ... and the development process characteristics. The

most significant code characteristic is size. Development process characteristics include engineering technologies and tools used and the level of expertise of personnel.... Fault removal depends on time, operational profile, and the quality of the repair activity. The environment directly depends on the operational profile. Since some of the foregoing factors are probabilistic in nature and operate over time, software reliability models are generally distinguished from each other in general terms by the nature of the variation of the random process with time. [1]

11.3.1 Objectives of Modeling

Applying modeling techniques to measure software reliability can help achieve the following objectives:

- Measure and predict software reliability in terms of its mean time to failure (MTTF);
- Determine optimal time to stop testing and release software;
- Provide data for making tradeoffs between test time, reliability, cost, and performance goals;
- Define realistic software reliability goals.

Many software organizations are making these decisions today using the gut feel (GF) model. As observed by Musa [1], a good software reliability model has several important characteristics:

- It predicts future failure behavior.
- It computes meaningful results.
- It is simple, widely applicable, and based on sound assumptions.

By properly applying a software reliability growth model we can get answers to the three questions presented at the beginning of this chapter.

11.3.2 Types of Models

As illustrated in Figure 11.2, there are two classes of models that can be applied. Empirical models involve fitting a curve to reliability growth data on a log-log scale. Mathematical models are based on modeling the reliability growth as a stochastic process. Both classes of models have advantages and disadvantages. (For a complete discussion of the different classes of models,

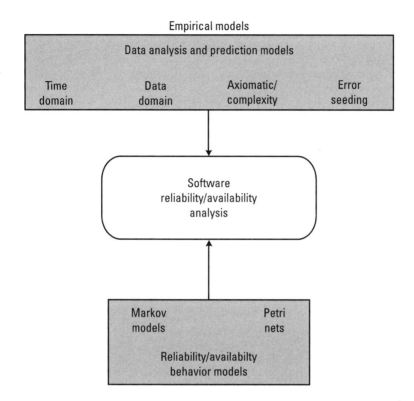

Figure 11.2 Types of models.

and other relevant topics, the reader is referred to Musa [1] and the *IEEE Guide for the Use of IEEE Standard Dictionary of Measures to Produce Reliable Software* [3].)

Since software reliability is a function of fault introduction, fault removal, and the environment, the discovery of a new fault is a random event. As a result, we can use data analysis and prediction models. More specifically, we can use models that operate in the time and data domains. These models are typically easier to use than many of the other types of models and can produce results that are just as accurate.

Examples of time and data domain models are listed below:

Jelinski-Moranda De-Eutrophication Model*

---

* Additional information on these models is included in Appendix J.

Shooman Exponential Model

Schick-Wolverton Model[*]

Goel-Okumoto Nonhomogeneous Poisson Process[*]

Goel Generalized Nonhomogeneous Poisson Process

Littlewood Bayesian Debugging Model

Brooks-Motley Model[*]

Goel-Okumoto Imperfect Debugging Model

Musa Execution Time Model

Lipow's Extension Model

Generalized Poisson Model[*]

Rushforth, Staffanson, and Crawford Model

Duane Model

Moranda Geometric Model

Littlewood-Veral Bayesian Reliability Growth Model

Moranda Geometric Progression Model

Schneidewind Model

Littlewood Semi-Markov Model

Musa-Okumoto Logarithmic Poisson Execution Time Model

Thompson-Chelson Bayesian Reliability Model

11.3.3   Model Assumptions

All models make assumptions. The process of selecting a model (discussed in Section 11.3.4) has much to do with the assumptions that models make.

There are three types of assumptions:

1. *Universal assumptions.* Assumptions made by all models, for example:
   a. Time between failures is independent.
   b. Testing is representative of actual use.
   c. Faults are of similar severity.
   d. Time is used as basis of failure rate.
2. *Criteria assumptions.* Assumptions made by some models, for example:
   a. The number of potential faults is fixed and finite.
   b. Detected faults are fixed immediately.

c. Individual fault occurrence times are recorded (versus fault occurrences grouped by time intervals).

d. New faults can be introduced as a result of fixing existing faults.

3. *Particular assumptions.* Assumptions made by individual models, for example:

a. There are a fixed number of errors in the code.

b. No new errors are introduced through the bug fixing process.

c. The program size is constant (no new code is being added).

d. The detection of errors is independent.

e. The testing is performed in a manner that is similar to intended usage.

f. The error detection rate is proportional to the number of errors remaining in the code.

In addition to assumptions, each model has specific data requirements. That is, you may need to collect specific information that is needed for the model. Model assumptions and data requirements are usually clearly defined in the description of the model.

11.3.4 Model Selection Process

There are several factors to consider before selecting a particular model to use.

- There is no one best model.
- Each model has pros and cons.
- The model's assumptions should be matched to the software development process.
- More than one model should be used to validate results.
- Models use data based on actual faults obtained as a result of software validation testing.

With this in mind, we can now describe a general process for selecting a model.

- Use criteria assumptions to select a group of candidate models.

- Compare each model's particular assumptions with your software development process and narrow down the list of candidates to two or three.

- Identify the data requirements for each of the selected models and determine how to collect this data.

- Once the data is collected, apply the models to the data.

- Perform goodness-of-fit test and determine if each model meets your goodness-of-fit criteria.

- Rank the models based on goodness-of-fit criteria.

11.3.5   Applying the Selected Model

After selecting a model, the next step in the process is collecting the required data. This data will usually be collected during the validation testing phase of a project. As an example, if you chose the Duane model, you would need to collect (1) cumulative testing time and (2) time to each fault. Collection of this information should be automated if possible. If it is not possible to automate the collection of the data, then use lab notebooks to record testing time and time to each fault.

As faults are detected during validation testing, the information is entered into the model. Periodically, a graph similar to that shown in Figure 11.3 can be created, which shows progress toward reaching a reliability goal.

The reliability goal can, for example, be expressed as a number of faults found by customers that require immediate correction.

Once a model has been selected and applied, the results produced from the model need to be validated against actual experience. This requires that you collect actual failure data once the product is released and see how the actual data compares with that predicted by the model.

11.3.6   Reliability Modeling Tools

Statistical Modeling and Estimation of Reliability Functions for Software (SMERFS) [4, 5] contains a collection of several reliability models including:

- Littlewood-Veral Bayesian Model (see Appendix J)
- Musa Execution Time Model
- Geometric Model

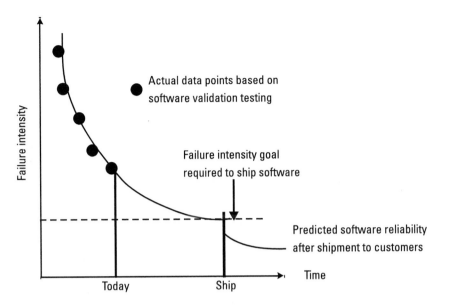

Figure 11.3 Software reliability growth model.

- Nonhomogeneous Poisson Model for Execution Time Data
- Musa Logarithmic Poisson Execution Time Model
- Generalized Poisson Model for Interval Data
- Nonhomogeneous Poisson Model for Interval Data
- Brooks-Motley Discrete Software Reliability Model (see Appendix J)
- Schneidewind Maximum Likelihood Model
- Yamada S-Shaped Reliability Growth Model

Let us look at one example of a SMERFS model, the generalized Poisson model. The following assumptions can be made:

- The expected number of errors occurring in any time interval is proportional to the error content at the time of testing and to some function of the amount of time spent testing.
- All errors are equally likely to occur and are independent of each other.
- Each error is of the same order of severity as any other error.

- The software is tested in a manner similar to intended usage.

- The errors are corrected at the ends of testing intervals without introduction of new errors into the program.

- Errors discovered in one testing interval can be corrected in others; the only restriction is that corrections be made at the end of an interval.

- The data requirements for this model are as follows:

- The length (time) of each testing interval;

- The number of errors corrected at the end of each testing interval;

- The number of errors discovered in each testing interval.

11.4 Summary

Software reliability growth modeling provides management with another piece of quantitative data to use in making key decisions regarding product quality, especially for embedded software products. This data can be extremely helpful in determining when to stop testing and release a product.

The key points regarding software reliability growth are:

- There are many software reliability models.

- The accuracy of models varies widely.

- Significant differences in results can be achieved from using different models.

- There isn't one best model.

- It is possible to obtain an accurate reliability prediction using these models if the selection process is followed.

- As many models as possible should be tried, with the goal of selecting the one(s) that provides the best result.

- Data collection is usually the most difficult problem.

- Software reliability growth modeling, like anything else, must be subject to continuous process improvement.

References

[1] Musa, J. D., A. Iannino, and K. Okumoto, *Software Reliability Measurement, Prediction, and Application*, New York: McGraw-Hill, 1987.

[2] IEEE Standard 610.12-1990, IEEE Standard Glossary of Software Engineering Terminology, © 1990 by IEEE, Inc.

[3] IEEE Standard 982.2-1988, IEEE Guide for the Use of IEEE Standard Dictionary of Measures to Produce Reliable Software, © 1988 by IEEE, Inc.

[4] Farr, W. H., "Statistical Modeling and Estimation of Reliability Functions for Software (SMERFS) Library Access Guide," NAVSWC TR-84-371, Revision 3, 1993.

[5] Lyu, M. R., *Handbook of Software Reliability Engineering*, Los Alamitos, CA: IEEE Computer Society Press, 1996.

Web Resources

Information on SMERFS can be found at the following Web sites:

- http://www.cse.cuhk.edu.hk/~lyu/book/reliability/smerfs.html

- http://technology.nasa.gov/scripts/nls_ax.dll/w3TechBrief(15;NPO-19307@;0;0)

Note: URLs cited were accurate as of April 2001.

Part IV
Predictable Software Development

If you always do what you've always done, you'll always get what you've always gotten. [1]

To maximize the return on investment of the software V&V activities described in Parts I through III, software development organizations must learn to behave in a predictable manner. Common sense would dictate that increases in efficiency are achieved by increasing an organization's ability to behave in such a manner.

In Part IV, we explore management's role in changing an unpredictable, inefficient organization that produces poor-quality products that are delivered late (if at all) into an efficient organization that consistently meets commitments to customers and delivers high-quality products on time. This transformation can only occur with the direct involvement of and commitment from all levels of management.

Software V&V activities, if applied effectively, can have a significant positive impact on the quality of products released and on the company's bottom line. Management must learn to recognize this and play an active role in fostering the use of these techniques across software development projects.

At this point you may be thinking, how does predictability relate to software V&V? The effectiveness of the software V&V techniques discussed in Parts I through III of this book can be significantly increased when an organization learns to behave in a more predictable manner. For example, software validation testing in an unpredictable organization that does not have effective change control can be ineffective, costly, and time consuming.

In Part IV, we look at topics related to predictable software development. The chapter titles of this section are self-explanatory:

Chapter 12: Motivation for Becoming Predictable

Chapter 13: Balancing Quality, Features, and Schedule

Chapter 14: Accurate Estimating and Scheduling

Chapter 15: Balancing People, Process, and Product

Chapter 16: Managing Commitment and Risk

While Parts I through III of this book are written primarily for practitioners, Part IV is written primarily for managers. For without the understanding, commitment, and active participation of management, the changes the organization must make in order to behave in a more predictable manner will not happen.

Reference

[1]   Author unknown, quoted in J. O'Toole, *Forming the Future: Lessons from the Saturn Corporation*, Cambridge, MA: Blackwell Publishers, 1996.

12

Motivation for Becoming Predictable

How often have you heard the expression, "We never have the time to do it right but always have the time to do it over"? This theme is unfortunately common for many companies developing software. While this mode of operation may have been acceptable in the past, the global economy of the new millenium is forcing companies to become more efficient. Those organizations unable or unwilling to learn how to do it right the first time are going to be left in the dust.

Software development in the twenty-first century is changing dramatically. New paradigms such as "Extreme Programming" [1] and developing software on "Internet time" [2] are putting increasing pressure on organizations to develop better software more quickly with fewer resources.

Do more with less. Software development organizations are developing more products that are more complex and more difficult to create. To staff up for new projects, organizations are competing, fiercely at times, for a limited pool of experienced people. The tight labor market for software developers and QA professionals is expected to continue well into the first decade of the twenty-first century, since the demand for qualified people is expected to far exceed available resources [3, 4]. Doing more with less means that there are fewer people available for testing. So the testing that is done must be that much more effective.

Do it faster. As a result of the global economy, many organizations are now facing competition from new players in other parts of the world. These new players are developing products faster and at lower cost. Further, the ability to develop products on Internet time is affecting all businesses, not just those that are developing software for the Web. Product development, testing, and release cycles that once took years are being compressed to months and sometimes weeks. So, not only do organizations have to do more with less, they also have to do it faster. Doing it faster means that the verification and validation activities have to be completed in less time.

Do it with higher quality. Customers are becoming more demanding and more selective in deciding which software products to buy. Unreliable products with exotic features are less attractive than products that contain the features customers actually need and are very reliable. Compressed schedules and understaffed projects, coupled with the need to release very reliable products, result in extraordinary pressures on people within development organizations.

Organizations need a way to cope with these conflicting demands. Doing more with less, doing it faster, and doing it with higher quality all mean that there is little room for error. More than ever before, organizations must learn how to get it right the first time. A predictable development process is crucial to getting it right the first time.

The goal of predictable software development is simply to delight your customers by consistently delivering what you promised when you promised it.

Now let us look at why this is so important.

12.1　Introduction to Predictable Software Development

For every software project, management wants to know three things: (1) when will coding be done; (2) when will testing be done; and (3) when will the product be released?

These are legitimate questions for management to ask. Unfortunately, when an organization is unpredictable, it is very difficult to provide accurate answers to these questions. Why? Well, knowing with certainty when a product will be released requires, among other things:

- A clear definition of what "done" means with respect to coding and testing;

- A process for writing and reviewing requirements (so that developers know what features to code and testers know what features to test);

- A process for designing software;

- A process for planning, estimating, and scheduling software development activities;

- A process for planning, estimating, and scheduling software verification and validation activities;

- A process for controlling changes to requirements, designs, code, and tests;

- A staff that has been trained in critical skills such as accurate estimating and scheduling, requirements writing, project management, inspections, verification and validation, and testing;

- A commitment from management to follow the process agreed to for the project.

New projects often begin with great optimism—a naive expectation that somehow this project is going to be different, that it will be successful. For some reason, management expects that the outcome for new projects will be different, even though the organization continues to use the same unpredictable processes that resulted in failure on earlier projects.

After the initial euphoria ends, the hard reality sets in. The project team quickly recognizes that the same unpredictable processes used on the last unsuccessful project are being applied yet again to the new project. Lessons learned from the previous failure have not resulted in any changes to the process, because there was no management commitment to improve. Managers and executives need to understand that having a predictable software development process is vitally important to the long-term success of their business.

Many software development organizations lack discipline. These organizations either do not have or have but do not follow a written software development process. As a result, they are not able to accurately predict when key events (such as code complete, test complete, and product release) will occur. What many companies fail to recognize is that various parts of the organization need to know when things will happen so that:

- Marketing can plan product-rollout events;

- Customer service can alert customers to new software updates;

- Training can prepare updated course materials and schedule new training sessions;

- Technical writers can prepare updates to online help and have printed manuals ready for product launch;

- Managers can plan resource assignments for the next project.

As a result of the inability to predict when things will happen, many software development organizations suffer from a lack of credibility. No one believes dates from the development group, because it has never met a date. As a result, management frequently sets (or allows to be set) unrealistic release dates for products and makes (or allows to be made) unreasonable commitments to customers.

As you might expect, the unrealistic dates set by management are rarely met. This creates a lose-lose situation—your customers lose, since their plans may be predicated on your unrealistic schedules and unreasonable commitments, and your employees lose, since no one wants to be associated with a project that fails.

On projects with unrealistic schedules, the schedule can only be reduced so much (the time required to get the minimum feature set coded and tested). Developers, being eternal optimists, fail to anticipate problems, and coding frequently takes longer than expected. QA engineers fail to accurately estimate how many tests are needed and how long it will take to write and execute them. This problem occurs because most people have never been trained in how to develop accurate estimates and build realistic schedules. When development time expands, time for software V&V activities is reduced (usually owing to a commitment made to a key customer to ship on a certain date). When V&V tasks are cut from projects, the organization will find fewer bugs and customers will find more bugs. This makes the QA staff frustrated and customers unhappy. It also means that the organization will need to do unplanned bug-fix releases.

Simply stated, the more predictable an organization is, the more likely the software V&V activities discussed in Parts I–III of this book will be performed. When those activities are performed, they will significantly increase the ability of the organization to find and fix bugs before the software is shipped to customers, thereby decreasing the need for unplanned, expensive bug-fix releases.

Lack of predictability impacts your bottom line. Unplanned bug-fix releases represent a significant cost to the organization, as shown in Figure 12.1. Management determines how to use scarce and expensive resources. You can decide to use these resources to deliver bug-fix releases,

How do you want to use your scarce, expensive engineering resources?

Develop new products   OR   Rework existing products

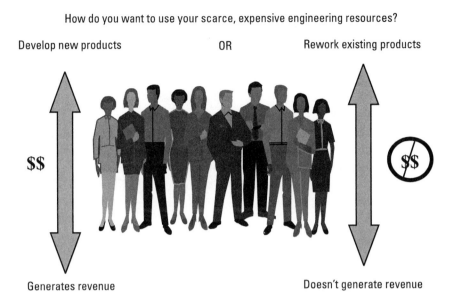

Generates revenue   Doesn't generate revenue

Figure 12.1 The real cost of unplanned bug-fix releases.

which typically don't generate any revenue, or to work on new features and new products, which do generate revenue. The choice is yours to make.

Lack of predictability negatively impacts customers. In unpredictable organizations, customers are unsure of when new products and updates to existing products will be released. This makes it hard for customers to plan to migrate to new software releases. Further, since unpredictable organizations are unable to develop accurate schedules, they tend to release software with far too many bugs, adding to customer dissatisfaction.

Lack of predictability negatively impacts employees. No one wants to be associated with projects that fail. In unpredictable organizations, failed projects are the norm. And experience has shown that there is a very strong correlation between customer satisfaction and employee satisfaction.

Predictable software development can be achieved when management takes the lead to change the behavior of the organization. Management needs to be focused on the elements identified in Figure 12.2.

To become predictable, organizations need to learn how to balance quality, features, and schedule. While tradeoffs are made all the time, organizations need to understand and assess the implications of these tradeoffs. Further, organizations need to learn how to balance the needs of people,

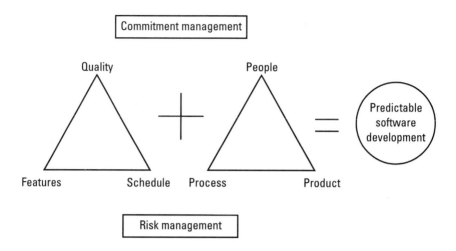

Figure 12.2 Elements of predictable software development.

process, and product. Tradeoffs here affect productivity as well as customer and employee satisfaction.

Also required is the ability to manage commitments and to manage risks. Managing commitments (internal and especially external) is essential so that the organization can consistently exceed commitments. Many complex software projects are fraught with risks. Risks on many software projects may be tacitly understood, but all too often they are not actively managed. Effective risk-management skills can make the difference between success and failure.

12.2   Characteristics of Unpredictable Organizations

How can you tell if your organization is unpredictable? Listed below are some characteristics of unpredictable organizations.

- The organization frequently over-commits and under-delivers.
- Project schedules are consistently not met.
- Customer perception of product quality is low.
- It is difficult to plan for new product releases and product rollout.
- It is difficult to plan the resources required for future products.

- Customer satisfaction is low and probably not being measured regularly.
- Employee satisfaction and employee morale are low.
- Many unplanned bug-fix releases are needed.
- Revenue projections are frequently not met.

From working with dozens of companies, I have identified several root causes of unpredictable behavior. These include:

- *Unrealistic schedules.* Unrealistic schedules can result from several causes, including lack of training in estimating and scheduling, allowing other organizations to set development and validation schedules, and not keeping or using information from past projects to help develop more accurate estimates.
- *Poor project management.* Software project management is a difficult and unrewarding job. Project managers frequently become scapegoats for failed projects. Good project managers are rare and worth their weight in gold. Without a doubt, one of the most frequent reasons that projects fail is due to poor project management. In many cases, the root cause of this problem is not the project manager, but rather, how management measures the project manager's performance. Usually, project managers are measured on their ability to get products released. Therefore, they will do whatever it takes to get the product released, including cutting features and reducing quality.
- *Crisis mentality.* For many organizations, working in "firefighting" mode is the norm. These organizations move from one crisis to the next. It is a mystery how anything gets done. What we should have learned by now is that working from crisis to crisis is not the most effective way to use scarce, expensive resources. This mode of working frequently leads to burnout and frustration.
- *Rewarding of wrong behaviors.* In many organizations, management's goals and objectives are not aligned with the individual performance goals and objectives of the staff. For example, in organizations where management complains about poor product quality, you would likely not find any mention of the word "quality" in the performance plans for the staff. Rather than encouraging the behavior that is desired, management knowingly or unknowingly does the opposite. For example, management inadvertently encourages firefighting

behavior by rewarding "heroes" who resolve the crisis-du-jour. In fact, in organizations that work in crisis mode most of the time, in many instances it is the so-called "heroes" who frequently cause the crises in the first place.

- *Lack of measurement.* Many organizations are unable to measure the amount of effort required to develop, document, and test a software release. Some organizations are unable to answer basic questions, such as how big is the product (using any particular size metric); how long did it take to develop and release; and how many bugs were found?

12.3   Characteristics of Predictable Organizations

Predictable organizations exhibit the following characteristics:

- Under-commit and over-deliver;
- Master skills for estimating tasks and building realistic schedules;
- Use project postmortem information to refine estimating and scheduling skills;
- Make effective use of scarce, expensive resources;
- Rarely operate in firefighting mode;
- Require few unplanned bug-fix releases;
- Follow a documented software development process;
- Actively manage risks and commitments;
- Measure quality and customer satisfaction regularly;
- Measure employee satisfaction regularly;
- Recognize the connection between customer satisfaction and employee satisfaction.

These characteristics will be discussed further in subsequent chapters.

12.4   Management Can Change the Organization

Being a parent who has helped raise two children, I learned the value of positive reinforcement—rewarding and recognizing good behavior and providing negative incentives for bad behavior. I adapted these principles to managing technical people and found that they worked just as well with adults as they did with children.

Management has the ability to change the organization. Management controls the organization's human resources, determines how resources are allocated to projects, and most importantly, determines how people are evaluated and measured. What management often fails to recognize, however, is that to change the culture, you need to change the way people behave. In most organizations, the way people behave is directly related to how they are measured.

This is particularly true for software engineering organizations, where technical challenge and peer recognition are very important. The notion that management can change the culture of an organization by changing the way people are measured is not new. It has been acknowledged for many years [5, 6]. Unfortunately, in many organizations, management hasn't recognized it.

The following are some specific actions management can take to help create an organization that behaves in a more predictable manner.

- *Measure individual performance based on objectives that are directly related to overall corporate goals.* Most organizations have general corporate goals such as increasing market share and improving quality and customer satisfaction. Frequently, management fails to define specific goals and objectives for individuals that are based on the corporate goals. Setting individual goals and objectives is vitally important, since we know from experience that people will be conscientious about those things that they are being measured on.

  A client having quality problems asked me to come up with recommendations for improvements. I asked to see the performance plans for the software engineering staff. Not one person had "improve code quality" or " reduce defects" as an objective. My recommendation was to incorporate such objectives into the performance plans. The client did this and over time the quality problem disappeared.

- *Learn to develop accurate, realistic schedules, and then meet them.* The literature is full of horror stories about project failures, cost overruns, and missed schedules [7]. The ability of an organization to define an accurate and realistic schedule is critical. Yet few organizations know how to do this. Why? Well, there are probably many reasons, but what I have observed is that most people have never been trained, while in school or on the job, in how to accurately estimate a task, build an accurate schedule, and then meet that schedule. Even in those organizations that conduct project postmortems, there is little or no improvement in the organization's ability to develop accurate schedules that can be met. Skills required to develop accurate estimates and build realistic schedules are discussed in Chapter 14.

- *Follow a documented software development process.* One of the reasons that organizations are unpredictable is that either they don't have a documented software development process or they don't follow the process they do have. We know from experience that to successfully develop complex products you need to rely on a proven process. This is as true for software as it is for any complex product. For software, the process must address both development activities and verification and validation activities, as described in Chapter 3 and Appendixes G and H.

  Without a documented process, people will spend a significant amount of time arguing about what to do. It will be harder to develop accurate estimates and schedules. Groups like software QA and documentation that need to have specific information will not know if or when that information will be available. Further compounding the problem is the claim from some software engineers that having to follow a process will diminish their ability to be creative. Nothing could be further from the truth. Ask hardware engineers if following a process diminishes their ability to innovate. It doesn't. I've found that software engineers who resist following a process do so out of fear that they will actually be held accountable for some task (such as writing a design specification) when they would rather spend all of their time writing code. This topic will be further discussed in Chapter 15.

- *Hold people accountable.* Accountability is a concept that is totally foreign to many in the software industry. However, it is essential for those organizations that want to become predictable. Everyone in the organization, from the CEO on down, needs to be held accountable for doing his or her job. On a project team, people need to be held accountable for meeting their schedule, assuming of course that the people doing the work set their schedules. Development should be held accountable for delivering what was promised, not just to the external customers but to internal customers (such as software QA and technical documentation) as well. Software QA should be held accountable for writing and executing tests based on the SRS and for performing the testing as defined in the schedule.

Management needs to give people the responsibility for defining what they will do and when they will do it by. Once this happens, people need to expect to be held accountable for delivering what they promised. When people miss their commitments, managers need to understand the reason and determine how to get things back on track by working collaboratively and cooperatively with everyone involved.

Note that accountability extends to managers as well. Oftentimes management is responsible for providing resources, buying equipment and tools, and taking care of other things that project teams need to meet their commitments. This topic will be further discussed in Chapter 16.

- *Proactively manage risk.* Most software development projects are fraught with risk, yet few project managers proactively manage risk. On projects where risk management is ignored, I frequently see several "replanning" activities. Replanning is often just a euphemism for dealing with something that wasn't expected but could possibly have been avoided. Many times, replanning activities can be prevented if proactive risk management is used from the outset. Proactively managing risk not only helps ensure that development and software QA will meet their schedule, it increases the likelihood that the project will be successful. Risk management is further discussed in Chapter 16.

- *Manage internal and external commitments.* In many organizations, salespeople frequently make unrealistic commitments to customers in order to sell product. This often results in undue pressure on project teams to deliver. When they can't deliver (because the commitments were unrealistic), customers become unhappy. Meanwhile, the salesperson has received their commission check and is off with other customers making more unrealistic commitments.

The underlying problem here is an organizational one. There is a disconnect between sales and development. And it all goes back to how salespeople are measured. In many organizations, salespeople are measured on the dollar amount of sales they book, not on meeting commitments to customers. In fact, some customers have finally smartened up and have signed agreements that have penalty clauses in them based on agreed-to delivery dates and feature sets.

Surprisingly, even with these financial incentives in place, management still has failed to hold salespeople accountable.

Management needs to manage commitments made to external and internal customers. One way to do this is to set expectations lower. By doing this, the organization has a much better chance of meeting or exceeding expectations. All too often, organizations set expectations unrealistically high and frequently fail to meet them. As a customer, we are generally very satisfied when we receive exactly what we expect. If we receive more, we are very happy. If we receive less, we are usually not happy. Therefore, management should encourage the organization to undercommit and overdeliver.

In addition, people who make commitments to customers need to be held accountable for meeting those commitments. The same is true for commitments made to internal customers. Managing commitments is discussed in more detail in Chapter 16.

- *Measure what happens.* It goes without saying that in order to become more predictable, organizations need to measure what happens. A few simple measures that are tied to the overall corporate goals should be sufficient. For example, What is the average amount of schedule slippage on projects? How many known defects are products being shipped with? How many unplanned bug-fix releases were there last year? Measurement is discussed in Chapters 7, 10, 13, and 14.

Management must recognize that they have the ability to change the behavior of their organizations. By learning how to do this, management can significantly improve the organization's predictability.

12.5   Summary

As observed by Jones [8], "One of the most important topics in the entire software quality domain is the relationship between software quality and software project management. Indeed, Deming, Juran, and Crosby have asserted that the main source of quality problems can be assigned to management rather than to technical workers."

Management must provide leadership to help organizations behave in a more predictable manner. Management must understand that they can change how people behave by changing how people are measured. If you want to improve schedule accuracy, measure people on their ability to develop accurate schedules and then meet them. If you want to improve product quality, measure people on product quality. If you want to improve customer satisfaction, reward people based on achieving improvements in customer satisfaction.

Don't believe that this works? Jay Bertelli, CEO of Mercury Computer in Chelmsford, Massachusetts, challenged his management team in January 1999 to double the company's stock price by the end of the year. As an incentive to meet this goal, each executive was promised a new Porsche. By the end of 1999, the company's stock price had tripled. Bertelli had 20 Porsches delivered to the company's headquarters—one for each executive and two loaners for top performers among the staff [9].

References

[1] Beck, K., "Embracing Change with Extreme Programming," *IEEE Computer*, October 1999, pp. 70–78.

[2] Cusumano, M. A., "Software Development on Internet Time," *IEEE Computer*, October 1999, pp. 60–70.

[3] Schafer, M., "Hiring for Keeps (Or at Least for a While)," *Software Magazine*, April/May 2000.

[4] Wilkinson, S., "Hired Guns—Beating the IT Staffing Shortage with Contract Workers," *Datamation*, May 1999.

[5] Weinberg, G. M., *The Psychology of Computer Programming*, silver anniversary ed., New York: Dorset House, 1998.

[6] Lister, T., and T. DeMarco, *Peopleware: Productive Projects and Teams*, 2nd ed., New York: Dorset House, 1999.

[7] Yourdon, E., *Death March: The Complete Software Developer's Guide to Surviving "Mission Impossible" Projects*, Upper Saddle River, NJ: Prentice-Hall, 1999.

[8] Jones, C., *Software Quality: Analysis and Guidelines for Success*, Boston, MA: International Thomson Computer Press, 1997.

[9] *Boston Globe*, Business Section, April 27, 2000, page C4.

13

Balancing Quality, Features, and Schedule

Predictable organizations recognize the delicate balance that exists between quality, features, and schedule. While common knowledge seems to be that you can have "any two," in today's highly competitive market, it is essential to have all three. Managers must learn to work with their teams to identify acceptable tradeoffs among all three. Only then can organizations meet customer needs for quality, features, and schedule. The more factual information the organization has, the better able it will be to make informed decisions.

When an organization releases a poor-quality product, with fewer features than were promised, later than it was promised, there are no winners, only losers.

Your customers lose. They may have waited a long time for your product, only to discover that it is fraught with defects and doesn't have all the features they were promised. Often, your customers' success is dependent upon their ability to use your product effectively. When your product is defective, lacking important features, and delivered late, your customers may become less competitive in their markets.

Your employees lose. There is no pride in working on a team that delivers a poor-quality product behind schedule. When employees are dissatisfied, they are less productive. Eventually, dissatisfied employees may leave. Management is all too familiar with the costs associated with high turnover.

Predictable organizations reduce turnover by working to increase employee satisfaction. These companies have long since recognized the strong connection between employee satisfaction and customer satisfaction.

Your company loses. Releasing a poor-quality product that lacks important features, and doing so later than promised, negatively impacts your company's reputation and your bottom line (e.g., from lost sales to competitors, increased support costs). More important, your bottom line is further impacted by the need to divert costly and scarce engineering resources from work on new projects, which generates revenue, to fixing defects in current products, which typically generates no new revenue.

Management needs to understand the importance of relationships. A software project is a team effort consisting of software developers, software QA engineers, technical writers, project managers, and others. For a project to be successful, the project team must work well together and have a clear understanding of the tasks they are to accomplish. Furthermore, management must understand the complex relationships that impact a project team's ability to produce a quality product with the required features in the desired time frame. For software projects, these relationships are critical.

One of the most important relationships that management needs to understand is the delicate balance between quality, features, and schedule. These three attributes are tightly coupled—push on one and the other two are affected. Unpredictable organizations are often narrowly focused on only one or two of the three (features and schedule) to the detriment of the third (quality). As a result the effectiveness of the software V&V techniques discussed in Parts I through III can be diminished.

For example, in an unpredictable organization that lacks the ability to develop accurate schedules, it is likely that testing will be cut short as a result of pressures from unrealistic schedules. Since critical software V&V activities such as code inspections and testing are performed during the later part of the development process, such activities will be curtailed if the organization is unable to develop accurate estimates and schedules. Learning how to do this, then, is essential to ensure that these activities are not eliminated from projects.

In this chapter, we examine the issues related to balancing the conflicting demands of quality, features, and schedule. We begin by looking at each of these three critical parameters individually; then we will move on to a discussion of how they impact one another.

13.1 Quality

Software quality is difficult to define and hard to measure. People have defined quality in numerous ways. For example:

> When we examine an item based on its measurable characteristics, two kinds of quality may be encountered: quality of design and quality of conformance. *Quality of design* refers to the characteristics that designers specify for an item. The grade of materials, tolerances, and performance specifications all contribute to the quality of design. *Quality of conformance* is the degree to which the design specifications are followed during manufacturing. Again, the greater the degree of conformance, the higher the level of quality of conformance. [1]

> Quality: This term is among the most ambiguous words in the English language and is ambiguous in all other natural languages, too. For software, quality usually has a hybrid meaning that includes freedom from defects plus adherence to requirements plus other nuances such as fitness for use. There is no single, unambiguous definition. [2]

> The principal focus of any software quality definition should be the users' needs. Crosby [3] defines quality as "conformance to requirements." While one can debate the distinction between requirements, needs, and wants, quality definitions must consider the users' perspectives. The key questions then are, who are the users, what is important to them, and how do their priorities relate to the way you build, package, and support your products? [4]

> Wearing our consumer's hat, the first things we see when we put software quality under the microscope are:

> Reliability
>
> Usability
>
> Maintainability
>
> Adaptability [5]

[T]he term quality will be used to mean software that has these six attributes:

1. Low levels of defects when deployed, ideally approaching zero defects.

2. High reliability, or the capability of running without crashes or strange results.

3. A majority of users expressing satisfaction with the software when surveyed.

4. A structure that minimizes bad fixes or insertion of new defects during repairs.

5. Effective customer support when problems do occur.

6. Rapid repairs for defects, especially for high-severity defects [2].

From the definitions above, it should be clear that software quality refers to more than an absence of defects. When asked to define software quality, most people answer, "I can't define it but I know it when I see it." Further compounding the problem is the fact that many organizations don't know what level of quality their customers are willing to pay for and wait for. Nor do they know what level of quality they are capable of delivering.

The measurement program identified in Chapter 7 as well as the software validation metrics identified in Chapter 10 can provide objective data that helps assess product quality.

13.1.1 The Impact of Poor Quality

Management needs to understand that software is a handcrafted product. Each line of code is individually devised, usually based on incomplete, ambiguous, and inconsistent requirements. Humphrey [6] has collected data that shows that experienced programmers make one mistake for every 10 lines of code they write. At this rate, a software product with a million lines of code would have 100,000 defects. Humphrey states that about 95% of these defects are typically found before the product is released. This means that there could be as many as 5,000 defects in the released product, yielding a defect rate of 5%.

Table 13.1 applies a 5% defect rate to other things we are familiar with in order to provide some perspective on the magnitude of the software quality problem. Clearly, we would not accept a 5% defect rate in other areas of everyday life.

Jones [2] has studied thousands of software development projects at hundreds of companies and reports that the U.S. average for software quality ranges from 75% to 85%, yielding a defect rate of from 15% to 25%.

While there are many companies that consistently develop high-quality, feature-rich software on time, there are many more companies that

Table 13.1
A 5% Defect Rate, in Perspective

Item	At a 5% defect rate...
Of the approximately 900,000 prescriptions [7] written per year by U.S. doctors...	45,000 prescriptions would be incorrect
Of the approximately 3 million parts [8] in a Boeing 767 airplane...	150,000 parts would be defective
Of the approximately 2 million checks [9] processed per day by the Federal Reserve Bank of Boston...	100,000 checks would be deducted from wrong accounts

develop poor-quality software, cut features late into the project, and deliver the product late, if at all. While the quality of software generally improved during the 1990s, the gap between best and worst widened. Yourdon reports that at the beginning of the 1990s the gap between the best and worst companies was about 10:1. For every company producing high-quality software, there were 10 companies producing poor-quality software. Today, the gap between best and worst has increased to about 100:1 [10].

Even though it may be hard to define what we mean by high-quality software, we unfortunately have many real-life examples of poor-quality software. For example:

The fiasco surrounding the delayed opening of the Denver International Airport was probably one of the most visible and publicized examples of how costly poor quality software can be. The opening of the airport was delayed for over a year at a cost of about $1 million per day directly as a result of software defects in the highly automated baggage handling system. [2]

For more examples of serious software failures, see Collins [11] and Weiner [12]. Poor-quality software has caused significant financial losses. Consider what happened to the Bank of New York in 1985. A defect surfaced in software used at the bank to track government securities transactions from the Federal Reserve Bank. The Federal Reserve Bank would debit the Bank of New York for each transaction, but the defect prevented the Bank of New York from determining who owed it how much for which securities.

After running up a staggering debt of $32 billion in just 90 minutes, the Bank of New York managed to shut this system down. The bank had to borrow over $23 billion from the Fed and pay $5 million in interest in addition to pledging all of its assets to cover the loss [12].

There aren't many businesses that can survive the effects of a $5 million defect. Poor-quality software has also caused physical harm and even loss of life. In 1991, during the Gulf War, an Iraqi Scud missile killed 28 American soldiers and wounded 98 others. The Scud missile might have been intercepted had it not been for a defect in the target acquisition software running in the Patriot Missile System. Engineers found the defect and sent over a fix. Unfortunately, the fix arrived the day after the incident [12].

Two cancer patients died from radiation therapy they received from the Therac-25 radiation therapy machine. Software was used to replace mechanical interlocks on the system. As a result of an operator error, the software interlock failed and the two patients were inadvertently given lethal overdoses of radiation [13].

Every day, in every part of the world, poor-quality software impacts businesses and people in many ways—from lost productivity and corrupted data to loss of life.

13.1.2 Quality and Risk

As customers, we need to determine the level of quality we need in the software products we buy. One way to do this is by considering the potential risk that using the software presents to developers and users. The higher the risk, the greater the need for quality. Kinds of risk include:

- Business risks, where a defective product may result in financial loss to either the developer or the user;

- Societal risks, where a defective product may adversely affect large groups of people;

- Safety risks, where a defective product may result in injury or death to users.

There is a valid business argument that says that the quality of the product should be consistent with the risk of using the product. Clearly, software for medical devices, such as an implantable pacemaker, presents a much higher risk than software for video games, and therefore should be developed with much higher quality requirements and much more rigorous V&V processes.

Figure 13.1 illustrates an overly simplified software quality spectrum. On this spectrum are examples (there are others) of methodologies that could be used to achieve a level of quality commensurate with the risk associated with use of the software.

Work by Yourdon and Bach [10, 14–16] has stimulated debate on the notion of how much quality is enough. While Yourdon's notion of "just enough quality" [17] is not applicable to safety-critical software, it can be applied to a wide spectrum of non-safety-critical products. Just enough quality supports the business principle that quality should be commensurate with risk, and is based on the following important points:

- What most customers want is software that is cheap, fast, feature-rich, and available now [17].

- Customers would not be willing to pay for or wait for defect-free software, even if it were possible to produce defect-free software (which it isn't).

- Rigorous software development methods appropriate for safety-critical software may not be appropriate for software that is not safety critical.

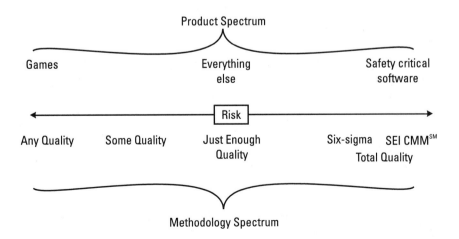

Figure 13.1 Software quality spectrum—an overly simplistic view.

Furthermore, experience has shown that:

- Customers can be very satisfied with software products that have defects, if they don't find those defects in their normal use of the product.
- Most companies start projects knowing full well that they will ship software with known defects.
- Zero-defect software, while a noble goal, is neither realistic nor practical.

In the real world, companies make decisions to ship software every day based on some notion (usually a gut feeling) of what is "good enough" for their customers. Most just haven't recognized or don't acknowledge that this is what they are doing.

13.2   Features

Many organizations are overly focused on functionality or feature richness. Sales and marketing people are keen on comparing their product's features against the competition's product features. Unfortunately, customers often use this comparison in making their purchasing decisions. This has resulted in software companies competing in "some kind of a heated 'feature race'. Each time a [company] releases a new gimmick in a product, all other [companies] do the same, and maybe add their own gimmicks as well. The result is massive suites of applications that take over 50 million bytes of storage and contain features that may be used less than 1% of the time by less than 1% of the users" [2].

The problem with the feature race is that it frequently leads to increasing complexity. The increasing complexity impacts the organization's ability to develop products on time and with a reasonable level of quality. From experience we have learned that there is a strong correlation between complexity and defects. As products grow, significantly more testing is required to find defects, because software engineers are not always aware of the impact coding changes can have on a product.

As observed by Brooks:

The besetting temptation for the architect of a general-purpose tool such as a spreadsheet or word processor is to overload the product with features of marginal utility, at the expense of performance and even ease of use. The appeal of proposed features is evident at the outset; the performance penalty is evident only as system testing proceeds. The loss of ease of use sneaks up insidiously, as features added in little increments, and the manuals wax fatter and fatter. [18]

Lastly, organizations need to know which features customers are actually using on a regular basis. Knowing this information is critical if organizations are to do a better job of focusing their testing effort on those features that are most frequently used.

13.3　Schedules

Building a suspension bridge is a pretty complex task—much more complex than say, building software. What does building bridges have to do with building software? Well, both are engineering-intensive activities, both are very complex, typically take a relatively long time, involve many people, and both must deal with many unexpected glitches encountered along the way.

In Chapter 8, I mentioned the Verrazano Narrows Bridge in New York City, which connects Staten Island to Manhattan. As one of the longest suspension bridges in the world, it is truly an engineering marvel. But what makes this bridge even more amazing is that, designed and built in 1959–1964, it was completed under budget and opened one month ahead of schedule.

The software projects most of us typically work on pale by comparison to the magnitude and complexity of the Verrazano Narrows Bridge project. However, many project teams consistently fail to deliver software products on time. And when the project team finally releases a product, more often than not, key features that customers need are left out and far too many defects are left in.

The track record of the software industry is dismal. Project teams consistently underestimate the magnitude of many software projects and management frequently promises customers more than can be delivered. The inability of many software organizations to develop accurate estimates and schedules has a negative impact on product quality and morale. Since validation testing is one of the last activities performed, it is often cut short when projects are behind. Shortchanging validation testing is shortsighted, since delivering a poor-quality product followed by several bug-fix releases is not cost-effective.

There are many factors that influence our ability to develop accurate estimates and stay on schedule. By looking at projects that fail to meet their schedules, we can identify some specific root causes, such as the following:

- Most projects are "scheduled-backwards."
- We don't teach the skills required for developing accurate estimates and schedules.
- We don't cultivate software project management skills.
- We don't manage risk and commitments.
- We don't manage change.

Let's look at each of these in some detail.

13.3.1   Most Projects Are Scheduled Backwards

Since many companies are unable to keep pace with the demand for new products, overly aggressive schedules for product development are the norm. Project teams are often pressured to deliver based on the desire to meet customer needs. Factors such as product complexity, the organization's capability, capacity, track record, resources, and difficulties related to staffing are frequently ignored when setting aggressive schedules. I have frequently seen projects that were under way with key roles identified only as TBH ("to be hired").

As a result, management frequently sets the release date without fully understanding the magnitude of the project, the resources required, and even what features the product must have.

When the release date is given, the project team has to "schedule backwards." This means that the project schedule is developed by starting with the release date and working back to the present day. It shouldn't be a surprise that scheduling backwards results in an unrealistic schedule. We know that this is the wrong way to develop schedules, yet we continue to do it and are always surprised when we miss the release date.

13.3.2   We Don't Teach Estimating and Scheduling Skills

Management should not be surprised that project teams do a poor job of estimating and scheduling, since these skills are rarely taught in school or on the job. And it isn't because it's difficult to learn how to do this. There are many techniques that can be used for accurate estimating and scheduling (some are discussed in Chapter 14). It's not hard to learn how to get better at estimating and scheduling. Management must create an environment that requires the organization to improve. Management must accept that the best way to get accurate estimates and realistic schedules is to involve the people who will actually be doing the work.

History is a great teacher—especially when it comes to estimating and scheduling. The best way to get better at estimating and scheduling is to learn from past projects. Unfortunately, this is an area in which we are also poor. We rarely ever look at our original estimates of tasks and compare them to how long the tasks actually took in order to understand why they are different. By reconciling the differences between the initial estimates and the actuals, people can learn to develop more accurate estimates and more realistic schedules.

13.3.3 We Don't Cultivate Software Project Management Skills

More often than not, the success or failure of a project hinges on the skill of the project manager. This is why savvy managers usually assign their best project manager to their most critical projects.

Not only does project management have a significant impact on the success or failure of a project, there is also a relationship between project management and software quality. When project management is weak or ineffective, software products more than likely will be behind schedule and of lower quality. In fact, Jones [2] has collected quantitative data on the relationship between project management techniques and software quality. Based on a sample of more than 100 companies and more than 1,000 software projects, Jones found the following management approaches to correlate with poor software quality:

- Use of manual project estimation methods;
- Use of manual project planning methods;
- Failure to estimate or consider software defect potentials;
- Failure to provide time for pretest inspections;
- No use of historical quality data from similar projects;
- Milestone tracking absent or perfunctory;
- Defect tracking absent or perfunctory;
- Management focus concentrated only on schedules.

When project management is weak or ineffective, software products are more likely to be behind schedule and of lower quality.

Organizations frequently fail to provide an environment that can help cultivate good project managers. Project managers need the support of management in applying these best practices in order to help them succeed.

13.3.4   We Don't Manage Risk and Commitments

Most software projects are fraught with risks. In fact, according to Jones [19], "Software has long been regarded as one of the most risk-prone of all engineering activities. Risks such as schedule slips and cost overruns tend to occur on more than 50% of all large systems. Even more severe risks, such as cancellation of the project prior to completion or serious quality deficiencies are not uncommon."

While we know that risks exist, we frequently ignore them, hoping that somehow they will go away. Unfortunately, this is never the case. Ignoring risks only makes the problem worse. By ignoring the risks present on every project, we significantly increase the likelihood that the project will be delivered late and with lower quality.

Similarly, many projects lack the human skills and internal discipline needed to manage both internal and external commitments. Management frequently commits to delivering more than can be delivered. In many organizations, management may not even be aware of commitments that salespeople make to customers in order to book sales (and earn their commissions).

Some customers, who have been burned in this way too many times, have smartened up and put penalty clauses in their contracts. Unfortunately, sometimes even penalties of thousands of dollars for every day, week, or month that the product is late are not enough to motivate management to change the process.

We discuss issues of managing risk and commitment in more detail in Chapter 16.

13.3.5   We Don't Manage Change

Does this sound familiar?

> A marketing or product manager, very late into a project, asks a young software engineer if he or she could "just add this one feature because the customer really wants it." Unfortunately, the young software engineer, wanting to be a team player, obliges and adds the new feature but doesn't tell anyone—like QA, the tech writer, or the person developing training materials. As you might expect, the implementation of the new feature isn't perfect and the software engineer inadvertently introduces new defect(s) into the product.
>
> Since QA doesn't know about it, the defect(s) is not caught during testing. Since the tech writer isn't aware of the new feature, it isn't described

in the user manual. Since the trainer isn't aware of the new feature, it isn't in the training materials. Since the new feature isn't in the user manual or training materials, customers aren't aware of it. When customers accidentally stumble across the new feature, they find the related defect(s) and are not happy about either the defect(s) or the fact that the feature isn't documented.

Allowing change to occur in a controlled manner is an essential organizational skill that is often lacking. This topic is addressed in Chapter 8.

13.4 Balancing Quality, Features, and Schedule

Now that we have looked at each of these parameters individually, let's see how they impact one another.

On most projects, tradeoffs between quality, schedule, and features are made implicitly and without considering the long-term impact on the product, the project team, and the customer. By recognizing that quality, features, and schedule are tightly coupled, organizations can make better decisions.

As an example, consider a typical project team that has determined, for a variety of reasons, that they will not make their release date. Assume that there is still time to do something about this problem. To balance the need for quality, features, and schedule, the project team identifies several alternatives, as shown in Table 13.2.

By assessing each option using the information above, project teams, project managers, and management can make better, more informed decisions about crucial tradeoffs between quality, features, and schedule. As a manager, when situations arise that impact these issues, you need to require that the project team provides options and alternatives, along with information similar to that shown in Table 13.2, so that the options can be evaluated and the best possible decision made.

13.5 Summary

A key component of a predictable software development process is balancing the conflicting goals of quality, features, and schedule. Learning how to balance these components can significantly improve the effectiveness of software V&V activities. Management must take the lead in helping the organization make informed decisions based on factual information.

Table 13.2
Balancing Tradeoffs Between Quality, Features, and Schedule

The Issue: The project is behind schedule and is at risk of missing the delivery date.
The possible options that the project team proposes to deal with the issue are:

	Option 1	Option 2	Option 3
Description	Add one developer and one QA person.	Drop features not implemented.	Negotiate an extension of the delivery date with the customer.
Risks	It will take time and effort for new people to get up to speed. May delay project even further.	Customers were promised some of these features. Will minimize the competitive value of release.	Customers may not be able to wait and may buy our competitor's product.
Quality Impact	Additional QA resource could help perform more testing.	Dropping the features not implemented means that some code already written won't work. How will this be handled?	An extension to the schedule will allow all features to be coded and tested according to plan.
Feature Impact	Additional developer can help implement remaining features.	Customers were promised all of the features.	Customers were promised all of the features.
Schedule Impact	New people will take time from existing staff to get up to speed.	May shorten development time; impact on testing time is neutral.	Lengthening the schedule may not be acceptable to the customer.
Long-term Impact	Will help complete remaining features without impacting maintainability.	Dropping features means project "continues" after release, thereby delaying planned next release.	Lengthening the schedule will delay the date for the next release.

Table 13.2 (continued)

	Option 1	Option 2	Option 3
Pros	Will result in product delivered with features promised and acceptable quality.	Will result in shortened development schedule.	Will enable team to deliver all features properly tested.
Cons	Adding resources will ultimately delay the release further. Difficult to find qualified resources.	Code related to the dropped features may have to be excised or somehow disabled. Testing implications? Customers expecting all features.	Product will be delivered later than customer promised. Customers may choose to use competitor's product instead.

Key:

some positive impact

strong positive impact

some negative impact

−− strong negative impact

Description. States the alternative.

Risks. Describes risks that might be incurred were the option to be implemented.

Quality Impact. States what impact (or) the option has on the overall quality of the product.

Feature Impact. States what impact (or) the option has on the features that were supposed to be included in the product.

Schedule Impact. States what impact (or) the option has on the scheduled release date for the product.

Pros. Describes the advantages of this option.

Cons. Describes the disadvantages of this option.

Management must work to establish common definitions and measurable objectives for achieving quality in the products developed by the organization. These common definitions and objectives should be reflected in the individual performance plans of the staff and in the common objectives of project teams. Management can change the culture by holding people accountable (themselves included) for meeting specific goals and objectives related to desirable behaviors and product attributes. Individuals as well as project teams that meet specific quality goals should be rewarded.

Management must work to reduce the ever-increasing spiral of complexity resulting from feature wars. Developing robust products with a solid feature set may appeal to more customers than unstable products with exotic features. As products acquire more and more features, management must recognize that development time will increase (due to personnel changes and lack of architectural knowledge of the product) and testing time will increase (due to increased number of interactions between features and addition of new features). More often than not, support costs will also increase as a result of the decrease in usability that accompanies complex, exotic features.

Management must work to create an organization that is credible. Management must help the organization learn how to create accurate estimates, learn how to put these estimates together into a schedule, and learn how to manage projects to meet the schedule. Once this is done, the organization will become more credible and, as a result, more predictable.

Some specific actions that management can take to help make the organization more predictable are:

- Change individual performance goals and objectives throughout the organization to reflect those behaviors that are consistent with a predictable software development process.
- Require that the organization identify the features that customers need using techniques such as quality function deployment (QFD), conjoint analysis, focus groups, and no-tie ranking.
- Require that the organization define the level of quality customers require in measurable terms.
- Require that the organization determine when customers need the product as opposed to when they want it.
- Require that when project teams make tradeoffs between quality, features, and schedule, they consider the impact to all three in addition to the long-term impact to the product.

- Provide rewards and recognition for people and project teams that behave in the desired manner.

References

[1] Pressman, R. S., *Software Engineering: A Practitioner's Approach*, 4th ed. New York: McGraw-Hill, 1997.

[2] Jones, C., *Software Quality: Analysis and Guidelines for Success*, Boston, MA: International Thomson Computer Press, 1997.

[3] Crosby, P. B., *Quality Is Free*, New York: Mentor, 1980.

[4] Humphrey, W. S., *A Discipline for Software Engineering*, Reading, MA: Addison-Wesley, 1995.

[5] Dunn, R. H., *Software Quality: Concepts and Plans*, Upper Saddle River, NJ: Prentice Hall, 1990.

[6] Humphrey, W. S., "What If Your Life Depended on Software?" Carnegie Mellon University, SE 735-SI, 1996.

[7] *1997 World Almanac*, "Most Frequently Prescribed Drugs in the US for 1994," p. 973.

[8] Boeing Aircraft Company, Facts About the Boeing 767-400ER, available online at http://www.boeing.com/news/feature/767-400Erroll/funfacts.html (accessed February 2001).

[9] Federal Reserve Bank of Boston, Tour of Operations, Check Processing Department, available on-line at http://www.bos.frb.org/educate/html/checks.html (accessed February 2001).

[10] Yourdon, E., *Rise and Resurrection of the American Programmer*, Upper Saddle River, NJ: Prentice-Hall PTR, 1998.

[11] Collins, W. R., et al., "How Good Is Good Enough? An Ethical Analysis of Software Construction and Use," *Communications of the ACM*, Vol. 37, No. 1, January 1994, pp. 81–91.

[12] Weiner, L. R., *Digital Woes: Why We Should Not Depend on Software*, Reading, MA: Addison-Wesley, 1993.

[13] Leveson, N. G, and C. S. Turner, "An Investigation of the Therac-25 Accidents," *IEEE Computer*, July 1993, pp. 18–41.

[14] Bach, J., "A Framework for Good Enough Testing," *IEEE Computer*, Vol. 31, No. 10, October 1998, p. 124–126.

[15] Yourdon, E., *Death March: The Complete Software Developer's Guide to Surviving "Mission Impossible" Projects*, Upper Saddle River, NJ: Prentice-Hall PTR, 1997.

[16] Bach, J., "Good Enough Quality: Beyond the Buzzword," *IEEE Computer*, Vol. 30, No. 8, August 1997, pp. 96–98.

[17] Yourdon, E., "The Revolution for Just Enough Quality," Keynote speech, *10th Intl. Conf. Software Quality*, ASQ Software Division, New Orleans, LA, October 2000.

[18] Brooks, F. P., *The Mythical Man-Month*, 20th anniversary ed., Reading, MA: Addison-Wesley Longman, 1995.

[19] Jones, C., *Assessment and Control of Software Risks*, Upper Saddle River, NJ: Prentice-Hall PTR, 1994.

Selected Bibliography

Boehm, B. W., *Software Risk Management*, Los Alamitos, CA: IEEE Computer Society Press, 1989.

Brooks, F. P., Jr., *The Mythical Man-Month*, 20th anniversary ed., Reading, MA: Addison-Wesley, 1995.

DeMarco, T., and T. Lister, *PeopleWare Productive Projects and Teams*, 2nd ed., New York: Dorset House, 1999.

Jones, C., *Assessment and Control of Software Risks*, Upper Saddle River, NJ: Prentice-Hall PTR, 1994.

Leveson, N. G., *Safeware: System Safety and Computers*, Reading, MA: Addison-Wesley, 1995.

Weinberg, J., *The Psychology of Computer Programming*, Silver Anniversary ed., New York: Dorset House, 1998.

Note: URLs cited were accurate as of April 2001.

14

Accurate Estimating and Scheduling

> [I]ndustry surveys from organizations such as the Standish Group, as
> well as statistical data ... suggest that the average [software] project is
> likely to be 6 to 12 months behind schedule and 50 to 100 percent over
> budget. [1]

Learning how to create accurate estimates and build realistic schedules and
then meet them is a critical organizational skill required to achieve predictability. In this chapter, we will discuss the following topics related to accurate
estimating and scheduling:

- Why estimates and schedules are wrong most of the time;
- A typical scheduled backwards project;
- Best practices for estimating;
- Best practices for scheduling.

Developing accurate estimating and scheduling skills is critical for
many reasons, not the least of which is the impact on software V&V activities. When a project is behind schedule, what usually happens? Well, verification activities like code inspections are eliminated. And the time available for
software validation testing is often reduced. It is for these reasons that organizations must learn how to more accurately estimate tasks and build schedules

that can actually be met. And it is management's responsibility to see that this happens.

The objective of this chapter is twofold: (1) to provide insight into why estimates and schedules are usually wrong, and (2) to identify what management must do to help the organization improve its abilities to accurately estimate all of the tasks (development, QA, documentation) required, to use those estimates to build accurate and reasonable schedules, and then to meet those schedules.

14.1   Why Estimates and Schedules Are Wrong Most of the Time

From looking at many projects, I've found that there are several common factors that result in inaccurate estimates and missed schedules. Let's explore some of these.

1. *Organizations play ridiculous negotiating games.* Project managers often find themselves in a position where they must negotiate the project schedule with management. Frequently, this negotiation occurs at the beginning of a project, before all the requirements have been defined and all the variables identified. The negotiation usually continues throughout the project, as key milestones are missed. The negotiating games, many of which have been identified by Thomsett [2], are eloquently explained by Yourdon [1] in the list below.

   • *Double and add some.* In this game, the project manager comes up with an estimate for the schedule and then doubles it. For good measure, a few extra weeks or months are then added in.

   • *Reverse doubling.* Most managers are aware of the double-and-add-some game. They take the initial estimates from project managers and immediately cut them in half.

   • *Spanish inquisition.* In this game, the project manager walks into a meeting unaware that he or she will be asked to provide management with an on-the-spot, instant estimate. Usually, the schedule has already been determined and the unwitting project manager is coerced into accepting it.

   • *Low bid.* When outsourcing software, competitors often are encouraged to match or beat the competitor's schedule in order to win the contract. Of course, the competitor's schedule is not realistic, so the project manager must agree to match someone else's foolish time frame in order to get the contract.

- *"Guess the number I'm thinking of."* Management has decided what an "acceptable" schedule is but doesn't reveal it. The project manager meets with management and attempts to guess the end date by starting with a realistic estimate and negotiating until management's "acceptable" schedule is reached.

2. *Organizations overcommit and underdeliver.* Many organizations fail to manage commitments made to customers and frequently overcommit. This may be caused by many factors such as competitive pressure, failure to consult with development when making customer commitments, and so on. What happens when organizations overcommit? Well, usually the project manager will cut features and take whatever shortcuts he or she perceives is necessary to get a product out. More times than not, the product that is delivered is very buggy (as a direct result of those shortcuts) and has fewer features than the customer was promised. This results in unhappy customers and frustrated employees.

Effectively managing commitments to customers (internal as well as external) is discussed in more detail in Chapter 16.

3. *Projects start with predetermined release date.* Kickoff meetings for new projects are exciting events. There's lots of hoopla, food, T-shirts, and optimism. The feeling is upbeat. Most projects are begun with a predetermined release date that has been communicated to customers. And the release date is often set before the requirements are defined. How is it possible to commit to a delivery date before the requirements are defined? It's like buying a new house without detailed architectural drawings. How will you know what kind of house you are buying? Without these drawings, how can the contractor give you an accurate completion date? How can the carpenters, electricians, and plumbers actually build the house? They can't. Yet, we frequently ask software engineers, QA, and technical writers to build, test, and document a product *without* written requirements. Projects begun with a predetermined delivery date without written requirements will never complete on time. How can they?

4. *Tasks are estimated based on time available rather than time required.* When a project team commits to a delivery date before the

requirements are defined, the team members must schedule backwards—that is, start from the release date and work back to the present. When we do this, we generally tend to estimate tasks based on how much time is available rather than how much time the task actually requires. Estimating tasks based on time available rather than time required means that from the very beginning of the project, the estimates are incorrect and the schedule is not realistic.

5. *Task interdependencies are not identified.* Software development projects frequently require that several groups within the organization work together. Typically, these groups include software engineers, software QA, and technical writers. Often, other groups may be involved as well.

   On every software project, there are dependencies between the work performed by the various groups involved on these projects. For example, software engineers can't begin coding until requirements are defined and design work is completed. QA can't begin testing until tests are written and code is available. Technical writers can't do their job until requirements are defined and features are implemented.

   However, interdependencies between tasks are frequently ignored when scheduling backwards. Why? Because even if people took the time to identify them, the release date has already been determined so why do it. Anyone who has ever worked on a software development project understands the importance of identifying the interdependencies between tasks. Ignoring interdependencies guarantees that the schedule will not be met.

6. *Unexpected things that always happen on every project are ignored.* Every software project has unexpected things happen. When developing a schedule, we frequently ignore this fact. Again, when scheduling backwards people don't bother to take this into account since they will likely push the release date out and they know that is not acceptable. Here are some of the unexpected things that we know from experience happen on every project:

   • The requirements change.

   • Key member(s) of the project team leave, get sick, take maternity or medical leave, win the lottery, and so on.

   • A key assumption about the product proves wrong.

   • Training for new tools or new technology is not provided.

- Dependencies arise that were previously unknown or ignored.
- Key resource(s) are pulled off to fight the most recent "fire."

By not planning for unexpected things, we create unrealistic schedules right from the start.

14.2 A Typical Scheduled Backwards Project

Now let's take a look at what happens on a typical scheduled backwards project—a project that starts with a predetermined end date usually resulting from one of the negotiating games listed in the previous section. Scheduling backwards always leads to an unrealistic schedule, because:

1. When you schedule backwards, task estimates are made based on the time available rather than the time required. Activities such as decomposing tasks to understand the total scope of the problem and identifying intertask dependencies are not done. Since the release date is already set, why bother?

2. When you schedule backwards you assume that nothing will go wrong and that nothing unexpected will happen. Since this is not very realistic, neither is the schedule.

By not acknowledging the complexity, organizational capabilities, resource requirements, task interdependencies, and the unexpected things that always happen, the schedule quickly becomes meaningless.

So what happens on a scheduled-backwards project? Well, sooner or later, a critical task will be very late or, worse, unable to be completed. And then the ripple effect begins. The test plans, documentation, and coding all take longer than expected because the tasks were never fully understood from the outset, dependencies between tasks were never identified, contingency plans for staffing were never implemented, and so forth.

When it becomes obvious that the project team will not meet the schedule, the project manager panics because his or her performance is based on releasing a product "on time." Customers have already been promised that the product would be released on time. Given this situation, the project manager has no choice but to take shortcuts.

First, the project manager abandons whatever process the team was following in the hope this will somehow speed things up. The project team's focus is shifted to paring down features and cranking up coding. Verification activities such as design reviews and code inspections are now viewed as unnecessary and are eliminated. The time planned for validation testing is drastically cut since testing is always one of the last activities on the schedule.

Some project managers add more people in a desperate attempt to meet the schedule, ignoring the advice of Dr. Fred Brooks [3], who early on recognized that the relationship between time and people on software projects is not linear. According to Brooks, adding people to a late project just makes it later.

No design reviews, no code inspections, less testing, and much more hurrying all add up to a poor-quality product. The product eventually gets released, usually weeks or months after the scheduled date. The project team is demoralized since they worked extremely hard to get the product released and know that customers will not be satisfied because it is missing key features and has far too many defects. And in fact, even prior to shipping, there's usually a team already at work on the ubiquitous bug-fix release. The most amazing thing about this scenario is that no matter how many times this happens, management is still appalled at the high support costs, upset that so many defects were missed, and quick to blame the team for doing shoddy work.

Another critical factor related to project schedules has to do with how project managers are measured and evaluated. If a project manager's salary increase is based on getting a product released, then release the product is what he or she will do, regardless of quality and of whether or not critical features are included. Since the project team is usually aware of this, there is no incentive to do it right the first time.

Clearly, focusing only on time to market or only on quality or only on features, to the exclusion of other factors, is not desirable. Having a high-quality product that is months late and as a result does not sell is just as bad as releasing a poor-quality product on time.

14.3   Software Estimating Techniques

There are several excellent techniques for estimating either the size or cost of a software project. These include:

- Function points and feature points;
- Constructive cost model (COCOMO II);
- Wideband delphi method.

A brief overview of each method is included below. Additional resources for some of these methods are included at the end of this chapter.

14.3.1 Function Points and Feature Points

Function points are a way of estimating how big a software product will be based on functionality from the user's perspective. Function points were developed initially for information systems. The feature point extension [4] applies a similar method for other types of software, such as real-time software, embedded software, and communications software.

The method for counting either function points or feature points has been well documented in the literature [5–8]. The training required to learn how to count function points takes about two days. To ensure consistency in counting, the International Function Point Users Group (IFPUG) publishes and periodically revises function point counting rules. IFPUG also offers counting certification exams.

Once function points are counted for a proposed system, an extensive body of empirical data can be used to relate function points to productivity and size of the product. Jones [9] also claims that function points can be useful for such things as normalizing defect data and estimating tests required and number of test runs.

14.3.2 COCOMO II

COCOMO II is a mathematical modeling and estimation tool that helps estimate the cost, effort, and schedule of a software development activity. The original COCOMO model was developed by Boehm [10]. COCOMO II [11] has reflected the numerous changes in software development that have occurred since the publication of the original model in 1981.

The first version of the COCOMO II tool was released in 1997 and was calibrated to 83 data points that represent historical software development projects, using a 10% weighted average approach that blends empirical data with expert opinion. Experience with COCOMO has shown that if an organization calibrates the model to its own empirical data, the accuracy of the results can be greatly improved over the generic calibration described above.

The COCOMO model has been widely used in large organizations, especially those doing work for the U.S. government.

14.3.3   Wideband Delphi Method

This method was developed at the Rand Corporation in 1948 and is useful for estimating attributes of complex tasks or projects—that may or may not have anything to do with software. This method helps improve the accuracy of estimates because:

- It requires that several experienced people estimate the same task.
- It requires that a detailed breakdown of the work be prepared.
- It is an iterative process based on consensus.

I have found that this technique is most effective when estimating tasks (such as building a new driver or incorporating new technology) being done for the first time. The process of task estimation using the wideband delphi method is shown in Figure 14.1.

The process typically includes the project manager, who acts as the facilitator for the process, and from three to five experienced engineers, who act as estimators. The process begins with a planning phase. During this phase, the problem statement is prepared and broken down into smaller, more manageable parts, as appropriate.

During the planning phase, the team meets to review the problem statement and decide if and how to decompose the problem into smaller parts. Once this is done, the team reviews and agrees on assumptions and constraints. The project manager documents the assumptions and constraints. Lastly, the team agrees on what they will be estimating and the units—development effort in person-hours, cost in dollars, or size in lines of code, etc.

Once the planning phase is completed, the estimators get to work. They review the problem statement(s) and start estimating. They must do

Wideband Delphi Process Flow

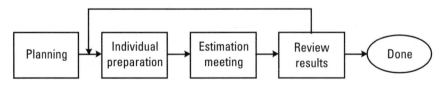

Figure 14.1 Wideband delphi process flow.

this in a manner that is free from management influence of any kind. For this reason, it is best that the anonymity of the estimators is preserved.

Each estimator should identify all tasks related to the problem, such as writing and reviewing specifications, design reviews, testing, quality assurance, configuration management, bug fixing, and documentation. Each assumption made by an estimator is recorded along with a justification.

When estimating, the estimators should make the following assumptions:

- That all of the tasks will be performed;
- That the tasks will be completed sequentially even though some concurrent work could be done;
- That work on each task will be uninterrupted;
- That known events (such as trade shows and planned vacations) may interrupt activities.

The estimation is done in a series of several rounds. Typically, two to four rounds are necessary. In each estimating round, the estimators discuss such things as assumptions, constraints, and justifications. Once the estimators complete their preparation (typically in three to five days), they provide the project manager with a copy of their estimation worksheet, similar to that shown in Table 14.1. The project manager convenes a meeting and the individual estimates are plotted on a graph similar to that shown in Figure 14.2. This illustrates that there was a wide variation in the estimates. The variation is usually due to differences in assumptions and perspectives.

The group discusses assumptions and constraints and begins the second round. Based on discussions, the estimators change their estimates anonymously and provide the project manager with their revisions using the worksheet shown in Table 14.1. The round 2 estimates are graphed and discussed.

This process continues until the variation decreases to an acceptable amount (determined in advance) and the estimators reach consensus. This is illustrated in Figure 14.2. When this happens, the process is completed and the project team uses the final estimate.

Completion criteria for the process are as follows:

- An overall task list has been defined;
- A complete list of assumptions has been documented;
- The estimators have reached consensus on the final estimate.

Table 14.1
Wideband Delphi Estimating Worksheet

Problem #1	Round 1 Estimate	Round 2 Estimate	Round 3 Estimate	Round 4 Estimate	Final Estimate
Task 1					
Task 2					
Task 3					
Change					
Total					

From: Weigers [12]. Used with permission.

Lastly, it is critically important for the estimators to compare their individual estimates to the actual results once the project is completed in order to reconcile differences and improve their estimating skills. This is true regardless of the estimating technique being used.

14.4   Scheduling Techniques

In this section we discuss the following scheduling techniques: the program evaluation and review technique (PERT), the critical path method (CPM), and the yellow sticky method.

14.4.1   PERT and CPM

Most of us are familiar with PERT and CPM charts for software projects. At one time or another, anyone who has managed software projects has had to create schedules using these tools.

The important point to note about PERT and CPM is that they are a means, not an end. They both depend on people creating information based on their knowledge of the project and the tasks that software engineering, QA, and other groups must perform. There is no substitute for this information. Too often, I've seen project managers starting out on a new project creating PERT and CPM charts before anyone has had a chance to identify and estimate tasks. The techniques of estimation described earlier must precede the creation of PERT and/or CPM charts.

Before creating a PERT or CPM chart, the following information must be clarified:

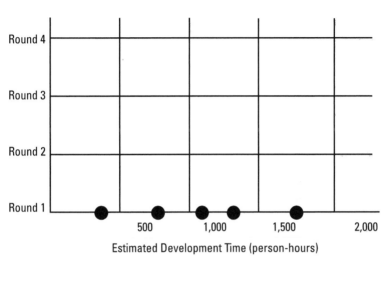

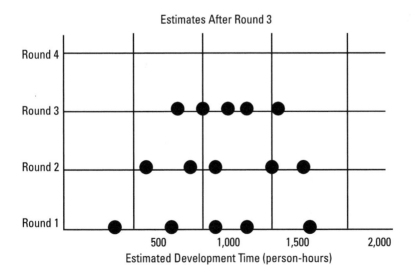

Figure 14.2 Task estimation using wideband delphi.

- Decomposition of product function;
- Identification of all tasks required to be performed;
- Estimates of effort for each task;
- Interdependencies between tasks;
- Assignment of specific resources to tasks.

Once this information is available, building schedules using either PERT or CPM tools can begin.

The product decomposition and task list is often referred to as a work breakdown structure (WBS). Once the WBS is identified, a timeline or Gannt chart can be created to show the overall timeline for the project.

14.4.2   The Yellow Sticky Method

The yellow sticky method[1] has been used successfully for many years in other industries. I first learned this method several years ago from a small software company. I was impressed by both its simplicity and by the accuracy of the resulting schedules. The experiences of this software company piqued my interest. What was it about this method that enabled teams to develop schedules that they actually met? By examining the process closely and observing teams using it, I soon learned why this method works so well.

The yellow sticky method helps people develop more accurate, realistic estimates of tasks they themselves will perform. It also includes identification of dependencies between tasks. By starting with more accurate estimates and including the dependencies, it is a rather simple and straightforward process to create a project schedule that is accurate, realistic, and can actually be met.

The method is based on the following simple principles:

- Know what you are being asked to deliver.
- People who will be doing the work create the task estimates and help build the schedule.
- Project team members critique each other's estimates.
- Everyone is held accountable for meeting his or her commitments.

---

1. I did not create the yellow sticky method. I have looked far and wide to find the person(s) deserving credit, but as yet I have not found anything in print. If you know who created the yellow sticky method, please send an email to info@swqual.com.

- Customers are promised less than what can realistically be delivered (undercommit and overdeliver).
- Everyone on the project team (developers, software QA, technical writers, and project managers) is trained in the method.
- Management has "bought into" the process.

A project team for a given software project would typically include people from project management, software engineering, QA, technical documentation, and training. Other groups may also be involved.

For a complete description of how to use the yellow sticky method, refer to Appendix K.

14.5 Summary

The track record of the software industry with respect to meeting schedules is abysmal. In an unpredictable organization, management's responsibility is to recognize that:

- To continue to use the same mechanism for estimating and scheduling will result in continued inability to meet schedules.
- The organization needs to find an estimating and scheduling process that works.
- People who will be doing the work are best able to estimate how long the work will take.
- The organization needs training in good estimating and scheduling practices.
- The people doing the work must be given the ability to set the schedule and then be held accountable for meeting it.
- The way to improve estimating skills is to learn from past estimates.
- People who create accurate estimates and schedules and then meet them should be rewarded.

In order for the organization to become more predictable, the organization must learn how to create accurate estimates and schedules. Management plays a key role by creating a culture based on developing accurate, realistic schedules. By helping to establish a more predictable development process, management will be increasing the effectiveness of software V&V activities, which will have a positive impact on the company's bottom line.

References

[1] Yourdon, E., *Death March: The Complete Software Developer's Guide to Surviving "Mission Impossible" Projects*, Upper Saddle River, NJ: Prentice-Hall PTR, 1997.

[2] Thomsett, R., "Double Dummy Split and Other Estimating Games," *American Programmer*, June 1996.

[3] Brooks, F. P., *The Mythical Man-Month*, 20th anniversary ed., Reading, MA: Addison-Wesley, 1995.

[4] Jones, C., *Applied Software Measurement*, New York: McGraw-Hill, 1991.

[5] Garmus, D., and D. Herron, *Measuring the Software Process: A Practical Guide to Functional Measurement*, Upper Saddle River, NJ: Prentice-Hall, 1995.

[6] Dreger, B., *Function Point Analysis*, Upper Saddle River, NJ: Prentice-Hall, 1989.

[7] Function Point Counting Practices Manual, Release 4.0, International Function Point Users Group (IFPUG), 1994.

[8] Pressman, R. S., *Software Engineering: A Practitioner's Approach*, 4th ed., New York: McGraw-Hill, 1997.

[9] Jones, C., *Software Quality: Analysis and Guidelines for Success*, Boston, MA: International Thomson Computer Press, 1997.

[10] Boehm, B., *Software Engineering Economics*, Upper Saddle River, NJ: Prentice-Hall, 1981.

[11] Boehm, B., et al., *Software Cost Estimation with COCOMO II*, Upper Saddle River, NJ: Prentice-Hall, 2000.

[12] Wiegers, K., "Stop Promising Miracles," *Software Development*, February 2000.

Selected Bibliography

Pressman, R. S., *Software Engineering: A Practitioner's Approach*, 4th ed. New York: McGraw-Hill, 1997. (For further reading on function points and feature points.)

Putnam, L., and W. Myers, *Measures for Excellence*, Englewood Cliffs, NJ: Yourdon Press, 1992. (Contains helpful information on project planning.)

Web Resources

More information on function points and feature points and COCOMO II can be found at the IFPUG and COCOMO Web sites:

- http://www.ifpug.org

- http://sunset.usc.edu/research/COCOMOII/cocomo_main.html

Note: URLs cited were accurate as of April 2001.

15

Balancing People, Process, and Product

Management plays a central role in making tradeoffs that affect people, process, and products. In this chapter, we discuss issues related to balancing the needs of people (employees, organizations, and customers), process (in the form of "best practices"), and product (did we build the right product and does the product meet customer needs?).

Tradeoffs with regard to people, process, and product impact the effectiveness of the software V&V activities described in Parts I–III. Management must balance the often-conflicting needs of people, process, and product in order to help the organization behave in a more predictable manner.

15.1 Process

In working with many companies, I have found that management is sometimes reluctant to impose "process" upon the organization. Management, encouraged by a small, vocal segment of the software engineering community, is led to believe that somehow process gets in the way of progress, that somehow process diminishes creativity, even though instinct says otherwise. In some companies, the process is viewed with much disdain. In fact, I've been confronted with the attitude that "Real programmers don't need a written process!" on more than one occasion.

If you pick any industry and find the most competitive, profitable, and efficient companies in that industry, you will find that most every one of them is dependent upon a written process. Clearly, these industries have learned how to use process to their advantage.

Within the software industry, as observed by Jones [1], "there are thousands of ways to fail when building software applications, and only a few ways to succeed. It is an interesting phenomenon that the 'best in class' companies in terms of quality all use essentially similar approaches in achieving their excellent results."

There will be more on this later. Let's look briefly now at the economic motivation for process.

15.1.1 Economic Motivation

In working with organizations that are not "process-oriented," I am often asked the question "We're profitable operating the way we do, why should we change?" A good question. The answer is simple.

First, whether or nor the process is written down, there is a process. If it's not written down, then it resides in someone's head. If that person leaves, the process and knowledge about the process leaves with that person. Having worked as a developer for several years, I've found that there are some software engineers and some software QA people who prefer to not have any written process, since it would force them to be accountable. While there are few of these people around, they nonetheless are vocal and persistent. In most every other organization within companies, process is not only accepted, but required. Why should software development be different than other engineering disciplines?

Second, in my view, companies that lack a basic set of written processes are less efficient then they could be and are inherently unpredictable. By defining and following a written process that's appropriate for your business, commensurate with the type of product you develop and the risk it engenders, your organization will become more predictable and, as a result, more cost-effective.

Lastly, if your company is profitable operating without any written process, your company can be more profitable if you define and follow an appropriate set of basic processes. This fact often is lost in the sometimes-heated discussions regarding process.

The objectives of a product development process should be to:

- Increase competitiveness by alignment with overall business goals and objectives;

- Reduce risk (and therefore liability) by ensuring that the product development process is commensurate with the business risk of developing the product and the potential risk of using the product;

- Increase predictability of the organization by establishing common terminology, clearly defined work products, and a concise means for measuring project progress.

Given these objectives, let us now look at what it means for an organization to be process-oriented.

15.1.2 The Process-Oriented Organization

To become predictable, organizations need a written product development process. The notion of a written software development process was introduced in Chapter 3. Appendix G includes an example of what such a process might look like. This process should describe what must be done to create products that may include hardware, software, and related services. As such, it should incorporate procedures required of all engineering disciplines involved in product development. For example, it should include software engineering, software quality assurance, technical documentation, hardware engineering, customer support, training, and so on. By preparing one document (instead of separate documents for each technical discipline), it becomes possible to weave the activities of each discipline into one overall process. This enables the organization to work more efficiently and supports the principle of concurrent engineering.

All software companies have a business need for a minimum set of processes that need to be defined, documented, communicated, and followed. The specifics of these processes should be defined to be commensurate with business goals and product risk. That is, there needs to be a balance between process and risk. Developing life- or mission-critical systems clearly requires a more extensive product development process than developing video games. We need to avoid process for process' sake.

There are several important aspects of a product development process that management needs to understand:

- *The product development process must provide competitive advantage.* Why would an organization use a product development process that puts them at a competitive disadvantage? Clearly they wouldn't. Yet this is one reason why organizations that have written a product development process don't follow it.

Creating a process that provides competitive advantage can seem like a daunting task, especially for larger organizations with geographically dispersed development groups. In organizations like this, each product development group should create their own product development process and then work toward establishing a more common process, if that makes good business sense. This will only happen, however, if management at the highest levels truly believes in the value of creating such a process.

- *The product development process needs to be designed to be flexible.* A rigid, inflexible process is sure to be found on the shelf collecting dust. Flexibility means that project teams determine the amount of "process" appropriate for the project at hand. Flexibility doesn't mean ignoring process. Flexibility is essential since we know from experience that most software projects have unique constraints and business needs. (Note that in regulated industries the amount of flexibility is less than in nonregulated industries. However, some flexibility is still needed.)

Flexibility applies to software development tasks as well as software V&V tasks. One common reason that organizations don't follow their written product development process is that their process may be inflexible—every project must be done the same way, following the exact same procedures. While this approach is appropriate for manufacturing, it just doesn't work for software development.

- *The product development process needs to be tailored to meet the specific business needs of each project.* Part of the value of having a written product development process derives from the ability to tailor it to meet the specific and unique business and technical needs of each project. The concept of tailoring is extremely important because it provides the flexibility required by organizations and projects. The product development process should require that a project plan be written for each project. One of the primary purposes of the project plan is to describe which of the processes and procedures from the product development process will be used and which won't. For those that are not used, written justification (reviewed and approved by management) should be provided in the project plan.

Table 15.1 summarizes some "acknowledged" reasons why organizations fail to follow their product development process and the probable root cause.

15.1.3 Finding the Right Process

As stated by Jones, there are many ways to do it wrong but only a few ways to do it right. In Chapter 13, the concept of best practices was introduced; lists of best practices for software development and software quality assurance are included in Appendices L and M.

As a first step toward becoming process-oriented, your organization needs to select one or more software development life-cycle models (described in Chapter 2) and adapt them as necessary. Once this is done, your staff needs to then understand processes used by best-in-class companies, and then adapt them to your selected life-cycle model(s), products, and business objectives. By studying practices used at best-in-class companies, Jones [1] has found that while there are many differences, there are some similarities, as shown in Table 15.2.

Recently, Boehm and Basilli [3] reported on a study that identified ten of the most important techniques for reducing defects. Their so-called software-defect-reduction top-ten list is shown below.

Table 15.1
Why Product Development Processes Are Ignored

Acknowledged Reason	Probable Root Cause
The process makes it harder to get products to market.	The process ignores business objectives and risk.
The process is inflexible.	People with a manufacturing perspective probably wrote the process, since in a manufacturing environment it makes sense for the process to be the same for every product.
People other than those who must follow it created the process.	The process was probably developed by the "Process Police" and as a result, the people who must follow it have not "bought into" the process.
There is no accountability regarding process.	Management may not understand the importance of following a defined process and as a result, doesn't hold project managers accountable. Lack of accountability may be a systemic problem within the organization.
The process wasn't effectively communicated to all of the organization.	After the process was written and approved, it was never rolled out to the organization. Lack of effective communication across the organization may be a systemic problem.

Table 15.2
Practices Used By Best-in-Class Companies

Process	For more information, see...
Quality measurements	Chapter 10, Appendix L
Defect prevention techniques such as quality function deployment (QFD) and joint application design (JAD)	QFD—Pressman [2] JAD—Jones [1]
Defect and quality estimation automation	Jones [1]
Defect-tracking automation	Defect-tracking tools from several suppliers are available. See for example, Rational Software[*] at www.rational.com and Mercant[*] at www.mercant.com.
Complexity analysis tools	Pressman [2] Complexity tools are available from suppliers such as McCabe and Associates[*] at www.mccabe.com.
Test coverage analysis tools	Test coverage tools are available from suppliers such as Software Research[*] at www.soft.com.
Formal inspections	Chapters 5, 6; Appendixes A–D
Formal testing by test specialists	Chapter 9
Formal quality assurance group	Pressman [2] and Jones [1]
Executive and managerial understanding of quality	Jones [1]

[*]These tools are not necessarily endorsed by the author.

1. Finding and fixing a software problem after delivery is often 100 times more expensive than finding and fixing it during the requirements and design phase.

2. Current software projects spend about 40% to 50% of their effort on avoidable rework.

3. About 80% of the avoidable rework comes from 20% of the modules.

4. About 80% of the defects come from 20% of the modules, and about half the modules are defect free.

5. About 90% of the downtime comes from, at most, 10% of the defects.

6. Peer reviews catch 60% of the defects.

7. Perspective-based reviews catch 35% more defects than nondirected reviews.

8. Disciplined personal practices can reduce defect introduction rates by up to 75%.

9. All other things being equal, it costs 50% more per source instruction to develop high-dependability software products than to develop low-dependability software products. However, the investment is more than worth it if the project involves significant operations and maintenance costs.

10. About 40% to 50% of user programs contain nontrivial defects.

Management clearly must take a leadership role in helping the organization establish, define, and follow a written product development process that is focused on reducing defects and delivering high-quality products on time. Once established, management must continue to provide support for the development process by holding people accountable for following it and for allowing staff to continually look at possible improvements based on process effectiveness measures.

In summary then, management's role with regard to process is summarized in Table 15.3.

15.2 People

DeMarco and Lister's influential work *Peopleware* should be required reading for every manager and executive in the software industry. Here is but one bit of wisdom from this book: "The manager's function is not to make people work, but to make it possible for people to work" [4]. What does this mean? Well, it means that management needs to:

1. Create an environment based on trust that enables people to take pride in their work and do things right the first time;

2. Request factual information in a timely manner without recrimination;

3. Measure customer satisfaction on a regular basis—and make changes accordingly;

Table 15.3
Management's Role with Regard to Process

What to do...	How to do it...
Work to create a "process-oriented" culture within the organization.	Identify the processes (documented or not) that are currently being used to develop products.
	Define simple effectiveness measures that can be used to assess the effectiveness of these processes.
	Based on effectiveness measures, determine which processes need to be changed.
	Talk to staff about process and the importance to the organization of having an appropriate set of effective processes for product development.
Require the organization to establish a written process that is appropriate for your products and business goals and that is flexible so that it can be tailored to meet the specific needs of each project.	Meet with managers and staff to review issues related to process and risk.
	Establish a forum for staff to raise concerns about process (too much or too little).
	Encourage staff to consider best practices such as those included in the Appendices.
Require that the people who will have to follow the process be actively involved in creating it.	Establish "process definition teams" within the product development groups. Ensure that all groups are represented.
Ensure that the written process is communicated and understood. If necessary, provide training to ensure that people understand what is expected of them.	Formally introduce the process and schedule training sessions if appropriate.
	Ensure that everyone knows that following the process is part of his or her responsibility.
	Hold managers accountable for communicating the process to their group and for identifying training where appropriate.
Once the process is established, hold the organization accountable for following the process.	Hold project managers accountable for tailoring the process to meet specific project needs and then following the tailored process.
Require that the process be reviewed periodically and changed as a result of process effectiveness measures.	Meet with staff to discuss process issues and ways to improve effectiveness of processes.

4. Measure employee satisfaction on a regular basis—and make changes accordingly;

5. Acknowledge the relationship between customer and employee satisfaction;

6. Listen to your staff—they can tell you a lot about what is right and what is not;

7. Listen to your customers—they can tell you about their needs and concerns;

8. Ensure employees are properly trained for their job;

9. Ensure every employee has specific quality goals they must meet;

10. Reduce turnover by creating an environment of which people want to be a part.

From my own experience as a manager, I believe that the most important roles for management are to:

- Provide motivation;

- Reduce turnover;

- Build effective teams.

Let's look at each of these issues and see how it affects predictability.

15.2.1   Provide Motivation

What motivates your people? Surprisingly, it's not money.

> Money, benefits, comfort, and so on are "hygiene" factors—they create dissatisfaction if they're absent, but they don't make people feel good about their jobs and give them the needed internal generator. What does produce the generator are recognition of achievement, pride in doing a good job, more responsibility, advancement, and personal growth. [5]

As a manager for several years, I found that the best way to motivate people is to:

- *Set realistic, measurable goals.* For each employee, I prepared a plan that included written goals and objectives based on business objectives (i.e., planned projects). These goals and objectives were measurable (e.g., complete software validation of Release 1.2), and, more importantly, were aligned with the employees' interests and long-term career goals. We revisited the plan whenever a task was completed so that I could provide feedback as close to the completion of a task as possible. Adjustments to the plan were made as needed. In this manner, each person always knew exactly where they stood so that at performance review time, there were no surprises.

- *Establish career paths where they don't exist.* Several years ago I recognized that we had to takes steps to retain customer support engineers who were burning out. I also recognized that it was becoming increasingly difficult to find SQA engineers who had "domain knowledge." I could find testers but not testers that understood the product and how customers used the product. So, I worked with the customer support manager to create a new career path for customer support engineers. As a result I was able to build a core SQA group by encouraging customer support engineers to transfer to SQA. I provided these people with training in testing techniques and in a very short time, they became an extremely effective testing group.

Management must recognize that customer support people have an enormous amount of domain knowledge and that this knowledge is incredibly valuable to the organization. Since this knowledge can't be bought, management should take whatever steps are necessary (like creating new career paths) to retain as many of these people as possible.

- *Create a "Mentality of Permanence"* [4]. In the new millennium, it's a seller's market. People seem to change jobs as often as they change their clothes. As DeMarco and Lister stated, management needs to create a "mentality of permanence" rather than the ubiquitous revolving door.

At best-in-class organizations, management clearly takes a long-term view. Investing in people is why turnover is so low at these companies. People respond to the fact that management is willing to make significant investments in their future, through cross-training, the office environment, on-site child care, flex hours, job sharing, telecommuting, on-site fitness centers, and even on-site gardens.

By working to create a mentality of permanence, management provides a clear message: We value your abilities and we are willing to invest in you to make you more valuable to the company. People respond to this message because "there is a widespread sense that you are expected to stay" [4].

15.2.2   Reduce Turnover

Turnover is incredibly expensive. Average figures for the cost of turnover run as high as 20% of the total cost of labor [4]. But this is clearly only the tip of the proverbial iceberg. In organizations with high turnover, productivity is low, morale is low, and quality is, you guessed it, low. Why? Because most of the staff has taken a short-term view of their jobs. In fact, as reported by DeMarco and Lister [4], for organizations with high turnover, the reasons cited include:

- A "just-passing-through" attitude (people don't form a sense of long-term involvement or permanence in their jobs);
- A feeling of disposability resulting from the perception that management views workers as interchangeable parts;
- No sense of loyalty (who would be loyal to an organization that views people as interchangeable?).

Traditional techniques for reducing turnover were focused on the "hygiene factors" such as money—imagine saying to someone who has quit, "We'll pay you more not to leave"—or benefits—"We'll give you an extra week of vacation if you stay."

Frequently, management just doesn't understand the real reasons people leave. Many people are too frustrated to give honest answers at their exit interview and those that do are viewed as troublemakers or not a team player, so their reasons for leaving are often ignored if they are regarded at all.

In today's economy, management must become much more aggressive in reducing turnover, because there are so many more jobs than there are people to fill them. The traditional solutions for reducing turnover must give way to honest introspection and real change.

15.2.3   Build Effective Teams

There is nothing more gratifying for techno-geeks like us than working on an exciting, "bleeding-edge" project as a member of a cohesive, highly functional team. If we have just one experience like this in our career, we are considered fortunate. Some people never experience the joy, the wonder, the constant mind-stretching challenges, and the sheer electricity of such an experience. And from experience, we know that when the planets are aligned just so and one such team is formed, there is no telling what they can accomplish.

While there is no recipe for building teams like this, management must learn how to identify charismatic leaders, select people based on chemistry instead of politics, and empower rather burden. For most every company, much of the company's success (or lack thereof) is dependent upon having effective teams. And having such teams depends heavily on management's ability to form them and give them the freedom to work.

As observed by DeMarco and Lister, "In organizations with the best chemistry, managers devote their energy to building and maintaining healthy chemistry. Whatever their relationship to the work going on around them, they're certainly not *doing* any of it" [4].

Below are some elements of chemistry building that DeMarco and Lister [4] have identified as contributing to a healthy organization:

- Make a cult of quality—deliver higher quality than your customers expect.

- Provide lots of satisfying closure—people need reassurance they are headed in the right direction.

- Build a sense of eliteness—teams need to feel that they are special in order to achieve extraordinary performance.

- Allow and encourage heterogeneity—since teams are composed of individuals, each team will be very different.

- Preserve and protect successful teams—give people the option to continue to work together.

- Provide strategic but not tactical direction—the manager is not part of the team and therefore can only provide strategic direction.

Management is instrumental in forming cohesive, exciting teams. If management is lucky (or skilled) enough to form such a team, it needs to do what was stated earlier—remove as many roadblocks as possible and, most importantly, not become a roadblock itself. If management can do this, the results can be astounding.

15.2.4   Best Practices for Managing People

Many organizations have put a lot of time and money into process improvement by using some of the process improvement models identified in Section 1.4. Even with huge investments in process improvement, some organizations have come to the realization that continued improvement in productivity, quality, and time to market require significant changes in the management, development, and utilization of their people. Such changes are outside the scope of most process improvement models.

The idea that there could be a set of best practices for managing people is intriguing. The SEI recognized the need for such practices a few years ago and as a result, developed the People Capability Maturity Model (P-CMM^{SM}) [6]. The intent of the P-CMM^{SM} is to "provide guidance on how to continuously improve the ability of software organizations to attract, develop, motivate, organize, and retain the talent needed to steadily improve their software development organization" [6].

Work areas that are addressed by the P-CMM^{SM} include:

- Work environment;
- Communication;
- Staffing;
- Managing performance;
- Training;
- Compensation;
- Competency development;
- Career development;
- Team building;
- Culture development.

These areas are generally consistent with recommendations identified here and are intended to be used with the SEI CMM^{SM} (see Appendix L). For more information on the P-CMM^{SM}, see [6] or visit the SEI CMM Web site at www.sei.cmu.edu.

In summary, management's role with regard to people is as follows: Management must recognize that people have needs.

- People need to know that if they work hard they will be recognized and rewarded.
- People need to be part of a team that has a good chance of being successful.
- People need to know what is expected of them.

- People need appropriate training in tools and technology before being thrown onto projects.
- People need to have defined career paths with choices.
- People need to have written goals and objectives that they are measured against.
- People need a work environment based on trust.

Management must recognize that organizations have needs.

- Organizations need people with "domain knowledge."
- Organizations need people who can work well together.
- Organizations need people with specific skills.
- Organizations need to communicate effectively.
- Organizations need to be focused on customers.
- Organizations need to be constantly improving and constantly learning.
- Organizations need to be adaptable.
- Organizations need to change—constantly.

Management must recognize that customers have needs.

- Customers need suppliers they can count on.
- Customers need to build relationships with suppliers.
- Customers need tools that can help them get their job done.
- Customers need software products that work reliably.
- Customers need factual information in a timely manner.
- Customers need to make decisions in real-time.
- Customers need products that will give them an advantage.
- Customers need to be constantly improving and learning.

15.3   Product

In order for organizations to behave in a more predictable manner, management must be able to answer the following product questions:

- *Are you building the right product?* During the development process, it is important to have confidence that your team is building the right product—with features your customers want as defined by the requirements specification. The way to ensure that this is the case is to perform an inspection of the requirements specification (as described in Chapter 6) and to perform software validation testing (as described in Chapter 9).

- *Is the product "good enough"?* Clearly, customers have expectations for quality. It is imperative that these expectations be documented at the beginning of the project. Tests need to be created to ensure that the quality requirements are met as development proceeds.

- *Are measurable product release criteria defined for the product?* One of the most difficult decisions for a team to make is when to stop testing and release the product. Without measurable criteria, this decision can often become a contentious argument. As part of the test planning process outlined in Chapter 9, measurable completion criteria need to be defined and agreed to up front so that everyone knows where the bar is set with regard to releasing the product.

- *Does the product do what it is supposed to?* It may sound incomprehensible, but sometimes products are developed and released only to find out that they don't do what they were supposed to do. How does this happen? In organizations with no formal procedures for controlling change, frequently developers make changes to the product and neglect to communicate these changes to anyone else. When customers get the product, they are surprised to find that the product doesn't perform according to the user manual. Not surprising, since there may not have been time for SQA to test the user manual against the product. Another way this happens is described in Section 13.3.5 as when a product manager pressures a developer to slip in a new feature.

- *Does everyone (including your customers) know what the product is supposed to do?* It seems like printed user manuals are about as common as eight-track tapes. Without user manuals, how then do users know what features products are supposed to have? Usually this happens in a couple of ways: First, there is frequently on-line help included with the product that provides an explanation of features. Second, there may be internal documents prepared by the project team (like an SRS). And lastly, there is verbal communication from sales and marketing people.

The SRS and online help and can and should be tested as part of the software validation process described in Chapter 9. Communication from sales people is another issue, which is discussed in Chapter 16.

- *How are changes to product features communicated (internally and externally)?* During the development of a software product, many changes to the product may be made. It is absolutely essential for an organization to have a process that allows change to occur in a controlled manner. This process should ensure that changes are reviewed and approved, tested, and communicated to the organization and possibly to customers. More information on change control can be found in Chapter 8.

- *Are product installation, training, support, and maintenance issues considered part of the project?* Product installation (and possibly upgrading from previous versions), training of customers and support staff, and ongoing maintenance of products are critically important issues for organizations and customers. As such, these issues need to be addressed as part of the overall project plan and reviewed and approved by management so that sufficient resources are committed to the product.

The answers to these questions are critically important. Further, at product release time, there are several important activities that management should ensure occur: (1) project postmortem, (2) triage process, and (3) root-cause analysis.

Let's briefly look at each of these activities.

15.3.1 Project Postmortems

Postmortems can provide valuable insight into product development issues and project management (people) issues. Best-in-class organizations make effective use of postmortems to ensure that they learn as much as possible from each project. Unpredictable organizations may also conduct postmortems, but the lessons learned are frequently ignored, thus rendering the postmortem useless. As a result, many unpredictable organizations repeat the same mistakes over and over.

An interesting point about project postmortems is that you shouldn't necessarily wait till the end of the project to conduct one. Mini-postmortems can be planned at the end of each major phase of a project so that lessons learned can be instituted immediately rather than on the next project.

Conducting a postmortem is not difficult and should be a high priority. Details for planning and conducting a project postmortem are included in Appendix N.

15.3.2   Triage Process

A key problem for every organization is deciding which defects to fix. The organization has limited resources and usually many defects. Instituting a decision mechanism is critical because, if left to decide on their own, developers will fix those defects they are most interested in rather than those that are most critical to your customers.

To avoid this problem, predictable organizations use a triage process to review all reported defects and determine which ones are most critical and need to be fixed. This way, the organization's scarce resources can be applied to problems that will have a higher return on investment.

The triage process is simple. A team is formed consisting of a representative from development, QA, customer support, and project management. The team is chartered with reviewing reported defects and assigning them relative priority based on their perceived impact to customers (this is why a representative from customer support is part of the team). Developers are required to abide by the priorities set by the triage team when fixing defects. Management provides support for this approach.

The triage team meets as often as necessary based on the number of problems reported. It is usually a good idea to start the triage process before the product is released. This way, the team can help prioritize bug-fixing efforts on internally reported defects. Once the product is released, the triage team should continue by focusing on defects reported by customers. Defects reported by customers are critically important because they (1) reflect a gap in your testing process, (2) reflect a gap in your knowledge of how your customers use your product, and (3) represent an opportunity to improve customer satisfaction by fixing problems reported by customers.

The triage team not only helps improve effectiveness by prioritizing problems, it is also actively involved in root-cause analysis and in the root-cause-analysis review, as discussed below.

15.3.3   Root-Cause Analysis

Root-cause analysis is an effective tool that helps the organization understand why a defect exists. By understanding why defects exist, organizations can take corrective and preventive actions to not only fix the problem but change the process so similar problems don't occur again. The triage team is the focal point for performing root-cause analysis.

As a first step, organizations should consider performing root-cause analysis on all problems reported by customers. Once this is in place, the organization can then expand root-cause analysis to internally reported problems.

In order to determine the root cause of a problem, it can help to follow a systematic set of questions that will lead to the ultimate root cause. Once data is collected over a reasonable period of time, a root-cause-analysis review can be performed to identify process improvements that could eliminate one or more root causes. The process for performing root-cause analysis is described in Appendix O.

In summary, management's role with regard to product is as follows:

- Ensure project teams are building the right products with the right level of quality required by your customers.

- Require that project managers conduct postmortems on every project and that the results are published. Demonstrate your commitment to improvement by instituting corrective action within a reasonable time. Ensure that changes implemented are documented and communicated.

- Ensure that a triage team is in place following the release of a new product.

- Require that root-cause analysis be performed on customer reported defects.

- Reward project teams who perform postmortems, triage, and root-cause analysis.

15.4   Summary

Management has a delicate balancing act to perform. Balancing the needs of people, process, and product is no easy task. But then who said that management was supposed to be easy? While difficult, it's by no means insurmountable. To reap the benefits of predictable software development, management must demonstrate:

- An understanding of the issues related to efficient software development;

- A commitment to work with people to solve problems;
- Dedication to people (employees and customers);
- Follow-up and accountability.

With these attributes, management can help the organization become significantly more predictable and increase the effectiveness of software V&V activities.

References

[1]   Jones, C., *Software Quality: Analysis and Guidelines for Success*, Boston, MA: International Thomson Computer Press, 1997.

[2]   Pressman, R., *Software Engineering: A Practitioner's Approach*, 4th ed., New York: McGraw-Hill, 1997.

[3]   Boehm, B., and V. Basilli, "Software Defect Reduction Top 10 List," *IEEE Computer*, January 2001, pp. 135–137.

[4]   DeMarco, T., and T. Lister, *Peopleware: Productive Projects and Teams*, 2nd ed., New York: Dorset House, 1999, p. 34.

[5]   Herzberg, F., "One More Time: How Do You Motivate Employees?" *Harvard Business Review*, September–October 1987.

[6]   Curtis, B., et al., "People Capability Maturity Model[SM] Version 1.0," Software Engineering Institute, Pittsburgh, PA, CMU/SEI-95-MM-02, DTIC Number 300-822, September 1995.

16

Managing Commitment and Risk

Commitment and risk represent two important issues that, if not actively managed, can contribute to the demise of a project. Learning how to effectively manage commitment and risk are key skills required for organizations to become more predictable. Managing commitment and risk will result in fewer "unexpected surprises" on projects. With fewer unexpected surprises, planned software verification activities (like design reviews and code inspections) are less likely to be canceled or postponed, and the software validation testing can occur as planned.

16.1 Managing Commitments

> The role of the management system is to ensure that projects are successfully completed. This implies some organization-wide agreement on the meaning of the terms "success" and "completion." It also requires a continuing management focus on the progress of each project.... This involves managing commitments, project oversight, and contention. [1]

People make commitments every day. These commitments take many forms. For example, a commitment can be in the form of a work product, as in "I'll have that report on your desk by 5 P.M.," or an action, as in "I'll fix that bug in the next build," or a commitment can be in the form of a promise, as in when a salesperson tells a customer, "Release 5.2 will have the following features...." Commitments are often, but not always, made by the person who must fulfill the commitment, as in the first two examples above. Sometimes, commitments are made by someone other than the person or group that must fulfill the commitment, as in the third example above. Both kinds of commitments must be managed.

Commitments made by the person who must fulfill the commitment can be managed if those commitments are communicated and tracked. In the example above regarding the bug fix, there should be a list of bug fixes that are to be included in the next release along with the name of the developer assigned to do the work. By using such a list, management can actively "manage" the commitments made by people for their own work.

However, commitments made by people other than those who must fulfill the commitment are often harder to manage because:

- Frequently, the other person or group may not be aware that a commitment was made.

- Sales and marketing people frequently make commitments to prospective customers in order to book orders (and receive commissions). Sometimes these commitments are realistic. Sometimes they are not. Sometimes the commitment made to the customer is communicated back to the person or group that must fulfill it. Sometimes it isn't. Quite often the person making the commitment is not held accountable for seeing that it is fulfilled. Without accountability, unrealistic promises are frequently made.

Further complicating this picture is management's constant quest to get more done than can reasonably be expected. Management often pressures project teams into committing to deliver an ever-expanding list of features in an unrealistic amount of time with fewer people than are needed. Characterized by Yourdon [2] as "death marches," these projects often fail with many "casualties" among the project team.

As pointed out by Humphrey [1], what is needed is a discipline for managing commitments. This discipline should be based on a process that extends to the highest levels of management. The process should have the following elements:

- *Making Commitments.* At a personal level, a commitment is an agreement to do something. Commitments should not be taken lightly, since most every organization depends upon its people making and meeting their commitments. Humphrey [3] has identified the following points that each person should consider when making commitments:

1. The person making the commitment does so willingly.

2. The commitment is not made lightly, that is, the work involved, the resources, and schedule are carefully considered.

3. There is agreement between the parties on what is to be done, by whom, and when.

4. The commitment is openly and publicly stated.

5. The person responsible tries to meet the commitment, even if help is needed.

6. Prior to the committed date, if it is clear that it cannot be met, advance notice is given and a new commitment is negotiated.

Note that commitment management is a key component of the yellow sticky method for estimating and scheduling and is described in Appendix K.

- *Managing Commitments.* As stated by Humphrey [1], the active involvement of management is what motivates people to take commitments seriously. This involvement requires that:

  1. Management must create an environment based on honoring commitments, whether internal or external. Everyone (including management) must be accountable for meeting commitments to the best of his or her ability.

  2. All commitments made to customers for future delivery of products are reviewed and/or made personally by the organization's senior executive.

  3. Such commitments are made only after completion of a formal project review and assessment process in which management participates.

  4. Management is responsible for ensuring that formal project reviews and assessments are conducted.

  5. In the case of salespeople, commissions should be tied to delivery of the specified product, not taking of an order. This gives sales a stake in meeting commitments made to customers.

16.2   Risk

Software has long been regarded as one of the most risk-prone of all engineering activities. Risks such as schedule slips and cost overruns tend to occur on more than 50% of all large systems. Even more severe risks, such as cancellation of the project prior to completion or serious quality deficiencies are not uncommon. [4]

For software projects, risks are events that could have a negative impact on the project and/or the product. After surveying hundreds of projects, Jones identified the 10 most serious software risks:

1. Inaccurate metrics;
2. Inadequate measurement;
3. Excessive schedule pressure;
4. Management malpractice;
5. Inaccurate cost estimating;
6. Silver Bullet syndrome;
7. Creeping user requirements;
8. Low quality;
9. Low productivity;
10. Canceled projects.

Refer to Table 2.1 for Boehm's view of common software project risks. Some risk is present on every software development project. Many software organizations fail to recognize that risks are present and that they need to be dealt with. Sadly, a common risk management technique is to sweep them under the rug, pretend they don't exist, and won't impact the project. Common sense would tell you that if you ignore risks, they will cause problems. Unfortunately, when it comes to risk management, common sense isn't all that common.

16.3   Risk-Management Techniques

Risk management is an activity that needs to be performed throughout a project and is focused on the following three activities:

- *Risk Identification.* From experience, we have identified many types of risks that occur on software projects. Table 2.1 and the list in the previous section identify risks commonly observed on software projects. Clearly, the first task must be to try to identify as many potential risks that can be expected so that their impact can be assessed and a mitigation plan developed. To help to do this, Pressman [5] has created risk categories and questions that can be asked to determine if specific types of risk are present on a project. An example of several risk categories and the questions associated with each are shown in Table 16.1.

- *Risk Assessment.* Once risks are identified, their potential impact to the project needs to be assessed. A simple way to do this was developed by Boehm and is illustrated in Table 16.2. Each risk is listed in a table along with an assessment of the potential schedule and cost impact. Table 16.3 shows adding an additional piece of information, which is probability—how likely is it that this risk will occur—to the assessment. Then decide where to draw the line with regard to risk mitigation. In this way, project teams can decide which are the most important risks to address. Those risks in Table 16.3 above the line are actively managed while those below the line are not.

- *Risk Mitigation.* Once the risks are identified and assessed as to impact and probability, the next step is to determine mitigation strategies and a contingency plan should the risk occur. An example of this is shown in Table 16.4. Monitoring progress and status of risks is a task that should occur throughout the project, not just at the beginning.

- *Management's Role.* Management's role with regard to risk management should be as follows:

1. Create an environment where planning for and dealing with risk is part of the process;
2. Provide staff with training in risk management and risk avoidance techniques;
3. Require project managers to prepare risk management plans that address: risk identification; risk assessment; and risk mitigation, monitoring, and management;
4. Reward those project managers who proactively manage risks.

Table 16.1
Identifying Risk [5]

Risk Category	Risks
Technology	Is the technology new to your organization?
	Are new algorithms, input, or output technology required?
	Does the software interface with new/unproven hardware?
	Does the software interface with unproven third-party software?
	Do the requirements put excessive performance constraints on the product?
Staffing	Are the best people available?
	Do the people available have the right skills?
	Are enough people with the right skills available?
	Is staff committed for the duration of the project?
	Have staff members received necessary training?
	Will turnover likely affect the project?
Process	Does management support following a documented development process?
	Is there a documented development process?
	Is the documented process followed?
	Are published software standards provided to staff?
	Are formal inspections and/or design reviews included in the process?
	Has staff been trained in formal inspections?
	Are configuration management tools, procedures, and training in place?
	Is there a documented mechanism for controlling changes to requirements?
Development Environment	Is there a stable development environment that includes tools appropriate for the kind of development being considered?
	Does the development environment include bug tracking and configuration management tools?
	Are debugging, simulation, and performance analysis tools required? If so, are they available?
	Has everyone that needs training been trained?
Product Quality	Do we know what level of quality customers need?
	Are measures defined that are indicative of quality?
	What tradeoffs can be made with respect to quality?

Table 16.2

Risk Assessment [6]

	Rank	Impact	Cost	Schedule
Major	1	Project failure	Cost overrun of more than $x	Schedule slip of more than n
	2	Significant degradation of usefulness	Cost overrun of more than y but less than $x	Schedule slip of more than m but less than n
Minor	3	Significant reduction in desirable features	Cost overrun of more than z but less than $y	Schedule slip of more than p but less than m
	4	Minor reduction in desirable features	Cost overrun less than $z	Schedule slip of less than p
Negligible	5	—	—	—

Table 16.3

Rank Risks in Probability Order [6]

Risks	Rank	Category	Probability
Size estimate may be too low	1	Technology	65%
Customer will change requirements	1	Customer	50%
Project understaffed	1	Staffing	50%
Staff turnover will be high	2	Staffing	45%
Schedule not accurate	2	Process	40%
Lack of training on tools	3	Staffing	30%
Funding for project lost	5	Business	20%

Table 16.4

Example of a Risk-Mitigation Plan

Risk	Rank	Category	Probability	Mitigation	Monitoring	Contingency
Project understaffed	1	Staffing	45%	Mitigation strategies include more aggressive recruiting, actively recruiting internal transfers, and identifying potential reductions in scope.	Monitoring includes a weekly project team meeting to add an agenda item for staffing; and to check performance to schedule.	The management contingency plan is to outsource portions of the work.

16.4   Summary

In order for organizations to become predictable, management must play an active role in creating an environment that is focused on:

- Making commitments that can be met;
- Meeting those commitments;
- Proactively identifying and assessing risk;
- Using risk mitigation, monitoring, and management techniques.

Creating such an environment, while not easy, can be done if management believes that it is important. By doing this, management will help the organization achieve the goal of predictable software development.

References

[1]   Humphrey, W. S., *Managing the Software Process*, Reading, MA: Addison-Wesley, 1990.

[2]   Yourdon, E., *Death March: The Complete Software Developer's Guide to Surviving "Mission Impossible" Projects*, Upper Saddle River, NJ: Prentice-Hall PTR, 1997.

[3]   Humphrey, W. S., *Managing for Innovation—Leading Technical People*, Upper Saddle River, NJ: Prentice-Hall, 1987.

[4]   Jones, C., *Assessment and Control of Software Risks*, Upper Saddle River, NJ: Prentice-Hall PTR, 1994

[5]   Pressman, R., *Software Engineering: A Practitioner's Approach*, 5th ed. New York: McGraw-Hill, 2000.

[6]   Boehm, B. W., *Software Risk Management*, Los Alamitos, CA: IEEE Computer Society Press, 1989.

Appendix A:
Inspection Roles and Responsibilities

One of the most important aspects of the inspection process is that team members play specific roles. For the inspection process to be successful, it is essential that each team member know the role he or she is to play and the responsibilities of that role. It is expected that people eventually will play all the divergent roles as the inspection process becomes part of a company's culture.

A.1   Roles

An inspection team consists of three to six people who play the following roles:

- Moderator;
- Producer;
- Reader;
- Recorder (optional);
- Inspector.

The producer's immediate supervisor or manager, while not directly involved in the inspection process, does play a role in the inspection process. The manager's role and responsibilities are to participate in the decision of what to inspect; include inspections on project schedules; allocate resources for inspections; support inspection training; participate in the selection of moderators; and support the moderator in getting rework completed.

A.2   Responsibilities

Each inspection team member has specific responsibilities.

A.2.1   Moderator

The moderator is a key player in the inspection process. Selection of the moderator is crucial to the success of the inspection process. A good moderator will ensure that the inspection team is selected appropriately, is trained in the inspection process, is adequately prepared for the inspection, and abides by the guidelines for inspection meetings.

Selection of the moderator is, therefore, very important. The moderator is usually selected from a small group of senior people who have had prior experience as moderators and who are well respected for their technical skills as well as their people management skills.

The moderator must be able to:

- Understand the information being inspected;
- Lead the team in an effective discussion;
- Mediate disputes;
- Recognize key issues and keep the team focused on them;
- Maintain an unbiased view of the information being inspected;
- Assign responsibilities appropriately.

The specific responsibilities of the moderator are:

- To select inspection team members;
- To ensure that team members can devote sufficient time to the inspection and are not involved in other activities that could impair

their ability to spend the required amount of time preparing for the inspection;

- To ensure that the manager of the person whose work is being inspected is aware of the inspection;

- To schedule the inspection meeting and make the necessary logistical arrangements for conference rooms, review materials, and so on;

- To ensure that the inspection team is adequately prepared to conduct the inspection or, if the team is not prepared, to postpone the inspection meeting;

- To ensure that the inspection meeting is conducted in an orderly and efficient manner, starting promptly and ending on time;

- To ensure that all problems found during the inspection meeting are properly documented;

- To track each problem identified to closure;

- To prepare and distribute meeting minutes within two working days after the inspection meeting.

The moderator is usually selected by the producer and the producer's manager.

A.2.2 Producer

The producer is the person who prepared the information or work product that is to be inspected. Inspections are conducted for the benefit of the producer. The reward for the other inspection team members is the satisfaction gained from helping a peer improve the quality of the company's product. There is an implied understanding that they will be helped in return.

The producer's responsibilities are:

- To ensure that the work product to be inspected is ready for inspection;

- To make required information available on time;

- To support the moderator in making meeting arrangements, providing copies of materials, and helping to establish schedules for any required corrective action;

- To promptly resolve all problems identified by the inspection team;

- To remain objective and avoid becoming defensive.

The producer attends the inspection meeting to clarify any issues that are not clear to the inspectors. The producer does not justify why he or she developed the work product a certain way. Remember that the objective of the inspection is to determine if the work product, as it presently exists, meets established requirements.

A.2.3   Reader

The reader is responsible for paraphrasing portions of the work product being inspected so the inspection team can focus on small chunks of information. This helps divert attention away from the producer and toward the product. The reader is also an inspector and has the same responsibilities as inspectors.

The additional responsibilities of the reader are:

- To be thoroughly familiar with the work product being inspected;
- To identify logical chunks of information and to be able to paraphrase the information in each chunk, thereby allowing the moderator to keep the team focused on one chunk at a time;
- To support the moderator.

A.2.4   Inspectors

Inspectors are selected based on their knowledge and familiarity with the work product being inspected. Inspectors are also selected to represent a cross-section of skills. For example, at a code inspection, inspectors representing software engineering, marketing, and manufacturing may be selected. Inspectors are expected to devote the necessary time and effort to become thoroughly familiar with the work product. Their role is to look for discrepancies between the work product and the documentation and standards against which the work product is being inspected. Each inspector should expect that, at some future date, he or she will be in the role of the producer.

The inspector's responsibilities are:

- To be thoroughly familiar with the work product being inspected as well as the documents and standards against which the work product is being inspected;

- To identify discrepancies between the work product and the documentation and standards;
- To focus on identifying problems, not solving them;
- To remain objective;
- To criticize the product, not the producer;
- To support the moderator.

A.2.5 Recorder (Optional Role)

Recording information during an inspection can be a time-consuming task. Rather than burden the moderator with this task, many times a team member acts as the recorder. The recorder captures all issues and problems raised by the team, thus allowing the moderator to focus on leading the discussion. For each issue raised by the team, the recorder captures a complete description of the issue. The recorder is also an inspector and has the same responsibilities as inspectors.

The role of the recorder is optional. Depending on the size and the nature of the inspection, the moderator may assume the responsibilities of recorder.

The recorder's additional responsibilities are:

- To be thoroughly familiar with the work product being inspected;
- To record all issues raised by the team and ensure that they are recorded correctly;
- To provide additional information as requested by the moderator;
- To support the moderator.

A.2.6 Manager

The manager's role and responsibilities are:

- To help decide what to inspect;
- To include inspections in project schedules;
- To allocate resources for inspections;
- To support inspection training;
- To participate in the selection of moderators;
- To support the moderator in completing any required rework.

Appendix B:
A Sample Inspection Process

The second of the five basic elements of the inspection process is a documented process for conducting inspections. A documented process provides the basis for performing inspections in a manner such that everyone can understand the process and how they can contribute to its success. Having a written process also provides the basic materials required for training.

The inspection process has five steps:

1. Planning;
2. Overview meeting (optional);
3. Preparation;
4. Inspection meeting;
5. Follow-up.

This appendix discusses these steps in detail. For each step, the following information is included:

- Objectives: the purpose of the step;
- Entry criteria: the conditions that must be met to begin the step;
- Activities: the activities that occur as part of the step;
- Exit criteria: the conditions that must be met to complete the step;

- Metrics: the product and process data that should be collected.

B.1   Planning

B.1.1   Objectives

- To determine which work products need to be inspected;
- To determine if a work product that needs to be inspected is ready to be inspected;
- To identify the inspection team;
- To determine if an overview meeting is needed;
- To schedule the optional overview meeting and the inspection meeting.

B.1.2   Entry Criteria

The manager and the producer identify the work product to be inspected. Examples of work products are SRS, SDD, source code, and test procedures.

B.1.3   Activities

- Identify the work product to be inspected and determine if the work product is ready to be inspected (refer to Table 5.2).
- Select the moderator. The producer and the producer's manager select the moderator for the inspection.
- Identify inspection team members. Once the moderator has been selected and has accepted the assignment, the moderator and the producer determine the makeup of the inspection team. The nature of the work product being inspected determines if inspectors from other engineering disciplines are needed. For example, if the work product is communications software that interfaces with hardware, the engineer who designed the hardware should be on the team. A representative from the software QA group is invited to all inspection meetings. The minimum number of people required for an inspection is three (moderator, producer, and one inspector). The maximum number of people for an inspection should be limited to six or seven.

- The moderator ensures that all inspection team members have had inspection process training.

- The moderator obtains a commitment from each team member to participate. This commitment means the person agrees to spend the time required to perform his or her assigned role on the team. In some cases, approval from the team member's supervisor or manager may be required.

- The moderator and the producer decide if an overview meeting is required based on the inspection team's familiarity with the work product being inspected, the amount and complexity of information the team must review to be prepared for the inspection, and the complexity of the work product being inspected.

- The moderator schedules meetings and distributes review materials. The moderator communicates the date, time, and location of the meetings to the inspection team. If an overview meeting is held, the moderator can distribute the review materials at that meeting.

- The moderator and the producer identify the review materials required for the inspection (see Chapter 5). The moderator ensures that the review materials are distributed (and received) at least five working days before the inspection meeting, so the inspection team has sufficient time to prepare for the inspection.

- Inspection meetings should be limited to two hours in duration. Studies have shown that the effectiveness of the inspection diminishes after two hours. Inspection meetings also should be limited to two per day. Use the following guidelines to estimate the amount of material that can be inspected in two hours:

  - Work product is a document: 10 to 20 pages per hour;

  - Work product is code: 100 to 200 source statements per hour (based on C).

B.1.4 Exit Criteria

The planning phase is complete when the following tasks have been accomplished:

- The inspection team has been selected and trained and its members are committed.

- Review materials have been identified and distributed at least five working days in advance.
- An overview meeting, if required, has been scheduled.
- The inspection meeting has been scheduled.

B.1.5 Metrics

The process metric that should be recorded during the planning phase is the time spent by each person in the planning phase measured in person-hours.

B.2 Overview Meeting (Optional)

B.2.1 Objective

The objective of the overview meeting is to educate the inspection team on the work product being inspected and to discuss the review materials.

B.2.2 Entry Criteria

- The work product is ready to be inspected (see Chapter 5).
- The producer has prepared an overview of the work product and the review materials.
- The review materials are ready to be distributed.

B.2.3 Activities

- The moderator distributes the work product and the review materials.
- The producer describes the information contained in the review materials and the relationship to the work product.
- The producer provides the context for the work product and how the work product fits into the big picture.
- Team members ask questions to facilitate their understanding of the work product and the information in the review materials.

B.2.4 Exit Criteria

The overview meeting has been held and all questions have been resolved.

B.2.5 Metrics

- Preparation time by the producer;
- Duration of the overview meeting.
- The moderator multiplies the number of participants by the meeting duration and enters that number in the appropriate place on the Inspection Process Summary Report (see Appendix C). The measure is person-hours.

B.3 Preparation

B.3.1 Objective

To prepare for the inspection meeting by critically reviewing the review materials and the work product.

B.3.2 Entry Criteria

- The work product is ready to be inspected.
- The overview meeting, if required, has been held.
- The review materials and the work product have been distributed to the inspection team members.

B.3.3 Activities

B.3.3.1 Inspectors

- Review prompting checklists and internal standards and conventions before reviewing work product to create mental list of things to look for;
- Become very familiar with review materials and work product;
- Review the work product against the review materials, and record any discrepancies on an Inspection Problem Report form (see Appendix C);
- Keep track of preparation time and bring that information to the meeting.

B.3.3.2   Reader

- Performs same activities as inspectors;
- Breaks down the work products into chunks and then paraphrases or summarizes those chunks in his or her own words.
- Keeps track of preparation time and brings that information to the meeting.

B.3.4   Exit Criteria

Each team member is prepared for the inspection meeting.

B.3.5   Metrics

Preparation time, measured in person-hours.

B.4   Inspection Meeting

B.4.1   Objective

The objective of the inspection meeting is to identify errors and defects in the work product being inspected.

B.4.2   Entry Criteria

The inspection team members have completed the required preparation.

B.4.3   Activities

- The moderator calls the meeting to order promptly.
- The moderator reviews the ground rules for the meeting: (1) The objective of the inspection meeting is to find problems, not solve them; (2) criticism is to be focused on the product, not the producer; (3) the producer is present to clarify, not justify; and (4) the meeting duration is set at two hours.
- The moderator determines if the inspectors are prepared. One way to determine if the team is prepared is to ask each inspector to write down how much time he or she spent preparing for the meeting. If,

in the moderator's opinion, the team is not adequately prepared, the moderator postpones the meeting.

- If the moderator is satisfied that the team is adequately prepared, the inspection begins. The reader starts by paraphrasing the first chunk of information from the work product.

- The moderator then goes around the table and solicits any potential errors or defects from the team. Each potential error or defect is discussed, and the team reaches consensus as to whether a potential problem should be recorded as an error or a defect.

- Each potential problem is recorded on an Inspection Problem Report form for consistency.

- The producer can provide clarification but not justification.

- The recorder ensures that the information entered on the Inspection Problem Report forms is complete and accurate and reflects any team discussions and clarifications.

- After the reader has completed paraphrasing the entire work product, the moderator asks the recorder to read back all the Inspection Problem Report forms to ensure they were recorded correctly.

- The team decides if the severity of the problems found warrants another inspection or if the moderator can review the corrective action without another inspection meeting.

- The recorder records the meeting duration information on the Inspection Process Summary Report form (see Appendix C).

- If another meeting is required, the moderator schedules it.

- The moderator adjourns the meeting.

B.4.4   Exit Criteria

- The inspection meeting has been held.

- Errors and defects identified at the meeting are documented on the Inspection Problem Report forms.

- The Inspection Process Summary Report form has been completed.

- The meeting minutes are published and distributed within two working days after the inspection meeting.

B.4.5   Metrics

- Time spent by each team member during the inspection meeting, measured in person-hours;
- Size of work product being inspected, measured in number of pages (for documents) or KLOCs (for code);
- Number of problems identified.

B.5   Follow-Up

B.5.1   Objective

To ensure that corrective action has been taken to correct problems found during an inspection.

B.5.2   Entry Criteria

The producer has completed the necessary rework.

B.5.3   Activities

- The producer and the moderator agree on the schedule for completing corrective action.
- The producer resolves the problems identified by the inspection team.
- When all rework has been completed, the moderator inspects the rework and records the resolution of each problem on the Inspection Problem Report form or reschedules a follow-up inspection meeting, as determined by the team.

B.5.4   Exit Criteria

- All reported problems have been corrected and reviewed by the moderator.
- The moderator completes the rework section of the Inspection Problem Report form.
- The moderator issues a follow-up report informing inspection team members of the completed rework.

B.5.5 Metrics

- The producer records the time spent in rework for each problem, measured in person-hours.
- The moderator records the elapsed calendar time from when the inspection meeting was held to completion of follow-up, measured in days.

Appendix C: Inspection Process Forms

Tables C.1 and C.2 display the Inspection Problem Report Form and the Inspection Process Summary Report, respectively.

Table C.1   The Inspection Problem Report Form

INSPECTION PROBLEM REPORT	Report No. _____

Inspector

Item Information: Date _____

Item inspected: _____   Inspector: _____

Defect description: Defect location: _____

_____

_____

_____

Recorder

Meeting Decisions:

❏ Accepted-Planned Resolution date: _____
❏ Duplicate of Problem Report No. _____
❏ Rejected-Reason: _____
❏ Deferred-Reason: _____

Impact:	Category:	Type:	Origin:
❏ Local	❏ Missing	❏ Procedure/logic	❏ Requirements
❏ External	❏ Wrong	❏ Interface	❏ Code
	❏ Extra	❏ Data definition	❏ Design
	❏ Unclear	❏ Documentation	❏ Test
	❏ Suggestion	❏ Other: _____	❏ Other: _____

Producer

Resolution: Date: _____

Description:_____

_____

_____

Items changed:_____

_____

Verifier

Verification: Date: _____

Verified by: _____

Items checked:_____

_____

Comments:_____

Table C.2 The Inspection Process Summary Report

INSPECTION PROCESS SUMMARY REPORT
Inspection Information: Moderator: Inspection Meeting date: _____   _____
Product Information: Item Identification_____   Errors detected: _____ errors   _____   (Total problems caused by activities in the   process which led to this inspection)   Item size: _____ KLOC or pages   (Code inspection units: thousand lines   Defects detected: _____ defects   non-commented source code.   (Total problem caused by activities prior to   Document inspection units: pages)   the process which led to this inspection)
Resource Measures: Planning: _____ person-hours   Preparation: _____ person-hours   (Include time spent by all involved in   (Sum of preparation time for all inspectors)   planning the inspection)   Overview meeting: _____ person-hours   (Meeting duration x number of participants)   Inspection meeting: _____ person-hours   (Meeting duration x number of participants

Meeting Decision:
 	
 ❑ Item accepted. No errors or defects found.
 ❑ Meeting rescheduled. Reason: _____
 ❑ Item rejected. No re-inspection required.
      Rework verification scheduled to be completed by date: _____
 ❑ Item rejected. Re-inspection required.
      Re-inspection meeting date: _____

Verification of Rework:
 	
 ❑ Accepted. All errors and defects corrected.
 ❑ Rejected. Additional rework required.
      Additional rework to be completed and verified by date: _____
      Verifier: _____   Date: _____

Appendix D:
Inspection Checklists

The inspection checklists included in this appendix can help inspectors prepare for an inspection.

D.1   Requirements Inspection Checklist

1. Do the requirements exhibit a clear distinction between functions and data?
2. Do the requirements define all the information that is to be displayed to the user?
3. Do the requirements address system and user response to error conditions?
4. Is each requirement stated clearly, concisely, and unambiguously?
5. Is each requirement testable?
6. Are there ambiguous or implied requirements?
7. Are there conflicting requirements?
8. Are there areas not addressed in the SRS that need to be?
9. Are performance requirements (such as response time and data storage requirements) stated?

10. If the requirements involve complex decision chains, are they expressed in a form that facilitates comprehension (decision tables, decision trees, etc.)?

11. Are requirements for performing software upgrades specified?

12. Are there requirements that contain an unnecessary level of design detail?

13. Are the real-time constraints specified in sufficient detail?

14. Are the precision and accuracy of calculations specified?

15. Is it possible to develop a thorough set of tests based on the information contained in the SRS? If not, what information is missing?

16. Are assumptions and dependencies clearly stated?

17. Does the document contain all the information called out in the SRS outline?

D.2   Design Inspection Checklist: High-Level Design

Assumption: Detailed-level design done using SA/SD methodology.

General Requirements and Design

1. Has the review of the design identified problems with the requirements, such as requirements that are missing, ambiguous, extraneous, untestable, or implied?

2. Is the design consistent with the requirements? For example, are there functions that are missing, extraneous, imprecise, ambiguous, or incorrect?

3. Are deviations from the requirements documented and approved?

4. Are all assumptions documented?

5. Have major design decisions been documented?

6. Is the design consistent with those decisions?

7. Does the design adequately address the following issues?

   • Real-time requirements;
   • Performance issues (memory and timing);
   • Spare capacity (CPU and memory);
   • Maintainability;
   • Understandability;

- Database requirements;
- Loading and initialization;
- Error handling and recovery;
- User interface issues;
- Software upgrades.

Functional and Interface Specifications

8. Is the Process Spec (P-spec) for each process accurate and complete?
9. Is the P-spec specified in precise, unambiguous terms? Does it clearly describe the required transformations?
10. Are dependencies on other functions, operating system kernel, hardware, etc., identified and documented?
11. Are human factor considerations properly addressed in those functions that provide a user interface?
12. Are design constraints, such as memory and timing budgets, specified where appropriate?
13. Are requirements for error checking, error handling, and recovery specified where needed?
14. Are interfaces consistent with module usage? Missing interfaces? Extra interfaces?
15. Are the interfaces specified to a sufficient level of detail that allows them to be verified?

Conventions

16. Does the design follow the established notation conventions?

D.3   Design Inspection Checklist: Detailed Design

Assumption: Detailed-level design done using SA/SD methodology.

Requirements Traceability

1. Does the detailed design of this module or interface fulfill its part of the requirements?

2. Has inspection of this module or interface identified problems in the SRS? For example, are any requirements missing, ambiguous, conflicting, untestable, or implied?

3. Does the detailed design of this module or interface meet its high-level design requirements?

4. Has inspection of the detailed design identified problems in the high-level design?

5. Are all functions completely and accurately described in sufficient detail?

6. Are all interfaces completely and accurately described, including keyword or positional parameters, field descriptors, attributes, ranges, and limits?

7. Are the detailed design documents complete and consistent within themselves, i.e., data with logic; all internal data defined; no extraneous data?

Structure and Interfaces

8. At the system and subsystem levels, have all components or modules been identified on a system architecture model?

9. Is the level of decomposition sufficient to identify all modules?

10. Will further decomposition result in identification of more modules?

11. Have all interfaces between system/subsystem elements and modules been clearly and precisely identified?

12. Do successive levels of decomposition result in successive levels of detail?

13. Are modules performing more than one specific function?

Logic

14. Are there any logic errors?

15. Are all unique values tested? All positional values tested? Increment and loop counters properly initialized? Variables and data areas initialized before use?

16. Has the module been inspected for correct begin and end of table processing? Correct processing of queues across interrupts? Correct decision table logic? Correct precision and accuracy of calculations?

17. Are message priorities allocated properly to ensure the correct execution of code?

18. Is the message processing sequence correct?

19. Are there errors in handling data, data buffers, or tables; incorrect field updates; conflicting use of data areas; incomplete initialization or update; inconsistent or invalid data attributes?

20. Are procedure call and return interfaces correctly defined? Call and return parameters defined correctly? Syntax correct?

Performance

21. Are memory and timing budgets reasonable and achievable?

Error Handling and Recovery

22. Is there adequate error condition testing?

23. Are error conditions defined where the probability of an error is high or results of an error would be fatal to the system?

24. Are return codes documented?

25. Are return messages understandable?

26. Does the program allow for successful error recovery from module or process failures? From operating system failure? From interrupts? From hardware failures?

Testability and Extensibility

27. Is the design understandable (i.e., easy to read, to follow logic)? Maintainable (i.e., no obscure logic)? Testable (i.e., can be tested with a reasonable number of tests)?

Coupling and Cohesion

28. Evaluate the design using standard coupling and cohesion criteria, if appropriate.

D.4   Code Inspection Checklist for C Code

1. Is the design implemented completely and correctly?
2. Are there missing or extraneous functions?
3. Is each loop executed the correct number of times?
4. Will each loop terminate?
5. Will the program terminate?
6. Are all possible loop fall-throughs correct?
7. Are all CASE statements evaluated as expected?
8. Is there any unreachable code?
9. Are there any off-by-one iteration errors?
10. Are there any dangling ELSE clauses?
11. Is pointer addressing used correctly?
12. Are priority rules and brackets in arithmetic expression evaluation used as required to achieve desired results?
13. Are boundary conditions considered (null or negative values, adding to an empty list, etc.)?
14. Are pointer parameters used as values and vice versa?

Interfaces

15. Is the number of input parameters equal to the number of arguments?
16. Do parameter and argument attributes match?
17. Do the units of parameters and arguments match?
18. Are any input-only arguments altered?
19. Are global variable definitions consistent across modules?
20. Are any constants passed as arguments?
21. Are any functions called and never returned from?
22. Are returned VOID values used?
23. Are all interfaces correctly used as defined in the SDD?

Data and Storage

24. Are data mode definitions correctly used?

25. Are data and storage areas initialized before use and correct fields accessed and/or updated?
26. Is data scope correctly established and used?
27. If identifiers with identical names exist at different procedure call levels, are they used correctly according to their local and global scope?
28. Is there unnecessary packing or mapping of data?
29. Are all pointers based on correct storage attributes?
30. Is the correct level of indirection used?
31. Are any string limits exceeded?
32. Are all variables explicitly declared?
33. Are all arrays, strings, and pointers initialized correctly?
34. Are all subscripts within bounds?
35. Are there any noninteger subscripts?

Maintainability and Testability

36. Is the code understandable (choice of variable names, use of comments, etc.)?
37. Is there a module header?
38. Is there sufficient and accurate commentary to allow the reader to understand the code?
39. Does the formatting and indenting style add to the readability of the code?
40. Are coding conventions followed?
41. Is tricky or obscure logic used?
42. Is the code structured to allow for easier debugging and testing?
43. Is the code structured so that it can be easily extended for new functions?
44. Are there any unnecessary restrictions due to code structure?

Error Handling

45. Are all probable error conditions handled?
46. Are error messages and return codes used?

47. Are the error messages and return codes meaningful and accurate?

48. Are the default branches in CASE statements handled correctly?

49. Does the code allow for recovery from error conditions?

50. Is range checking done where appropriate to isolate the source of an error?

D.5   A C++ Code Inspection Checklist

Copyright © 1992 by John T. Baldwin. Complete information regarding copyright permission, sources, and distribution appears in Section D.5.20.

D.5.1   Variable Declarations

D.5.1.1   Arrays

Is an array dimensioned to a hard-coded constant?

```
int intarray[13];
```

should be

```
int intarray[TOT_MONTHS+1];
```

Is the array dimensioned to the total number of items?

```
char entry[TOTAL_ENTRIES];
```

should be

```
char entry[LAST_ENTRY+1];
```

The first example is extremely error prone and often gives rise to one-by-one errors in the code. The preferred (second) method permits the writer to use the LAST_ENTRY identifier to refer to the last item in the array. Instances that require a buffer of a certain size are rarely rendered invalid by this practice, which results in the buffer being one element bigger than absolutely necessary.

D.5.1.2   Constants

Does the value of the variable never change?

```
int months_in_year = 12;
```

should be

```
const unsigned months_in_year = 12;
```

Are constants declared with the preprocessor #define mechanism?

```
#define MAX_FILES 20
```

should be

```
const unsigned MAX_FILES = 20;
```

Is the usage of the constant limited to only a few (or perhaps only one) class? If so, is the constant global?

```
const unsigned MAX_FOOS = 1000;

const unsigned MAX_FOO_BUFFERS = 40;
```

should be

```
class foo {

public:

    enum { MAX_INSTANCES = 1000; }

private:

    enum { MAX_FOO_BUFFERS = 40; }

};
```

If the size of the constant exceeds int, another mechanism is available:

```
class bar{

public:

    static const long MAX_INSTS;
```

```
};
```

```
const long bar::MAX_INSTS = 70000L;
```

The keyword static ensures there is only one instance of the variable for the entire class. Static data items are not permitted to be initialized within the class declaration, so the initialization line must be included in the implementation file for class bar.

Static constant members have one drawback: You cannot use them to declare member data arrays of a certain size. That is because the value is not available to the compiler at the point that the array is declared in the class.

D.5.1.3 Scalar Variables

Does a negative value of the variable make no sense? If so, is the variable signed?

```
int age;
```

should be

```
unsigned int age;
```

This is an easy error to make, since the default types are usually signed.

Does the code assume char is either signed or unsigned?

```
typedef char SmallInt;
```

```
SmallInt mumble = 280; // WRONG on Borland C++ 3.1 // or
                        MSC/C++ 7.0!
```

The typedefs should be

```
typedef unsigned char SmallUInt;
```

```
typedef signed char SmallInt;
```

Does the program unnecessarily use float or double?

```
double acct_balance;
```

should be

```
unsigned long acct_balance;
```

In general, the only time floating-point arithmetic is necessary is in scientiWc or navigational calculations. It is slow and subject to more complex overflow and underflow behavior than integer math is. Monetary calculations can often be handled in counts of cents and formatted properly on output. Thus, acct_balance might equal 103446 and print out as $1,034.46.

D.5.1.4 Classes

Does the class have any virtual functions? If so, is the destructor nonvirtual?
Classes having virtual functions should always have a virtual destructor. This is necessary since it is likely that you will hold an object of a class with a pointer of a less derived type. Making the destructor virtual ensures that the right code will be run if you delete the object via the pointer.

Does the class have any of the following:

- Copy-constructor;
- Assignment operator;
- Destructor.

If so, it generally will need all three. (Exceptions occasionally may be found for some classes having a destructor with neither of the other two.)

D.5.2 Data Usage

D.5.2.1 Strings

Can the string ever not be null-terminated?

Is the code attempting to use a strxxx() function on a nonterminated char array, as if it were a string?

D.5.2.2 Buffers

Are there always size checks when copying into the buffer?

Can the buffer ever be too small to hold its contents?

For example, one program had no size checks when reading data into a buffer because the correct data would always fit. But when the file it read was accidentally overwritten with incorrect data, the program crashed mysteriously.

D.5.2.3   Bitfields

Is a bitfield really required for this application?

Are there possible ordering problems (portability)?

D.5.3   Initialization

D.5.3.1   Local Variables

Are local variables initialized before being used?

Are C++ locals created, then assigned later?

This practice has been shown to incur up to 350% overhead, compared to the practice of declaring the variable later in the code, when an initialization variable is known. It is a simple matter of putting a value in once instead of assigning some default value, then later throwing it away and assigning the real value.

D.5.3.2   Missing Reinitialization

Can a variable carry an old value forward from one loop iteration to the next?

Suppose the processing of a data element in a sequence causes a variable to be set. For example, a file might be read, and some globals initialized for that file. Can those globals be used for the next file in the sequence without being reinitialized?

D.5.4   Macros

If a macro's formal parameter is evaluated more than once, is the macro ever expanded with an actual parameter having side effects? For example, what happens in the following code?

```
#define max(a,b) ( (a) > (b) ? (a) : (b) )

max(i++, j);
```

If a macro is not completely parenthesized, is it ever invoked in a way that will cause unexpected results?

```
#define max(a, b) (a) > (b) ? (a) : (b) result = max(i, j) + 3;
```

This expands into:

```
result = (i) > (j) ? (i) : (j)+3;
```

See the example for the first question in this section (D.5.4) for the correct parenthesization.

If the macro's arguments are not parenthesized, will this ever cause unexpected results?

```
#define IsXBitSet(var) (var && bitmask) result = IsXBitSet( i
|| j );
```

This expands into:

```
result = (i || j && bitmask); // not what expected!
```

The correct form is:

```
#define IsXBitSet(var) ((var) && (bitmask))
```

D.5.5   Sizing of Data

In a function call with arguments for a buffer and its size, is the argument to sizeof different from the buffer argument? For example:

```
memset(buffer1, 0, sizeof(buffer2)); // danger!
```

This is not always an error, but it is a dangerous practice. Each instance should be verified as (1) necessary and (2) correct and then commented on as such.

Is the argument to sizeof an incorrect type? Common errors include:

- sizeof(ptr) instead of sizeof(*ptr)
- sizeof(*array) instead of sizeof(array)

- sizeof(array) instead of sizeof(array[0]) (when the user wanted the size of an element)

D.5.6   Dynamic Allocation

D.5.6.1   Allocating Data

Is too little space being allocated?
Does the code allocate memory and then assume someone else will delete it?
This is not always an error, but it should always be prominently documented, along with the reason for implementing it in this manner. Constructors that allocate, paired with destructors that deallocate, are an obvious exception, since a single object has control of its class data.

Is malloc(), calloc(), or realloc() used in lieu of new?
C standard library allocation functions should never be used in C++ programs, since C++ provides an allocation operator.

If you find you must mix C allocation with C++ allocation, is malloc, calloc, or realloc invoked for an object that has a constructor?
Program behavior is undefined if that is done.

D.5.6.2   Deallocating Data

Are arrays being deleted as if they were scalars?

```
delete myCharArray;
```

should be

```
delete [] myCharArray;
```

Does the deleted storage still have pointers to it?
It is recommended that pointers are set to NULL following deletion or to another safe value meaning "uninitialized." This is neither necessary nor recommended within destructors, since the pointer variable itself will cease to exist upon exiting.

Are you deleting already deleted storage?

This is not possible if the code conforms to the answer to the preceding question. The draft C++ standard specifies that it is always safe to delete a NULL pointer, so it is not necessary to check for that value.

If C standard library allocators are used in a C++ program (not recommended), is delete invoked on a pointer obtained via malloc, calloc, or realloc?

Is free invoked on a pointer obtained via new?

Both these practices are dangerous. Program behavior is undefined if you do them, and such usage is specifically deprecated by the ANSI draft C++ standard.

D.5.7 Pointers

When dereferenced, can the pointer ever be NULL?

When copying the value of a pointer, should it instead allocate a copy of what the first pointer points to?

D.5.8 Casting

Is NULL cast to the correct type when passed as a function argument?

Does the code rely on an implicit type conversion?

C++ is somewhat charitable when arguments are passed to functions: If no function is found that exactly matches the types of the arguments supplied, it attempts to apply certain type conversion rules to find a match. While this saves unnecessary casting, if more than one function fits the conversion rules, it will result in a compilation error. Worse, it can cause additions to the type system (either from adding a related class or from adding an overloaded function) to cause previously working code to break!

See Section D.5.17 for an example.

D.5.9 Computation

When the value of an assignment or computation is tested, is the parenthesization incorrect?

```
if ( a = function() == 0 )
```

should be

```
if ( (a = function()) == 0 )
```

Can any synchronized values not get updated?

Sometimes, a group of variables must be modified as a group to complete a single conceptual "transaction." If that does not occur all in one place, is it guaranteed that all variables get updated if a single value changes? Do all updates occur before any of the values are tested or used?

D.5.10   Conditionals

Are exact equality tests used on floating point numbers?

```
if ( someVar == 0.1 )
```

might never be evaluated as true. The constant 0.1 is not exactly representable by any finite binary mantissa and exponent; thus, the compiler must round it to some other number. Calculations involving someVar may never result in it taking on that value.

The solution is to use >, > =, <, or < = depending on which direction you want the variable bound.

Are unsigned values tested greater than or equal to zero?

```
if ( myUnsignedVar = 0 )
```

will always evaluate true.

Are signed variables tested for equality to zero or another constant?

```
if ( mySignedVar ) // not always good
```

```
if ( mySignedVar = 0 ) // better!
```

```
if ( mySignedVar 0 ) // opposite case
```

If the variable is updated by any means other than ++ or − −, it may miss the value of the test constant entirely. That can cause subtle and frightening bugs when code executes under conditions that were not planned for.

If the test is an error check, could the error condition actually be legitimate in some cases?

D.5.11 Flow Control

D.5.11.1 Control variables

Is the lower limit an exclusive limit?

Is the upper limit an inclusive limit?

By always using inclusive lower limits and exclusive upper limits, a whole class of one-by-one errors is eliminated. Furthermore, the following assumptions always apply:

- The size of the interval equals the difference of the two limits.

- The limits are equal if the interval is empty.

- The upper limit is never less than the lower limit.

- For example, instead of saying x > = 23 and x < = 42, use x > = 23 and x < 43.

D.5.11.2 Branching

In a switch statement, is any case not terminated with a break statement?

When several cases are followed by the same block of code, they may be stacked and the code terminated with a single break. Cases may also be exited via return.

All other circumstances requiring "drop-through" cases should be clearly documented in a strategic comment before the switch. This should be used only when it makes the code simpler and clearer.

Does the switch statement lack a default branch?

There should always be a default branch to handle unexpected cases, even when it appears that the code can never get there.

Does a loop set a boolean flag to effect an exit?

Consider using break instead. It is likely to simplify the code.

Does the loop contain a continue?

If the continue occurs in the body of an if conditional, consider replacing it with an else clause if it will simplify the code.

D.5.12   Assignment

D.5.12.1   Assignment Operators

Does a += b mean something different than a = a + b?

The programmer should never change the semantics of relationships between operators. For the example here, the two statements are semantically identical for intrinsic types (even though the code generated might be different), so for a user-defined class, they should be semantically identical, too. They may, in fact, be implemented differently (+ = should be more efficient).

Is the argument for a copy constructor or assignment operator non const?

Does the assignment operator fail to test for self-assignment?

The code for operator =() should always start out with:

```
if (this == &right_hand_arg )

return *this;
```

Does the assignment operator return anything other than a const reference to this?

Failure to return a reference to this prevents the user from writing (legal C++):

```
a = b = c;
```

   Failure to make the return reference const allows the user to write (illegal C++):

```
(a = b) = c;
```

D.5.12.2   Use of Assignment

Can this assignment be replaced with an initialization?

See the second question in Section D.5.3.1.

Is there a mismatch between the units of the expression and those of the variable?

For example, you might be calculating the number of bytes for an array when the number of elements was requested. If the elements are big (say, a long or a struct!), you would be using way too much memory.

D.5.13 Argument Passing

Are nonintrinsic-type arguments passed by value?

```
Foo& do_something( Foo anotherFoo, Bar someThing );
```

should be

```
Foo& do_something( const Foo& anotherFoo, const Bar& some-
Thing );
```

While it is cheaper to pass an int, a long, and such by value, passing objects that way incurs significant expense due to the construction of temporary objects. The problem becomes more severe when inheritance is involved. Simulate pass-by-value by passing const references.

D.5.14 Return Values

Is the return value of a function call being stored in a type that is too narrow?
See Section D.5.18.

Does a public member function return a non const reference or pointer to member data?

Does a public member function return a non const reference or pointer to data outside the object?
This is permissible, provided the data were intended to be shared, and that fact is documented in the source code.

Does an operator return a reference when it should return an object?

Are objects returned by value instead of const references?
See the question in Section D.5.13.

D.5.15 Function Calls

D.5.15.1 Varargs Functions (printf and Other Functions With Ellipses)

Is the FILE argument of fprintf missing? (This happens all the time.)

Are there extra arguments?

Do the argument types explicitly match the conversion specifications in the format string? (printf and friends.)

Type checking cannot occur for functions with variable length argument lists. For example, a user was surprised to see nonsensical values when the following code was executed:

```
printf( %d %ld \n , a_long_int, another_long_int);
```

On that particular system, int s and long s were different sizes (2 and 4 bytes, respectively). printf() is responsible for manually accessing the stack; thus, it saw "%d" and grabbed 2 bytes (an int).

It then saw "%ld" and grabbed 4 bytes (a long). The two values printed were the MSW of a_long_int, and the combination of a_long_int's LSW and another_long_int's MSW.

The solution is to ensure that types explicitly match. If necessary, arguments may be cast to smaller sizes (long to int) if the author knows for certain that the smaller type can hold all possible values of the variable.

D.5.15.2   General Functions

Is this function call correct? That is, should it be a different function with a similar name (e.g., strchr instead of strrchr)?

Can this function violate the preconditions of a called function?

D.5.16   Files

Can a temporary file name not be unique? (Surprisingly enough, this is a common design bug.)

Is a file pointer reused without closing the previous file?

```
fp = fopen(...);

fp = fopen(...);
```

Is a file not closed in case of an error return?

D.5.17 Errors Due to Implicit Type Conversions

Code that relies on implicit type conversions may become broken when new classes or functions are added. For example:

```
class String {

public:

String( char *arg ); // copy constructor operator const char*
() const;

...

};

void foo( const String& aString );

void bar( const char *anArray );
```

Now, we added the following class

```
class Word {

public:

Word( char *arg ); // copy constructor

...

};
```

need another foo that works with "Words"

```
void foo( const Word& aWord );

int gorp()

{

foo( hello ); // This used to work! Now it breaks! What gives?
```

```
String baz =  quux ;

bar(baz); // but this still works.


}
```

The code worked before class Word and the second foo() were added. Even though there was no foo() accepting an argument of type const char * (i.e., a constant string like "hello"), there is a foo() that takes a constant String argument by reference. And (un)fortunately, there is also a way to convert a Strings to a char * and vice versa. So the compiler performed the implicit conversion.

Now, with the addition of class Word and another foo() that works with it, there is a problem. The line that calls foo("hello") matches both:

```
void foo( const String& );

void foo( const Word& );
```

Since the mechanisms of the failure may be distributed among two or more header files in addition to the implementation file, along with a lot of other code, it may be difficult to find the real problem.

The easiest solution is to recognize while coding or inspecting that a function call results in implicit type conversion and either (1) overload the function to provide an explicitly typed variant or (2) explicitly cast the argument.

Option 1 is preferred over option 2, because option 2 defeats automatic type checking. Option 1 can still be implemented efficiently, simply by writing the new function as a forwarding function and making it inline.

D.5.18   Errors Due to Loss of "Precision" in Return Values

Functions that can return EOF should not have their return values stored in a char variable. For example:

```
int getchar(void);

char chr;

while ( (chr = getchar()) != EOF ) { ... };
```

should be:

```
int tmpchar;

while ( (tmpchar = getchar()) != EOF ) {

    chr = (char) tmpchar; // or use casted tmpchar throughout

};
```

The practice in the first example is unsafe because functions like getchar() may return 257 different values: valid characters with indexes 0–255, plus EOF (–1). If sizeof(int) > sizeof(char), then information will be lost when the high-order byte(s) are scraped off prior to the test for EOF. This can cause the test to fail. Worse yet, depending on whether char is signed or unsigned by default on the particular compiler and machine being used, sign extension can wreak havoc and cause some of these loops never to terminate.

D.5.19 Loop Checklist

The following loops are indexed correctly and are handy for comparisons during inspections. If the actual code does not look like one of these, chances are that something is wrong or, at least, could be clearer.

Acceptable forms of for loops that avoid off-by-one errors are:

```
for ( i = 0; i max_index; ++i )

for ( i = 0; i sizeof(array); ++i )

for ( i = max_index; i>= 0; - -i )

for ( i = max_index; i ; - -i )
```

D.5.20 Copyright Notices

Some of the questions applicable to conventional C contained herein were modified or taken from *A Question Catalog for Code Inspections,* Copyright 1992 by Brian Marick. Portions of his document were Copyright 1991 by Motorola, Inc., which graciously granted him rights to those portions.

In conformance with his copyright notice, the following contact information is provided below:

Some questions and comment material were modified from Program-
ming in C++, Rules and Recommendations, Copyright 1990–1992 by
Ellemtel Telecommunication Systems Laboratories.
In conformance with their copyright notice:

Finally, all modifications and remaining original material are:

D.6   Test Procedure Inspection Checklist

1. Does each test have a header that identifies the author, revision
date, test objectives, required configuration, and initial setup?
2. Is each test traceable to a specific requirement defined in the SDD
or the SRS?
3. Does the test procedure define the exact sequence of steps required
to execute the test?
4. For each test, are the expected results clearly defined?
5. Are the expected results consistent with the SRS and the SDD?
6. Are the test objectives achievable?

Appendix E:
Attributes of Good Requirements
Specifications

Good requirements specifications have the following attributes:

- *Unambiguous.* The SRS is unambiguous if and only if every requirement has only one interpretation.

- *Complete.* The SRS is complete if it contains all signficant requirements that relate to functionality, performance, timing, design constraints, attributes, external interfaces, and so on. A complete SRS also contains a definition of the response of the software to all known classes of inputs in all known situations.

- *Verifiable.* The SRS is verifiable if and only if every requirement is verifiable. A requirement is verifiable if and only if there is some finite, cost-effective process by which a human being or a machine can verify that the software correctly implements the stated requirements.

- *Consistent.* The SRS is consistent if and only if individual requirements do not confict.

- *Modifiable.* The SRS is modifiable if its structure and style are such that unanticipated changes can be made easily, completely, and consistently.

- *Traceable.* The SRS is traceable if each requirement is clearly traceable to a statement contained in the preceding document and if the SRS facilitates the referencing of requirements to subsequent documents (such as the SDD).
- *Usable.* The SRS must provide sufficient information to be usable during the maintenance phase of the product life cycle since it is likely that different people will be involved with product maintenance activities.

Appendix F:
Sample Criteria for Selecting Modules
for Code Inspection

You can use the following sample criteria to help select modules for code inspection. Revise this list based on criteria important to your project or organization.

- *Criticality.* The module performs a function or functions critical to the correct operation of the end product.

- *Complexity.* The module is determined to be more complex than other modules based on an evaluation by a complexity metric, such as the McCabe cyclomatic complexity or Halstead software science metric.

- *Past history.* In the past, a relatively high number of bugs have been found in modules that perform similar functions.

- *Experience level of software engineer.* The software engineer who wrote the code is relatively inexperienced.

Appendix G:
Sample Software Development Process Based on the Waterfall Model

For each phase of the process, the following information is included:

- Purpose;
- Activities;
- Deliverables;
- Tools;
- Exit Criteria;
- Metrics.

G.1 Requirements Analysis Phase

Purpose

- Develop product concept;
- Allocate requirements to hardware and software (if appropriate).

Activities

- Conduct market research;
- Write business plan;
- Write product concept document;
- Create RTM.[*]

Deliverables

- Product concept document;
- Business plan.

Tools

- Requirements tracing tool;
- Market research tools (e.g., conjoint analysis).

Exit Criteria

- Concept specification reviewed and approved;
- Business plan reviewed and approved;
- RTM created.

Metrics

- Person-hours expended to date;
- Number of testable requirements identified;
- Number of untestable requirements identified.

---

[*] Software V&V-related items are indicated with an asterisk.

G.2   Requirements Definition Phase

Purpose

- Define requirements to be implemented by software.[*]

Activities

- Refine requirements contained in concept specification;
- Define user interface metaphors (if appropriate);
- Write SRS;
- Conduct a requirements inspection on the SRS[*];
- Update the RTM.[*]

Deliverables

- SRS;
- User interface metaphors (if appropriate; can be expressed in the form of a style guide);
- Software development plan;
- Software V&V plan.[*]

Tools

- Performance analysis tools;
- Structured analysis and information modeling tools;
- Requirements tracing tool.

Exit Criteria

- SRS, software development plan, and software V&V plan approved;
- Requirements inspection held on SRS;
- User interface style guide prepared (if appropriate).

Metrics

- Completeness of RTM[*];
- Number and type of errors and defects found during requirements inspection of SRS.[*]

G.3   Design Phase

Purpose

- Develop a clear, concise, and consistent design;
- Establish a controlled environment for the coding phase.

Activities

- Develop overall software architecture;
- Develop high-level software design;
- Develop detailed software design;
- Conduct design inspections[*];
- Develop software architecture, high-level software design and detailed software design specifications;
- Begin development of software validation test procedures based on SRS[*];
- Develop software reliability growth plan[*];
- Evaluate and select SCM and SPR tracking tools[*];
- Evaluate and select automated software validation testing tools[*];
- Update RTM.[*]

Deliverables

- Software architecture, high-level design specification(s), detailed design specifications;
- Software validation test procedures[*];
- SCM plan[*];
- Software validation test plan[*];

- Software reliability growth plan[*];
- Alpha and beta test plans (if appropriate).[*]

Tools

- Structured design and information modeling tools;
- Detailed design tools (data flow diagrams, state transition matrices, etc.);
- Performance analysis tools;
- Configuration management tools;
- Automated software validation testing tools;
- Software problem report tracking tool;
- Requirements tracing tools.

Exit Criteria

- Software architecture reviewed and approved;
- Software design specifications approved;
- Design inspections held[*];
- SCM plan reviewed and approved[*];
- SCM tools selected and in place[*];
- Software validation test plan and alpha and beta test plans reviewed and approved.[*]

Metrics

- Completeness of RTM[*];
- Number and type of errors and defects found during design inspections.[*]

G.4   Coding Phase

Purpose

- Write code that implements the requirements contained in the SRS as expressed by the overall architecture and further defined by the design specifications.

Activities

- Develop code;
- Conduct code inspections on selected modules[*];
- Perform unit and integration testing;
- Implement SCM procedures[*];
- Implement software problem reporting procedures[*];
- Implement software reliability growth tracking procedures[*];
- Apply selected software quality metrics to modules[*];
- Complete development of software validation test procedures based on SRS[*];
- Conduct software validation test procedure inspections[*];
- Develop software release procedures[*];
- Update product documentation (concept specification, SRS, and SDDs);
- Conduct software validation readiness review[*];
- Update RTM.[*]

Deliverables

- Source code;
- Software validation test procedures[*];
- Software reliability growth procedures[*];
- Software release procedure[*];
- Software problem reports.[*]

Tools

- Coding tools (compilers, debuggers, lint, etc.);
- Quality metric tools (e.g., code complexity);
- SCM tools;
- Software problem report tracking tools;
- Automated software validation test tools;
- Software reliability growth tracking tools;
- Requirement tracing tools.

Exit Criteria

- Coding completed;
- All source code under configuration management control;
- Software problem report tracking in place[*];
- Software reliability growth tracking in place[*];
- Software validation readiness review held[*];
- Software validation test procedures approved[*];
- Test procedure inspections held[*];
- All software validation test procedures executed at least once.[*]

Metrics

- Number and type of errors and defects found during code inspections[*];
- Number and type of errors and defects found during test procedure inspections[*];
- Complexity and quality metrics for each module[*];
- Size of each module (lines of source code)[*];
- Size of final executable (number of bytes)[*];
- Completeness of RTM.[*]

G.5   Testing Phase

Purpose

- To determine if the software meets requirements defined in the SRS.

Activities

- Execute software validation test procedures[*];
- Track and resolve problems identfiied as a result of executing tests[*];
- Perform regression testing as required[*];
- Fix bugs and release new versions for validation testing.

Deliverables

- Software validation test report[*];
- Final version of software for release.

Tools

- Automated software validation testing tools;
- Software problem report tracking tool;
- SCM tools;
- Coding and debugging tools;
- Requirements traceability tools.

Exit Criteria

- Software validation testing completion criteria met[*];
- Software validation test report reviewed and approved.[*]

Metrics

- Find-and-fix time for bugs[*];
- Test coverage metrics[*];

- Software reliability growth metrics.[*]

G.6   Maintenance Phase

Purpose

- Provide ongoing product support after release.

Activities

- Fix known defects;
- Change software to correct deficiencies in other parts of the product;
- Add new features or enhance existing features;
- Extensive testing based on changes made.[*]
- Regression testing[*];
- Update product documentation (SRS, SDDs, test procedures, etc.).

Deliverables

- New releases of software;
- Updated product documentation.

Tools

- Same tools used in earlier phases.

Exit Criteria

- Decision made to discontinue supporting the product.

Metrics

- Number and type of bugs reported by customers;
- Number and type of new features requested by customers;
- Find-and-fix time for bugs.

Appendix H:
Document Outlines

Included in this appendix are outlines for the following documents:

1. Product Concept Document
2. Software Requirements Specification (SRS)
3. Software Design Description (SDD)
4. Software Development Plan (SDP)
5. Software Quality Assurance (SQA) Plan
6. Software Validation Test Plan
7. Software Validation Test Procedure
8. Software Validation Test Report
9. Software Validation Test Script
10. Software Configuration Management Plan
11. Software Release Procedure

H.1   Product Concept Document

Purpose

The purpose of the product concept document is to define overall product goals as well as high-level requirements that the product must meet.

Outline

1. Overview
   a. Product Features and Benefits
   b. Market Requirements
   c. Target Markets
   d. Competitive Analysis
   e. Desired Launch Window
2. Product Goals
   a. Usability Goals
   b. Reliability Goals
   c. Upgradeability Goals
   d. Serviceability Goals
   e. Maintainability Goals
3. Product Functional Requirements
   a. Functional Requirements
   b. Performance Requirements
   c. Timing Requirements
4. Financial Requirements
   a. Cost Requirements
   b. Projected Selling Price

H.2   Software Requirements Specification (SRS)

Purpose

The purpose of this document is to define the requirements that have been allocated to software. By far, this document is the most important document written for a software development effort. It forms the basis for the software design, for software validation, and for development of technical manuals and training materials, among other things.

Outline

Reference: IEEE-Standard-830-1998

1. Product Overview

    a. Product Perspective. This section places this product into perspective with regard to other products and/or projects. Dependencies between this product and other products and/or projects should be clearly stated. Include block diagrams showing major components, external interfaces, and interconnections where appropriate.

    b. Product Functions. Provide a brief summary of the product functions and categorize these functions into related groups for ease of understanding. A key element to include in this section is the feature release plan. This plan identifies specific features that will be included in a sequence of planned releases.

2. General Constraints. This section describes items that limit the available options for software design. For example:

    - Hardware limitations;
    - Interface requirements to other systems and/or products;
    - Communication protocols that must be supported;
    - Criticality of operations;
    - Conformance to accepted standards.

3. Assumptions and Dependencies. Identify specific assumptions and dependencies that impact requirements.

4. User Interface. Describe in detail the user interface for the product. This should include screen layouts for all expected screens, and all anticipated user interaction and input devices. If necessary, a User Interface Style Guide may need to be developed for a new or radically different user interface.

5. Specific Requirements. This section contains the functional requirements that the software must implement. There are many ways to organize the information in this section. Use the method most appropriate for the users of the document.

    a. Introduction

(1) Inputs. Describe sources of inputs, quantities, ranges and limits, accuracy and tolerance, timing issues, and units.

(2) Processing. Describe all operations performed on the input data and intermediate parameters to obtain the desired output. Include: equations, algorithms, logical operations, validity checks on input data, sequences of operations, and timing issues. Also, address responses to abnormal situations, such as buffer overflow and communications failures. Provide requirements for degraded operation, if required.

(3) Outputs. Describe in detail: destination/use of outputs, quantities, units, timing issues, range of valid outputs, and error handling.

 b. Performance Requirements
 c. Diagnostics Requirements
 d. Security Requirements
 e. Maintainability Requirements
 f. Configurability Requirements
 g. Upgradeability Requirements
 h. Testability Requirements
 i. Installability Requirements

 6. Appendices

H.3 Software Design Description (SDD)

Purpose

The purpose of this document is to describe the design of the software.

Outline

Reference: IEEE Standard 1016-1998

The following is one of many ways to organize and format the information required for the software design description. Refer to the IEEE standard for alternatives more suited to your particular environment.

 1. Decomposition Description. The decomposition description records the division of the software into design entities. It describes the way the software has been structured. It also defines the purpose, function, subordinates, and type of each software design entity.

2. Dependency Description. The dependency description specifies the relationships among entities. It identifies the dependent entities, describes their coupling, and identifies the required resources.

3. Interface Description. The interface description provides everything designers, programmers, and testers need to know to correctly use the functions provided by an entity. This description includes details of the internal and external interfaces not included in the Software Requirements document.

4. Detailed Design. This section contains the detailed design for each of the entities identified above. These details include attribute descriptions for identification, processing, and data.

H.4 Software Development Plan

Purpose

The purpose of the Software Development Plan (SDP) is to document a common understanding of the software development activities that will occur during a development project. The plan describes the role of the software development team within the context of the development project, the process that will be used to develop the software, the inputs that must be provided to develop the software and what will be delivered as a result of following the SDP. The SDP also establishes the development schedule and the tools and staffing that will be required. The reason to document this understanding is to eliminate ambiguity and assumptions, provide a means of measuring progress and success, and a method for continuous improvement.

This plan is the primary document that will be used in conducting all audits of the software development process for the project. It should reference the company's Software Development Process wherever possible. If the project will deviate from the Software Development Process, the nature of the deviation must be described and justified in the Plan. For large or complex projects, the individual sections of the SDP can be handled as separate documents. These separate documents should then be referenced in the SDP.

Outline

1. Introduction
2. Project Definition

a. Goals. This section describes the overall goals of the Software. These goals include not only product specific goals, but also any other goals such as commonality, future projects, and staff development.

b. Deliverables. This section defines all of the deliverables from the Software Team.

3. Project Context

a. Project Teams. This section of the SDP describes all other teams working on the same project that directly influence the Software Development Plan. Entities to be considered include:

- Marketing;
- Manufacturing;
- SQA;
- Technical Publications;
- Training;
- Technical Support.

b. Team Interfaces. This section of the SDP defines the interfaces between the Software Development Team and other Project Teams detailed above.

4. Development Strategy

a. Process Model. This section describes the software development lifecycle to be used. This description includes dependencies, timing of reviews, baselines, deliverables, and milestones. If there are any timing requirements for input documentation, they should also be described here. This section should also describe any special mechanisms that will be used to control the software development process.

b. Target Environment. This section describes any assumptions made regarding the target environment for software development. Examples of assumptions to highlight include the number and type of processors being used, the user interface devices available, memory, and disk space.

c. Build Versus Buy. This section defines the criteria that will be used for determining what portions of the software system will be purchased, subcontracted, or developed in-house.

d. Team Organization. This section describes the organization of the software development team. This description includes the structure of the team, responsibilities of each part of the team, and formal reporting methods and frequency.

e. Constraints. This section describes any constraints on the software development that are not explicitly described elsewhere. These may include budgetary, timing, staffing, or operational constraints.

f. Metrics. This section describes the measurements that will be made to ensure adherence to this plan, for monitoring progress and for establishing the quality of the deliverables.

5. Methodologies. This section describes the methods, policies, procedures, and techniques to be used in the creation, modification, review, test, measurement, and maintenance of the deliverables.

6. Standards. This section of the SDP describes the technical standards to be applied to any and all deliverables from the development effort, and how adherence to the standards will be measured. For example, coding standards, naming conventions, notations, and requirements format.

7. Resource Requirements.

   a. Staffing Plan. This section of the SDP describes the staffing plan for the software development. It describes:

   - Skill set needed;
   - Whether skills will be developed internally or hired;
   - Number of people needed;
   - Ramp up and ramp down plans;

   b. Tools. This section describes the tools that will be used for the development of the software. Examples of the types of tools to be addressed include:

   - Development computers
   - Word processors
   - Compilers
   - CASE tools

- Revision control systems

- Debuggers

- Prototype target hardware

c. Support Functions. This section describes any and all support functions, either required by the Software Development team or provided by the Software Development team, not explicitly described elsewhere. Examples might include external integration testing support, external requirements traceability support and external revision control.

8. Schedules. This section provides an estimated schedule of the software development effort, describing the major activities called out in the process model, and the staffing levels required. For large projects, the schedule should be called out as a separate document, as it is likely to undergo a large number of changes during the course of the project.

9. Risks and Risk Management. This section describes the primary risk factors associated with the successful implementation of the plan, and how those risk factors will be managed. Where appropriate, contingency plans should also be included. Examples of risk factors to consider include:

- New technology;

- Target environment limitations;

- Human Resources;

- Budget;

- Schedules.

10. Appendix

    a. References

    b. Documents

    c. Standards

    d. Glossary and Acronyms

H.5 Software Quality Assurance Plan

Purpose

The purpose of this document is to define the processes and procedures used to ensure that software developed for a particular product is of the highest possible quality and meets all of its requirements.

The SQA Plan defines the software quality assurance tasks and when they are performed in relation to activities defined in the Software Development Plan. This plan also identifies the additional documents that need to be written. For example, the SQA Plan may call for separate plans to address Software Verification, Software Validation, and Configuration Management activities. Alternatively, these areas can be addressed within the structure of the SQA Plan.

Outline

Reference: IEEE-Standard-730.1-1995

1. Management

    a. Organization. Describe the organizational structure that influences and controls the quality of the software.

    b. Tasks. Describe the portion of the Software Lifecycle Model covered by this plan, the tasks to be performed, with emphasis on SQA activities, and the relationship between these tasks and major project milestones.

    c. Responsibilities. Identify the specific organizational elements responsible for each task.

2. Documentation. Identify the documents governing the development, verification, validation, use, and maintenance of the software; and identifies how these documents are checked for adequacy. This includes identification of the specific review or audit held to review each document.

3. Standards, Practices, Conventions, and Metrics. Identify the standards, practices, conventions, and metrics to be used, and state how compliance with these items is to be monitored and assured.

4. Reviews and Audits. Define the technical and managerial reviews and audits to be conducted, states how the reviews and audits are to be performed, and states what further actions are required and how they are to be implemented and verified.

5. Testing. State requirements for testing other than Software Validation Testing. Specifically, Unit Test, Integration Test, and Performance Test requirements should be identified. Software Validation Testing is described in the Software Validation Test Plan.

6. Problem Reporting and Corrective Action. Describe methods and procedures for problem reporting and corrective action as well as the organizational elements responsible for their implementation.

7. Tools, Techniques, and Methodologies. Identify special tools, techniques, and methodologies required.

8. Code Control. Define the methods and facilities used to maintain, store, secure, and document controlled versions of the identified software during all phases of the software lifecycle. For larger projects, this may be implemented by writing a Software Configuration Management Plan.

9. Media Control. Define the methods and facilities used to identify the media for each software product and to protect the physical media from unauthorized access, inadvertent damage, or degradation during all phases of the software life cycle.

10. Supplier Control. Define the process and procedures for assuring that software provided by Suppliers meets established requirements.

11. Records Collection, Maintenance, and Retention. Define the SQA documentation to be retained, the methods used to assemble, safeguard, and maintain this documentation, and shall designate the retention period.

12. Training. Identify the training required to meet the needs of the SQA Plan.

13. Risk Management. Define the methods and procedures used to identify, assess, monitor, and control areas of risk.

H.6   Software Validation Test Plan

Purpose

The Test Plan describes the process used to perform validation testing. This plan identifies the resources required for the proposed testing effort based on estimating the number of tests required. This estimate is derived from the

SRS. This plan also defines the Completion Criteria used to determine when to stop testing. This test plan is intended to be consistent with the requirements of the SQA Plan.

Outline

Reference: IEEE-Standard 1012-1998

1. Overview

    a. Organization. Describe the organization of the testing effort and the relationship of this organization to other organizations such as, development, project management, quality assurance, configuration management, and document control.

    b. Tasks and Schedules

    c. Responsibilities

    d. Tools, Techniques, Methods

2. Processes

    a. Management

    b. Acquisition

    c. Supply

    d. Development

    e. Operation

    f. Maintenance

3. Reporting Requirements

4. Administrative Requirement

5. Documentation Requirements

6. Resource Requirements

7. Completion Criteria. Define the criteria that will be used to determine when testing is completed. As an example, the following criteria should be considered:

    • All of the Test Scripts have been executed.

    • All SPRs have been satisfactorily resolved.

    • All changes made as a result of SPRs have been tested.

    • The projected software reliability growth meets reliability goal for software.

- The test coverage metric indicates that at least 95% of the code has been executed. A statement identifying the 5% of the code that hasn't been executed and why is included in the Test Report.

H.7   Software Validation Test Procedure

Purpose

The Test Procedure document contains the detailed test scripts that will be run.

Outline

1. Organization and Responsibilities
2. Overview of Test Scripts
3. Appendix
4. Detailed Test Scripts

H.8   Software Validation Test Report

Purpose

The purpose of this report is to document the results of software validation testing.

Outline

1. Organization and Responsibilities
2. Summary of Results
3. Summary by Software Version
4. Metrics
5. Conclusions and Recommendations
6. Appendices
7. Completed Test Scripts
8. Software Problem Reports

H.9 Software Validation Test Script

Purpose

The test scripts document the specific details of each test.

Test Script Header

Test Identifier: _____
Test Category: _____
Developed by: _____
Latest Rev: _____

Test Log:

Engineer	Date	Version	SPRs found	SPRs verified

Test Objectives:

1.
2.
3.

Hardware:

1.
2.
3.

Initial Setup:

1.
2.
3.

Test Script

Initial Test Setup

Detailed Steps

    1. Perform step 1   [Pass or Fail]
       Expected results for step 1

    2. Perform step 2   [Pass or Fail]
       Expected results for step 2

    3. Perform step 3   [Pass or Fail]
       Expected results for step 3

Notes and Observations:

H.10   Software Configuration Management Plan

Purpose

The purpose of this plan is to define the methods to be used to identify software products, control and implement changes, and record and report change implementation status. A Software Configuration Management Plan would normally be written for complex projects that involve a large number of software engineers.

Outline

Reference: IEEE-Standard-828-1998

    1. Management

        a. Organization. This section describes the organizational structure that influences the configuration management of the software during development.

        b. Responsibilities. This section describes the organization element responsible for each configuration management task.

        c. Interface Control. This section defines the methods used to:

- Identify interface specifications and control documents;

- Process changes to released documents;

- Provide follow-up on action items;

- Maintain status of interface specifications and control document;

- Control the interface between software and the hardware on which it is running.

d. Implementation. This section establishes the major milestones for the implementation of the Software Configuration Management Plan.

e. Applicable Policies, Directives, and Procedures. This section identifies all policies and procedures related to CM that are to be implemented as part of this plan.

2. Activities

a. Configuration Identification. This section defines the procedures for identifying software baselines.

b. Configuration Control. This section defines the procedures for controlling changes to software baselines.

c. Configuration Status Accounting. This section defines the procedures for accounting for changes to software baselines.

d. Audits and Reviews. This section defines the role of CM in audits and reviews.

3. Tools, Techniques, and Methodologies. This section describes the specific tools, techniques, and methodologies used to perform the CM functions.

4. Supplier Control. This section describes the procedure for assuring that vendor-supplied software meets the requirements of this plan.

5. Records Collection and Retention. This section defines the CM documentation to be retained, the methods used to assemble, safeguard, and maintain this documentation, and shall designate the retention period.

H.11   Software Release Procedure

Purpose

The purpose of this procedure is to define the process used to release software from Product Development to Manufacturing.

Outline

1. Organization and Responsibilities.

2. Overview of Software Release Process.

3. System Requirements. Identify the hardware and software required to create new baselines of software.

4. Configuration Management Requirements. Identify the configuration management requirements used to establish and control changes to each new baseline of software. Refer to the Software Configuration Management Plan if appropriate.

5. Procedure for Creating New Baselines. Describe the procedure for creating new baselines.

6. Software Validation Requirements. Describe the software validation testing performed on each baseline. Refer to the Software Validation Test Procedure and Software Validation Test Report.

7. Manufacturing Validation Requirements. Describe the validation activities performed by Manufacturing on each baseline received from Product Development. Refer to appropriate Manufacturing procedures.

8. Software Release Sign-off Requirements. Define the Software Release sign-off process. A form should be used with the appropriate signatures to attest to the fact that the requirements of this Software Release Procedure have been followed.

9. Appendix.

10. Software Release Sign-off Form.

Appendix I: Test Cases for the Triangle Program

This appendix describes test cases for testing the triangle program described in Chapter 9 [1].

Test Case Objective	Notes
1. Valid scalene triangle	Test cases such as 1, 2, 3 and 2, 5, 10 do not warrant a "yes" answer because there does not exist a triangle having such sides.
2. Valid equilateral triangle	
3. Valid isosceles triangle	Note that a test case specifying 2, 2, 4 would not be counted.
4. Test cases that represent valid isosceles triangles such that you have covered all three permutations of two equal sides	For example, 3, 3, 4; 3, 4, 3; and 4, 3, 3.
5. One side has a value of zero	
6. One side has a negative value	
7. Three integers greater than zero such that the sum of two of the numbers is equal to the third	If the program said that 1, 2, 3 represents a scalene triangle, that would be a bug.

Table I-1 (continued)

Test Case Objective	Notes
8. At least three test cases in category 7 such that you have tried all three permutations where the length of one side is equal to the length of the sum of the other two sides	For example 1, 2, 3; 1, 3, 2; 3, 1, 2.
9. Three integers greater than zero such that the sum of two of the numbers is less than the third	For example 1, 2, 4 or 12, 15, 30.
10. At least three test cases in category 9 such that you have tried all three permutations	For example 1, 2, 4; 1, 4, 2; and 4, 1, 2.
11. All sides zero	
12. Noninteger values	
13. Wrong number of values	For example two more than three.
14. Did you specify expected output for each test case?	

Reference

[1] Myers, G. J., *The Art of Software Testing*, New York: Wiley, 1976.

Appendix J :
Software Reliability Models

This appendix lists the basic assumptions of the following models:

- Jelinski-Moranda model;
- Geometric model;
- Schick-Wolverton model;
- Goel-Okumoto nonhomogeneous Poisson process;
- Generalized Poisson model;
- Brooks-Motley model.

This information is derived from a lecture sponsored by the Boston section of the IEEE Reliability Group titled *Software Reliability Measurement, Assessment, and Modeling,* presented by Dr. Michael Elbert and Dr. David Heimann, October–November, 1991.

J.1   Jelinski-Moranda Model

- There is a finite number of faults in the program.
- The failure rate $Z(t)$ is directly proportional to the number of remaining errors as follows:

$$Z(t) = K(N - (i - 1)) \qquad (\text{J.1})$$

where:
> N = the number of initial errors;
>
> i = the number of errors already detected and corrected;
>
> K = a constant $Z(t)$ reduction coeffcient;
>
> K and N are unknown.

- The failure rate $Z(t)$ is constant until an error is corrected, at which time $Z(t)$ is again constant, but at a reduced value.
- All errors are independent of each other and equally likely to occur.
- Each fault contributes equally to the unreliability of the program.
- Reliability growth occurs as a result of fixing faults.
- Faults are corrected instantaneously.
- Fixes are perfect and do not introduce new faults.
- All faults are of the same severity.

J.2   Geometric Model

- There is an infinite number of total errors (i.e., the program will never be error free).
- All errors do not have the same chance of detection (i.e., all errors are not equally likely to occur).
- The error detection rate forms a geometric progression and is constant between error occurrences.
- Software is tested in a manner similar to the operational usage.
- The detection of errors is independent.
- The hazard rate function $Z(t)$ is computed as:

$$Z(t) = (d)(k)^{i-1} \qquad (\text{J.2})$$

where:
> d = the initial hazard rate;
>
> k = a coefficient.

The hazard rate function is initially a constant (d) that decreases in a geometric progression ($0 < k < 1$).

J.3 Schick-Wolverton Model

- The hazard rate is proportional not only to the number of errors in the program, but also to the amount of testing time. The chance of error detection increases with increasing testing time.

- All errors are equally likely to occur.

- The errors are corrected instantaneously without introduction of new errors.

- The software is tested in a manner similar to actual usage.

- Each error is of the same order of severity.

- The hazard rate function $Z(t)$ is calculated as:

$$Z(t_i) = k(n - (i - 1))t \qquad (J.3)$$

where:

t_i = the amount of testing time between the $(i-1)$st error and the ith error;

k = the proportionality constant;

n = the total number of errors in the program.

J.4 Goel-Okumoto Nonhomogeneous Poisson Process

- The cumulative number of faults detected at time t is Poisson-distributed with mean $m(t)$.

- The mean number of detected faults $m(t)$ is bounded and nondecreasing and approaches limit a.

- The mean number of detected faults in a small time interval is proportional to the mean number of undetected faults, with constant of proportionality.

- There is a finite number of faults; therefore:

$$Pr = \frac{m(t)e^{-m(t)}}{n!} \qquad (J.4)$$

where Pr is the probability of n faults being detected in time t and

$$m(t) = a(1 - e^{-bt}) \qquad (J.5)$$

J.5   Generalized Poisson Model

- A generalization of the Jelinski-Moranda or Schick-Wolverton models, taken in a framework of error count per interval.

- The expected number of errors is proportional to the fault content at time of testing and to some function of the amount of time spent in testing.

- Not all faults are necessarily corrected upon detection.

- Fault correction takes place at the end of intervals, without the introduction of new faults.

- Let $E(f_i)$ be the expected number of faults detected during the ith time interval. Then:

$$E(f_i) = t[N - M_{i-1}]g_i(x_1, x_2, \ldots, x_i) \qquad (J.6)$$

where:

N = the initial number of faults;

M_{i-1} = the faults corrected after $i - 1$ time intervals;

t = proportionality constant;

$g_i(x_1, x_2, \ldots, x_i)$ is a function of the time spent testing.

J.6   Brooks-Motley Model

- New faults can be introduced when existing faults are corrected.

- The number of new faults is proportional to the number of faults corrected.

- The number of faults detected is proportional to the number of faults at risk for detection, which in turn is proportional to the number of remaining faults:

$$n_i = (N - aN_{i-1})q \qquad (J.7)$$

where:

n_i = the number of faults detected during the $(i-1)$th interval;

N = the number of faults in the program;

N_{i-1} = the number of faults detected through the $(i-1)$th interval;

a = the probability of correction without inserting new faults;

q = the error detection probability.

Appendix K:
The Yellow Sticky Method

The yellow sticky method helps people develop more accurate, realistic estimates of tasks that they themselves will perform. It also includes identification of dependencies between tasks. By starting with more accurate estimates and including the dependencies, it is a rather simple and straightforward process to create a project schedule that is accurate, realistic, and can actually be met.

The method is based on the following simple principles:

- Know in detail what you are being asked to deliver.
- People who will be doing the work create the task estimates and build the schedule.
- Project team members critique one another's estimates.
- Everyone is held accountable for meeting their commitments.
- Customers are promised less than what can realistically be delivered (undercommit and overdeliver).
- The project team commits to deliver at least what was promised and possibly more.
- Everyone is trained in the yellow sticky method.
- Management has "bought into" the process.

With these simple principles in mind, let us look at how to create accurate estimates and realistic schedules.

K.1   Start with a Complete Software Requirements Specification

In order to create accurate estimates and build a realistic schedule, the project team must have a relatively complete statement of what it is they are being asked to build. This information usually is written in the form of a software requirements specification (SRS). Regardless of what method is used to develop a schedule, having a relatively complete SRS is absolutely essential.

I have taught the yellow sticky method to thousands of people across the United States, and it never fails that when I mention the fact that a relatively complete SRS is required, people laugh. What I often hear is, "We never start projects with an SRS. We're lucky if the SRS ever gets written!"

What managers need to understand is how crucial this document is to the ultimate success of the project. Beginning a project without an SRS is akin to asking a carpenter to build you a house without architectural drawings. Of course, carpenters can build you a house, but will it be the house you wanted? Probably not. So the very first step in learning how to create accurate estimates and schedules is to start with an SRS.

K. 2   Group Requirements into "Must Haves" and "Wants"

Once the SRS is written, the requirements must be reviewed and grouped into "must haves" (the product is not worth introducing if it lacks these features) and "wants" (the features that customers want, but that could be put into a future release if necessary). Frequently, marketing people are involved in making these decisions, since they are supposed to be in close contact with customers and should be aware of customers' wants and needs.

Now, let's suppose that marketing goes through the SRS and determines that all the requirements are in the must-have group. Well, this is not an acceptable answer, since the yellow sticky method depends on the fact that some requirements will be more important than others. If this is the case, use the no-tie ranking method to force some ranking of requirements. Here, marketing (or whoever determined that all the requirements are in the must-have group) ranks each requirement according to importance to the customer from 1 to N, where N is the number of unique requirements. The team then determines that requirements numbered 1 through m are must haves and all the rest are wants.

K.3 Commit to Deliver Only the Must Haves, Not the Wants

Recall the overall goal of predictable software development: to delight your customer by delivering exactly what you promised when you promised it. The problem that many organizations have is committing to customers more than can be reasonably expected. (See Chapter 16 for a discussion on commitment management.)

For the yellow sticky method to be effective, management must be able to manage commitments made to customers. What this means is that management must be able to control the commitments made by salespeople, marketing people, and so on, in order to achieve the goal above. Management must get buy-in from the organization before making commitments to customers.

Again, when using the yellow sticky method, management commits to delivering only the must haves, not the wants. By only committing to deliver the must-haves, management is setting the customer's expectation lower so that it is more likely to be met. Setting the bar too high and consistently failing to meet it causes customers to become dissatisfied. If you doubt this, just recall the last time you as a consumer were promised delivery of some product or service and it arrived later than expected or was not what was expected. Were you satisfied? Probably not.

In planning the project tasks, the project team will plan to deliver a product that contains all the requirements— must-haves and wants. And by following the yellow sticky process, worst case, the team delivers exactly what was promised (i.e, the must-haves), and best case, the team delivers more than was promised (i.e, must-haves and some or all of the wants).

By following this approach, the organization undercommits and overdelivers. Set the bar low enough so that you can consistently deliver the minimum you promised when you promised it.

K.4 Yellow Sticky Estimating Rules

There are a few simple rules that need to be followed when preparing task estimates. These are:

- Each task should be short—not more than five working days. A larger number of short tasks are preferable to a smaller number of longer tasks.

- Tasks that take longer than five days should be decomposed into smaller subtasks. If there are longer tasks, break them down into several shorter-duration tasks. This provides better visibility and flexibility in building and managing the schedule.

- Apply the 80% rule. In a given week, most people don't have 40 hours to apply to project tasks. At most, people have 80% of that, or 32 hours. Why? Because people spend time in meetings, going to training classes, talking on the phone, surfing the Web, and other similar activities. Don't assume that people have more time than they actually do. Some people may actually have less than 80% to apply to a project because they may be working on two or three projects at the same time.

- Include in your estimate vacation, holidays, trade shows, and so on.

K.5   Identifying Tasks and Creating Initial Estimates

Once the project team has been trained in the yellow sticky method, they can begin to review the SRS. This review is conducted either individually (on smaller projects) or as a group within their own disciplines (on larger projects).

The purpose of this review is to identify every task that is required to develop, test, and document the product and determine who will be responsible for that task. Note that tasks are identified for all requirements—must-haves and wants.

After the tasks are identified, the person responsible for that task estimates how long (in days) it would take them to complete the task, assuming that they could work on that task uninterrupted.

The 80% rule is not used to determine how long a task takes, but rather, when the task will be complete, as discussed below. If the task is something that the organization has never been done before, use the wideband delphi method (discussed in Section 14.3.3) to develop a reasonable estimate.

Once the task duration is estimated, each person then identifies the dependencies for starting this task; that is, what task must be completed before this task can start.

All of this information is written onto a Post-it™ note (commonly referred to as a yellow sticky), as illustrated in Figure K.1. Different groups on the project team should use different color sticky notes so that they can be visually distinguished.

Each person goes through the process of completing an appropriately colored sticky note with the information shown in Figure K.1 for each task they have been assigned. The understanding with respect to the task estimates is that each person is making a personal commitment to complete that task in that amount of time. Because of this personal commitment, there is immediate buy-in to the schedule from each member of the project team.

It's a good idea to identify on each sticky note whether this task is related to a must-have or a want. (An "M" or "W" in the corner works well.) When everyone is finished with this part of the process, the project manager schedules a schedule-building session.

K.6   Building the Schedule Going Forward

The first schedule-building session includes the entire project team (everyone that has tasks assigned to them) and should occur at an off-site location. It's a good idea not to invite management to this session. The reason for this is that we want the team to come together and reach agreement on the best possible schedule before presenting it to management. More on this below.

The project manager should coordinate this activity. The room used for this activity should have a long wall upon which some plain chart paper can be affixed. Week marks (not dates) are indicated along the top of the chart paper. For simplicity, assume that every month has four weeks.

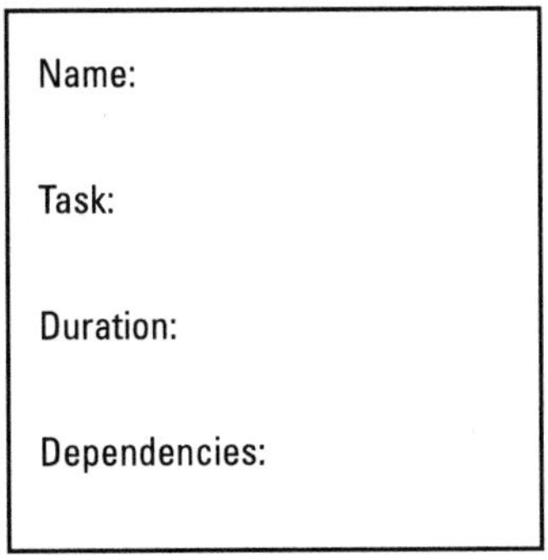

```
┌─────────────────────────────┐
│                             │
│  Name:                      │
│                             │
│  Task:                      │
│                             │
│  Duration:                  │
│                             │
│  Dependencies:              │
│                             │
└─────────────────────────────┘
```

Figure K.1 Yellow sticky information requirements.

The project team brings all of their colored sticky notes to the session. The process of building the schedule going forward is based on each task having at least one dependent task. When the project team is ready, they approach the chart paper with their sticky notes and start placing them on the chart in the location where the task should complete. Here is where the 80% rule is applied. Let's say you have identified a task that should take you five days (40 hours) to complete if you could work on it uninterrupted. By applying the 80% rule, a five-day task requires six working days to complete. So the sticky note is placed on the sixth day after it can begin. Refer to Figure K.2 for an example of what a schedule might look like.

Now this is where it gets very interesting and exciting. Recall that we have the whole project team in the room. Each person is now standing in front of this wall with a handful of colored sticky notes. As the sticky notes start to go up, discussions start happening. QA people talk to developers, developers talk to technical writers, everyone talks to the project manager. In addition, peers review one another's estimates. For example, a developer might put up a sticky note for a task with an estimate of three days. Another, perhaps more experienced, developer on the team may look at that estimate

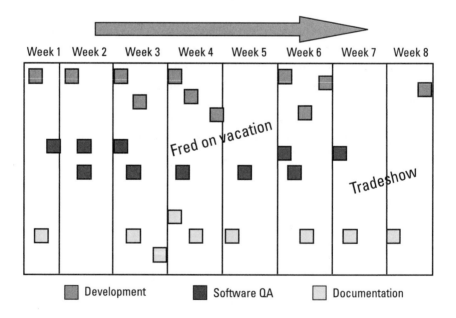

Figure K.2 Build the schedule going forward.

and say to the first, "You know, I did that task on the last project and it took me eight days, not three." Thus, with peers critiquing each other's estimates, the estimates get better.

Also, through discussion, team members identify tasks that may have been forgotten or overlooked. Frequently, many new stickies are created during the schedule-building process. This represents work that needs doing, but wasn't identified previously.

When placing tasks up on the chart, the team tries to place all of the tasks related to must-haves first and the tasks related to wants last. The reason for this will be apparent in the discussion below.

Finally, the team looks at the schedule they are building. The fact that they own the schedule is a powerful motivator. From talking with one another, sticky notes are put up and pulled off many times until the team as a whole is satisfied that this is the best possible schedule. Because each member of the project team contributed to the schedule and has made a personal commitment to completing their tasks on time, there is immediate buy-in to the schedule. Moreover, it should be obvious that people are much more motivated to meet schedules that they themselves determined.

K.7 Negotiate Based on Factual Information

Once the project team completes the task of building the schedule going forward, they will able to tell management when they can deliver the product. Frequently, management will not be pleased with this date and a negotiation session is usually required. Management will want to know how the delivery date can be pulled in. By looking at the chart with all of the colored sticky notes, the answers to this question will be fairly obvious. The choices that management has are to (1) change the requirements, or (2) add resources (people and equipment).

Two points need to be highlighted about this scenario. First, it is the people who will be doing the work telling management when they can deliver, and second, the negotiation can be conducted with factual information that everyone can see. For example, the chart will clearly highlight any resource bottlenecks (as evidenced by the lack of certain colored stickies in a particular area of the chart). The chart also has the estimates for each task.

During the negotiation, tradeoffs will be made between features, quality, and schedule. These negotiations can now be conducted with factual information that can result in an informed business decision being reached.

Once the negotiation is completed and everyone (management and the project team) is in agreement on the schedule, the information on the chart can then be entered into your favorite project management tool.

K.8   Manage the Project to the Schedule

Once everyone agrees to the schedule and the information from the chart is entered into a project management tool, the project manager now needs to manage the project to the schedule. This means that when a task is behind schedule, the end result is not a schedule slip. By scheduling forward, the project manager now has the following options:

- Work with the behind-schedule individual to understand if they can recoup lost time by working weekends or extra hours or by rearranging other tasks;
- Work with management to identify additional resources;
- Decide (as a last resort) to drop off a want (but not a must-have) to help keep the project on schedule.

Here then, is the reason why it is so important at the outset that the project team be able to categorize requirements as either must-haves or wants.

K.9   Benefits

Scheduling forward results in more accurate, realistic schedules that can actually be met. Worst case, you'll deliver exactly what was promised. Best case, you'll deliver more. People will work harder to achieve a schedule that they set for themselves. Scheduling forward helps your development process become more predictable

Appendix L:
Software Development Best Practices

A word of caution about best practices—they are only "best" if they work for your organization and in your environment. Instituting any practice without fully understanding the ramifications, without buy-in from the staff and without a plan for assessing effectiveness, is not recommended.

Two well-known sources of information on software engineering best practices are the Airlie Council and the Software Engineering Institute (SEI). In 1996 the Airlie Council [1], a group of prominent software engineering experts, considered over 170 best practices and from this list identified several principal best practices for software development. The principal best practices identified by the Airlie Council include:

- Define requirements first;
- Risk management;
- Peer reviews;
- Binary quality gates at the inch-pebble level;
- Project-wide visibility of project plan;
- Defect tracking against quality targets;
- People-aware management.

The Airlie Council's principal best practices are discussed below and are consistent with the SEI's Capability Maturity Model (CMM^{SM}) as illustrated in Figure L.1. For reference, the key process areas (KPAs) identified in CMM^{SM} are shown in the following list.

Key Process Areas Defined in the SEI CMM^{SM} [2]

Level 2 –KPAs

- Requirements Management
- Software Project Planning
- Software Project Tracking and Oversight
- Software Subcontract Management
- Software Quality Assurance
- Software Configuration Management

Level 3 –KPAs

- Organization Process Focus
- Organization Process Definition
- Training Program
- Integrated Software Management

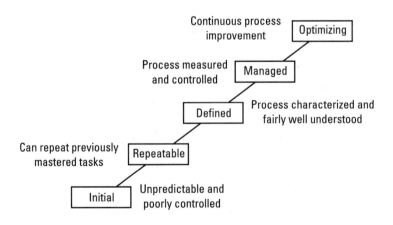

Figure L.1 SEI CMM^{SM}.

- Software Product Engineering
- Inter-group Coordination
- Peer Reviews

Level 4 –KPAs

- Quantitative Process Management
- Software Quality Management

Level 5 –KPAs

- Defect Prevention
- Technology Change Management
- Process Change Management

In addition to the Airlie Council and the SEI CMM^{SM}, Jones [3] has identified common practices performed by several organizations he determined to be best in class based on the quality of their products (see Table 15.2).

Table L.1 provides a comparison of these three sources of best practices, along with an assessment of how these practices impact software V&V activities.

Now we'll look at each of the Airlie Council's principal best practices and discuss management's role with respect to each.

L.1 Define Requirements First

I am still amazed at how many projects are begun these days without defined requirements. When faced with such a project, I ask these two questions: (1) If you don't know what the software is supposed to do, how can you build it; and (2) When you test software without defined requirements, what are you testing?

I often use the analogy of building a house to illustrate the problems of developing software without requirements. Imagine wanting to build a big, ornate home. What's the first thing you would do? Probably hire an architect to elicit your requirements and from these requirements, create blueprints

Table L.1
Comparison of Best Practices and Their Relationship to Software V&V Activities

Airlie Council best practice [1]	SEI CMM^{SM} KPAs [3]	Practices used by "best in class" companies as determined by Jones [7]	How this practice supports or enhances software V&V activities
Define Requirements First	Level 2: Requirements Management	Defect prevention techniques such as quality function deployment (QFD) and joint application design (JAD)	Provides documentation required for requirements inspections. Provides basis for effective validation testing.
	Level 2: Software Subcontract Management		Clarifies the role of subcontractors with respect to verification activities and validation testing.
	Level 2: Software Quality Assurance	Formal testing by test specialists; Formal quality assurance group; Complexity analysis tools; Test coverage analysis tools.	An effective software quality assurance function enables many V&V activities to be performed.
	Level 2: Software Configuration Management		Software CM provides mechanisms for change control, which are essential for effective software V&V activities.
Binary Quality Gates at the inch-pebble level	Level 2: Software Project Planning Level 2: Software Project Tracking and Oversight		Provides clear definition of what will and will not be completed at each gate. Can prevent wasted effort resulting from starting validation testing prematurely, before all required elements are completed.

Table L.1 (continued)

Airlie Council best practice [1]	SEI CMM^{SM} KPAs [3]	Practices used by "best in class" companies as determined by Jones [7]	How this practice supports or enhances software V&V activities
Risk Management			Increases the likelihood that verification activities such as inspections and peer reviews will not be curtailed due to unexpected events.
			Increases the likelihood that the time required for validation testing will not be reduced due to unexpected events.
			Increases the likelihood that project QA resources are adequate for defined tasks.
Peer Reviews	Level 3: Peer Reviews	Formal inspections	Identify problems earlier in the software development process, when they are easier and cheaper to fix.
			Increases the effectiveness of validation testing by eliminating many problems before testing starts.
	Level 3: Organization Process Focus	Executive and managerial understanding of quality	When ownership of the software development process rests with management, improvements in quality will follow.
	Level 3: Organization Process Definition		Having and following a written software development process is essential for effective use of limited resources and continued improvement in quality.

Table L-1 (continued)

Airlie Council best practice [1]	SEI CMM^{SM} KPAs [3]	Practices used by "best in class" companies as deter- mined by Jones [7]	How this practice supports or enhances software V&V activities
	Level 3: Training Program		Frequently, QA staff doesn't receive required training in software V&V activities.
			Providing this training will improve the effectiveness of the activities performed.
	Level 3: Integrated Software Management		Tailoring the defined software development process to meet the specific needs of projects is an essential tool for improving the effectiveness of soft- ware V&V activities and improving quality.
	Level 3: Software Product Engineering		Performing software development tasks in a consistent manner improves the effective- ness of software V&V activities.
Project-wide visibility of project plan	Level 3: Intergroup Coordination		Effective intergroup communication eliminates redundancy and avoids wasted effort.
			Ensures that all members of the project team are aware of where the project is at all times.

Table L-1 (continued)

Airlie Council best practice [1]	SEI CMM^{SM} KPAs [3]	Practices used by "best in class" companies as determined by Jones [7]	How this practice supports or enhances software V&V activities
Defect tracking against Quality Targets	Level 4: Software Quality Management	Quality measurements; Defect and quality estimation automation; Defect tracking automation.	Verification activities, such as testing and inspections, can help meet quality targets. Validation testing can help determine where the project and product is with respect to specific quality targets.
	Level 4: Quantitative Process Management		Process effectiveness data collected from peer reviews and inspections is used to drive process improvements.
	Level 5: Defect Prevention		Process effectiveness data collected from peer reviews and inspections is used to drive process improvements.
	Level 5: Technology Change Management		Assesses the impact of using new technology on product quality

that represent the house you want. You could then review the blueprints and make changes if needed.

Once you've approved the blueprints, a general contractor would be brought in to start work. How would the contractor know what kind of house to build? He or she would build the house described by the blueprints. The general contractor brings in carpenters, plumbers, electricians, and other tradespeople to perform tasks according to the requirements contained in the blueprints. How likely are you to get exactly the house you wanted? Pretty likely you'll get exactly what was specified.

When we switch from building houses to building software, the crucial first steps are often not done. Instead of defining what the software should do, many organizations start projects by bringing in the "carpenters" (or programmers). With only a sketchy outline of what this "house" is supposed to look like, how likely is it that the product they build resembles anything close to what the customer wanted? Not very likely.

Further compounding the situation is how many organizations view testing when requirements are not defined. Without written requirements to test against, all that the testers can do is demonstrate that the software does what it does. Does it do what it's supposed to do? Well, if you don't know what it's supposed to do, you can't answer that question. Many organizations fail to understand this basic fact. Are there problems with defining requirements first? Of course there are. Customers may not know what they want or they may frequently change their mind. However, there are solutions such as the "synchronize and stabilize" approach [4], rapid prototyping (discussed in Chapter 2) as a means to elicit requirements (not develop products), and having the customer or test team sign off on requirements prior to starting development.

Wiegers [5] has developed a list of requirements engineering good practices, shown in Table L.2a and b.

To briefly answer the questions I posed at the beginning of this section:

If you don't know what the software is supposed to do, how can you build it? You certainly can create software without knowing what it is supposed to do. However, there is a very good chance that under these circumstances, the software won't do what you intended or what your customer needs.

When you test software without defined requirements, what are you testing? When you test software without defined requirements, all you can do is prove that the software does what it does. Why? Because we don't know what it is supposed to do. Is this a good use of your scarce engineering resources? Probably not.

L.2 Binary Quality Gates at the Inch-Pebble Level

Here's a typical scenario: The project team realizes that there is a "crisis" but for various reasons, management isn't made aware of the situation for several months—when it's too late to do anything about it. This scenario is illustrated in Figure L.2.

Often, project teams intentionally create vague milestones. Since these milestones are not well defined, they are easy to meet. A vaguely defined

Table L.2a
Requirements Engineering Good Practices

Knowledge	Requirements Management	Project Management
Train requirements analysts. Educate user reps and managers about requirements. Train developers in application domain. Create a glossary.	Define change control process. Establish change control board (CCB). Perform change impact analysis. Trace each change to all affected work products. Baseline and control versions of requirements documents. Maintain change history. Track requirements status. Measure requirements stability. Use a requirements management tool.	Select appropriate life cycle. Base plans on requirements. Renegotiate commitments. Manage requirements risks. Track requirements effort.

milestone gives the impression that progress is being made. An example: most every project has this milestone: "Coding Complete." What does this mean? It means different things to different people. It could mean that the last line of code has been written, or that all the code is written and compiles without errors, or that developers have completed unit testing, or that they've completed unit testing and have fixed all the problems unit testing uncovered. Clearly, we need a precise definition of what "done" means. And this applies to every task, not just coding. Furthermore, task completion status must be binary. It's either done or it's not done. The concept of

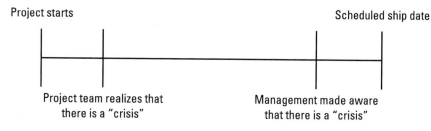

Figure L.2 Classic "crisis" scenario.

Table L.2b
Requirements Development

Elicitation	Analysis	Specification	Verification
Write vision and scope. Define requirements development procedure. Identify user classes. Select product champions. Establish focus groups. Identify use cases. Hold joint application development (JAD) sessions. Analyze user workflow. Define quality attributes. Examine problem reports. Reuse requirements.	Draw context diagram. Create prototypes. Analyze feasibility. Prioritize requirements. Model the requirements. Create a data dictionary. Apply quality function deployment (QFD).	Adopt SRS template. Identify sources of requirements. Label each requirement. Record business rules. Create requirements traceability matrix.	Inspect requirements documents. Write test cases from requirements. Write a user manual. Define acceptance criteria.

"partial credit" doesn't really apply. Depending on the project, for example, it may not be possible to begin certain tasks if dependent tasks are "almost done."

Management needs to beware of the "90% done" syndrome. This problem has plagued many projects. And it never fails that somehow completing that last 10% seems to always take more than 10% of the time. This problem is the result of poorly defined tasks, not having a clear definition of what "done" means, and not using binary measures for monitoring progress—either something is done or it's not done.

Another issue that management must deal with is deciding to proceed when defined tasks are not completed, or "inch-pebbles" have not been met. This can be a difficult situation to be in and frequently, business issues may enter into the decision process. But we need management to help make these tough decisions. Obviously, management needs to gather as much factual information as possible before making such decisions.

L.3 Risk Management

Every software project undertaken has some element of risk associated with it. Many organizations, however, ignore most risks until it's too late. The topic of risk management is discussed in Chapter 16.

L.4 Peer Reviews

The topic of peer reviews and formal inspections is discussed in Chapters 5 and 6 and in Appendixes A–D.

L.5 Project-wide Visibility of Project Plan

Frequently, real progress on projects is hard to discern. Project managers typically paint a rosy picture and report few problems. After all, they are being measured on the successful completion of the project. Unfortunately, management needs factual and timely information in order to avoid the situation illustrated in Figure L.2.

   To help provide more accurate information, project teams need to use a consistent set of terms with accepted definitions. Concisely defining terms and identifying evidence of task completion, like that shown in Table L.3, if used consistently, can help management understand where projects really are. Once a common set of terms and definitions are accepted, project status needs to be made visible to the project team and management.

L.6 Defect Tracking Against Quality Targets

By now, we should recognize that software defects are a primary indicator of quality. In fact, in 1996 there were over 200 million calls to technical support at an average cost to the software industry of about $23 per call [6].

   Of all the kinds of software defects, customer-reported defects are clearly the most important. These are the defects that directly affect customer satisfaction with your product. Organizations need to recognize the

Table L.3
Project Terms and Definitions

Term	Precise Definition	Evidence of Completion
Requirements complete	SRS conforms to standard. SRS reviewed and approved.	Requirements review held. SRS approved.
Design complete	SDD conforms to project standard. SDD reviewed and approved.	Design review held. SDD approved.
Code complete	All required features coded and checked into source control. All modules compile with no errors. Unit testing completed and all defects corrected.	All unit tests pass. All integration tests pass. All code checked into source control. Check-in of new modules decreased to 0.
Testing complete	All planned tests have been executed. Bugs reported from tests have been fixed and validated. Planned regression testing has been completed. Release criteria defined in the test plan have been met.	The test plan approved. Test report approved. Release report approved.

importance of customer-reported defects and define measures that will help them identify such defects prior to product release. Management needs to establish a small number of critically important quality measures that are tracked continuously. These quality measures need to be directly tied to corporate goals and objectives. Some examples of useful quality measures are illustrated in Figures L.3 through L.5.

Defect-removal percentage measures the number of defects that were found in each software baseline (see Figure L.4) prior to release. This measure can be used to help make decisions regarding process improvements, additional regression testing, and ultimate release of the software.

Defects reported in each baseline (see Figure L.3) measures the percentage of defects removed at release as compared with the previous release. It is computed by:

$$\left[\frac{\text{Number of bugs fixed prior to release}}{\text{Number of known bugs prior to release}} \right] \times 100 \qquad (\text{L.1})$$

Defects Reported In Each Baseline

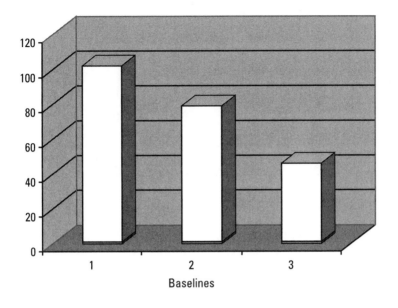

Figure L.3 Defects reported in each baseline.

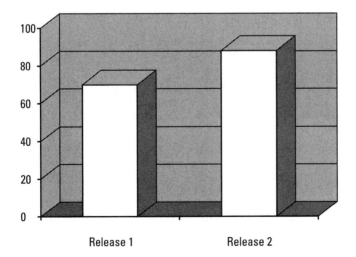

Figure L.4 Defect removal percentage at release.

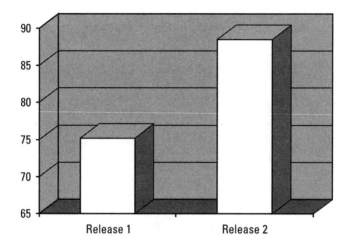

Figure L.5   Defect detection efficiency [7].

This measure can be used to help make decisions regarding process improvements, additional regression testing, and the ultimate release of the software.

Defect-detection efficiency [7] (see Figure L.6) measures how successful we are at finding those defects our customers are likely to find. It is computed by:

$$\left[\frac{\text{Number of unique defects we find}}{\text{Number of unique defects we find } + \text{ number of unique defects reported by customers}^*} \right] \times 100$$

This measure can be used to help make decisions regarding release of the product and the degree to which your testing is similar to actual customer use.

L.7   People-Aware Management

The subject of people-aware management is discussed in Section 15.2.

---

*   Based on at least three to six months of actual customer use.

References

[1]   Yourdon, E., *Rise and Resurrection of the American Programmer*, Upper Saddle River, NJ: Prentice-Hall, 1998.

[2]   Jones, C., *Software Quality: Analysis and Guidelines for Success*, Boston, MA: International Thomson Computer Press, 1997.

[3]   Jones, C., "Software Defect-Removal Efficiency," *IEEE Computer*, Vol. 29, No. 4, April 1996, pp. 94–95.

[4]   Cusumano, M., and D. Yoffe, "Software Development on Internet Time," *IEEE Computer*, October 1999, pp. 60–69.

[5]   Paulk, M. C., et al., *The Capability Maturity Model: Guidelines for Improving the Software Process*, Reading, MA: Addison-Wesley, 1995.

[6]   Wiegers, K. E., *Software Requirements*, Redmon, WA: Microsoft Press, 1999.

[7]   Kaner, C., "Article 2B and Software Customer Dissatisfaction," http://www.badsoftware .com/stats.htm, May 27, 1997.

Appendix M:
Software Quality Best Practices

A group of software quality experts have indirectly defined software quality "best practices" through the establishment of the Body of Knowledge for the Certified Software Quality Engineer (CSQE) exam. The Software Division of the American Society for Quality (ASQ) developed the CSQE Body of Knowledge and a certification examination as one of the requirements for achieving CSQE certification.

The Body of Knowledge is based on eight topic areas identified below. Within each topic area are a number of specifics that are included on the CSQE exam and thus indirectly represent best practices. Clearly, there is (and should be) some overlap between these topic areas and the software engineering best practices discussed in Appendix L.

For further information on the CSQE Body of Knowledge and exam, visit the ASQ Software Division Web site at www.asq-software.org or call ASQ at 1-800-248-1946 and request a copy of the CSQE exam brochure. At the end of this appendix is a Selected Bibliography that covers a significant portion of the Body of Knowledge. Cross-references to relevant information contained in this book are shown in parentheses.

General Knowledge, Topics, and Ethics

Tools such as:

Root-cause analysis (see Section 15.3.3 and Appendix O)
Pareto analysis (see Appendix O)
Risk management (see Section 16.2)
Fault tree analysis
Effective problem-solving skills
Effective written and verbal communication skills
Conflict-of-interest issues related to organizational independence
Software quality and product liability issues

Software Quality Management

Define customer quality requirements in measurable terms
Define supplier quality requirements in measurable terms
Track quality requirements throughout project development

Software Processes

Defect detection, prevention, and removal procedures
Software process effectiveness—measurement and assessment
Measurement-based process improvement

Software Project Management

Planning a testing activity—test estimating (see Chapter 9)
Project planning tools and techniques
Project estimating and scheduling (see Appendix K)
Managing to schedule (see Appendix K)
Requirement traceability matrix (see Table 9.3)

Software Metrics, Measurement, and Analytical Methods (see Chapter 7)

Measurement theory
Analytical techniques
Quality measurement—data collection and analysis

Software Inspection, Testing, and Verification and Validation

Inspection process, data collection, and analysis (see Chapters 5 and 6 and Appendixes A–D)
Testing methodologies (see Chapter 9)
Test planning and management (see Chapter 9)
Test strategies, testing levels, and types of tests (see Chapter 9)
Test design
Test coverage (see Chapter 9)
Test documentation
Testing third-party products
Methods for determining how much regression testing is appropriate
Requirements traceability (see Table 9.3)
Methods for evaluating software life-cycle products and practices
Methods for evaluating change control practices
Completion criteria (see Chapter 9)
Corrective and preventive action

Software Audits

Audit processes and procedures
Audit planning
Audit reporting and corrective action
Internal audits
External audits

Software Configuration Management (see Chapter 8)

Planning and configuration identification
Configuration control, status accounting, and reporting
Release process
Release planning
Release decision—criteria
Configuration management tools
CCB issues
Assessing impact of proposed changes

Selected Bibliography

Arter, D., *Quality Audits for Improved Performance*, ASQ Quality Press, 1994.

Dunn, R. H., *Software Quality Concepts: Practice and Plans*, Upper Saddle River, NJ: Prentice-Hall, 1990.

Humphrey, W., *Managing the Software Process*, Reading, MA: Addison-Wesley, 1990.

Kan, S., *Metrics and Models in Software Engineering*, Reading, MA: Addison-Wesley, 1995.

Kaner, C., et al., *Testing Computer Software*, New York: Van Nostrand Rheinhold, 1993.

Myers, G., *The Art of Software Testing*, New York: Wiley, 1979.

Paulk, M., et al., *The Capability Maturity Model: Guidelines for Improving the Software Process*, Reading, MA: Addison-Wesley, 1995.

Pressman, R., *A Manager's Guide to Software Engineering*, New York: McGraw-Hill, 1996.

———. *Software Engineering: A Practitioner's Approach*, 5th ed., New York: McGraw-Hill, 2000.

Schulmeyer, G., and J. McManus, *Handbook of Software Quality Assurance,* New York: Van Nostrand Rheinhold, 1992.

Software Configuration Management: An Overview, Osborne: National Computer System Labs, NIST Special Publication 500-161.

Appendix N:
Project Postmortems

A project postmortem is a tool for process improvement. It enables project teams to learn from past mistakes and change the process so that the same mistakes are not made again.

Remember that postmortems don't have to be "post-project." It is a good idea to plan and conduct mini-postmortems at the completion of each major project phase. That way, you can put lessons learned into practice immediately.

Keep in mind the following points about planning and conducting a postmortem:

- Start with a plan and a process.

- Remember that process helps focus the team on collecting factual information about what happened.

- Conduct a factual discussion of what happened—what worked well and what didn't work well.

- Publish the process for conducting the meeting so that everyone knows what to expect.

- Identify a few pieces of information that should be collected. Collect the same information each time that you conduct a postmortem.

- The data that you decide to collect should be recorded for future reference and for comparison. Collect the same data for each postmortem you conduct.

- Act on the information. Make a commitment to act within a reasonable amount of time.

- Prepare a report that outlines changes to be implemented as a result of the data collected. In this way, you'll get the message across that you're serious about process improvements.

- Have a disinterested third party act as moderator.

In addition to the "what worked well and what didn't" kind of information, the following list includes examples of additional information that should be collected. The actual information collected should be based on the specific process that was supposed to have been followed for the project.

- Development schedule: planned and actual;
- QA schedule: planned and actual;
- Requirements reviews: number of problems uncovered (if any) and whether they were corrected;
- Design reviews: number of problems uncovered (if any) and whether they were corrected;
- Code reviews: number of problems uncovered (if any) and whether they were corrected;
- Measurable release criteria defined and if they were met;
- Number of defects reported as a result of unit testing and integration testing;
- Number of complete QA testing cycles performed;
- Number of test scripts executed by QA: planned and actual;
- Number of defects found as a result of testing;
- Amount of time spent performing regression testing: planned and actual;
- Number of defects found as a result of regression testing.

Lastly, once the postmortem is completed, all of the information collected should be documented along with recommendations for improvements. Action items should be assigned to individuals where appropriate for implementation of process changes agreed to at the postmortem. Commitment from management is essential.

Appendix O:
Root-Cause Analysis

Root-cause analysis is a tool for discovering the underlying causes of software defects. This tool provides important information which can be used to drive process improvements that can eliminate the root cause of problems so that they don't recur in the future.

Developers can perform root-cause analysis as they find defects in their work. More importantly, the triage team (see Section 15.3.2) should perform root-cause analysis on all problems reported by customers, at a minimum, since these problems represent some gap in the organization's knowledge of customer use or some process deficiency.

As the triage team reviews problems reported by customers, they perform an initial assessment to determine if this is a new problem or a problem that has already been reported. If the problem has already been reported, the team determines if anything new can be learned from this report. The triage team approach can also be used for internally reported problems.

For new problems, the team goes through the questions in the list below and identifies information needed to determine the root cause. This could include test plans (was this situation tested?), documentation (was this situation documented?), and reviews (did we miss the problem in a review that was held?). Action items are assigned to team members to investigate issues further and report back at the next triage team meeting.

Initial Assessment for New Problems

- Is the problem reproducible? If not, root cause cannot be determined.
- Is the root cause of the problem obvious?
- Is there an environment, configuration, or installation issue?
- Is there an operating system, platform, or software version issue?
- Was the feature in question tested prior to release?
- Can the module(s) related to the problem be identified?
- Does a software requirements spec for the related module(s) exist?
- Does a design spec for the related module(s) exist?
- Is the design spec vague or subject to interpretation?
- Does the code implement the design correctly?
- Were applicable coding standards followed?

At the next meeting, the information identified is reviewed and determination made on root cause, if possible. Frequently, the triage team may have to ask "why?" several times before they reach the ultimate root cause of a problem. The following example (based on [1]) illustrates this point:

1. The requirement appears to have been missed in the test plan.
2. Why? Well, it seems that this particular requirement was changed after the SRS was signed off.
3. Why? Apparently, we learned that the customer wanted this changed in a conversation with product marketing that was captured in a memo but not circulated to the project team.
4. Why? Product marketing didn't realize this would impact testing.
5. Why? Product marketing doesn't understand that changes to requirements need to be communicated to the entire project team, not just developers.

It is possible and likely that there may be multiple root causes for one problem. All that are relevant should be checked. The triage team then creates a list of causes that represent the root causes of problems, as shown in Table O.1.

Table O.1

Example of Possible Buckets (Root Causes)

Bucket	Description
1	Feature was defined but not tested
2	Feature was defined but the test performed was inadequate
3	Feature was not defined—not included in SRS
4	Feature was not defined—in SRS not in use cases
5	Feature was not defined—in SRS, use cases but not user interface specification
6	Feature was not defined—not in technical specs
7	Feature was defined—Design was inadequate/inappropriate
8	Feature was defined—Coding was inadequate/incorrect
9	Feature was defined—Design review didn't catch it
10	Feature was defined—Code review didn't catch it
11	Installation/Environment/Version compatibility issue

Once a sufficient amount of data is collected, a root-cause-analysis review is performed to try to identify the most common root causes of problems and how they can be eliminated. A table similar to that shown in Table O.2 is created as part of this process.

The triage team performs a Pareto analysis (see [1]) on the root causes (to identify the 20% of root causes that account for 80% of the problems) and then uses this information to drive process improvements aimed at preventing those root causes from occurring in the future.

Table O.2

Root-Cause-Analysis Review

Problem Report #	Cause #1	Cause #2	Cause #3	Cause #4
403	✔	–	✔	–
508	–	✔	✔	–
990	–	✔	–	–
1112	✔	✔	–	–
Totals	2	3	2	–

Reference

[1] Arthur, L. J., *Improving Software Quality: An Insider's Guide to TQM*, New York: Wiley, 1993.

About the Author

Steven R. Rakitin received a B.S. in electrical engineering from Northeastern University and an M.S. in computer science from Rensselaer Polytechnic Institute. He has over 25 years of experience as a software engineer and software quality professional in a broad range of industries. He has earned certifications from the American Society for Quality (ASQ) as a software quality engineer and quality auditor. He is a member of the ASQ and the IEEE Computer Society. As president of Software Quality Consulting, Inc., he works with companies interested in creating a more predictable software development process. Visit http://www.swqual.com for more information or contact the author at info@swqual.com.

Index

Recent Titles in the Artech House Computing Library

Advanced ANSI SQL Data Modeling and Structure Processing, Michael M. David

Advanced Database Technology and Design, Mario Piattini and Oscar Díaz, editors

Business Process Implementation for IT Professionals and Managers, Robert B. Walford

Configuration Management: The Missing Link in Web Engineering, Susan Dart

Data Modeling and Design for Today's Architectures, Angelo Bobak

Demystifying the IPsec Puzzle, Sheila Frankel

Electronic Payment Systems for E-Commerce, Second Edition, Donal O'Mahony, Michael Peirce, and Hitesh Tewari

Future Codes: Essays in Advanced Computer Technology and the Law, Curtis E. A. Karnow

Global Distributed Applications with Windows® DNA, Enrique Madrona

A Guide to Software Configuration Management, Alexis Leon

Guide to Standards and Specifications for Designing Web Software, Stan Magee and Leonard L. Tripp

Information Hiding Techniques for Steganography and Digital Watermarking, Stefan Katzenbeisser and Fabien A. P. Petitcolas, editors

Internet Commerce Development, Craig Standing

Internet and Intranet Security, Rolf Oppliger

Managing Computer Networks: A Case-Based Reasoning Approach, Lundy Lewis

Metadata Management for Information Control and Business Success, Guy Tozer

Multimedia Database Management Systems, Guojun Lu

Practical Guide to Software Quality Management, John W. Horch

Practical Process Simulation Using Object-Oriented Techniques and C++, José Garrido

Secure Messaging with PGP and S/MIME, Rolf Oppliger

Security Fundamentals for E-Commerce, Vesna Hassler

Security Technologies for the World Wide Web, Rolf Oppliger

Software Verification and Validation for Practitioners and Managers, Second Edition, Steven R. Rakitin

Strategic Software Production with Domain-Oriented Reuse, Paolo Predonzani, Giancarlo Succi, and Tullio Vernazza

Systems Modeling for Business Process Improvement, David Bustard, Peter Kawalek, and Mark Norris, editors

User-Centered Information Design for Improved Software Usability, Pradeep Henry

Workflow Modeling: Tools for Process Improvement and Application Development, Alec Sharp and Patrick McDermott

For further information on these and other Artech House titles, including previously considered out-of-print books now available through our In-Print-Forever® (IPF®) program, contact:

Artech House	Artech House
685 Canton Street	46 Gillingham Street
Norwood, MA 02062	London SW1V 1AH UK
Phone: 781-769-9750	Phone: +44 (0)20 7596-8750
Fax: 781-769-6334	Fax: +44 (0)20 7630-0166
e-mail: artech@artechhouse.com	e-mail: artech-uk@artechhouse.com

Find us on the World Wide Web at:
www.artechhouse.com